D1124305

Criminal Justice

Recent Scholarship

Edited by
Marilyn McShane and Frank P. Williams III

A Series from LFB Scholarly

Police Coercion
Application of the Force Continuum

William Terrill

LFB Scholarly Publishing LLC
New York 2001

Library of Congress Cataloging-in-Publication Data

Terrill, William.
  Police coercion : application of the force continuum / William
Terrill.
      p. cm. -- (Criminal justice)
Includes bibliographical references (p.   ) and index.
  ISBN 1-931202-09-5
  1. Police discretion--United States. 2. Police
brutality--United States. 3. Resisting an officer--United
States. 4. Police-community relations--United States. 5. Police
discretion--Indiana--Indianapolis. 6. Police
discretion--Florida--Saint Petersburg. I. Title. II. Criminal
justice (LFB Scholarly Publishing LLC)
  HV7936.D54 T47 2001
  363.2'32--dc21

2001001150

ISBN 1-931202-09-5

Printed on acid-free 250-year-life paper.

Manufactured in the United States of America.

Table of Contents

Acknowledgments

Many people have contributed to the work contained in the following pages and I would like to acknowledge them here. My deepest thanks go to Steve Mastrofski, Roger Parks, Rob Worden, and Al Reiss, Jr., who made it possible for me to participate in the study that forms the basis for this research. In addition, I am indebted to many colleagues including, Lorraine Green Mazerolle, Candace McCoy, Elin Waring, George Kelling, Don Gottfredson, Jim Finckenauer, Manny Barthe, Dana Nurge, Rob Weidner, Justin Ready, Pat McManimon, Jack Morgan, Christina DeJong, John and Cynthia McCluskey, Mike Reisig, Chris Maxwell, Michael Maxfield, Kenna Davis Quinet, Roger Jarjoura, Ann Holmes, Hairam Yerac, John Ramirez, each of which have offered their time and effort at various points in my academic career. A number of others, Phyllis Schultze, Sandra Wright, Jean Webster, Shirley Parker, and David Petersen, have provided invaluable administrative support. Thanks are also due to the Indianapolis, Indiana, and St. Petersburg, Florida, police departments, as well as the National Institute of Justice who supported this work as part of Grant No. 95-IJ-CX-0071. Without their cooperation, especially Donald Christ, Darrel Stephens, and Goliath Davis, who provided access to their departments, and to the many patrol officers and support staff who permitted such a massive team of researchers to study them, this book would never have been possible. Of course, my warmest thoughts and thanks go to my entire family as well as my most treasured friends, Snapple, Christine, and Jesenia, who make it all worthwhile. While many of the shortcomings found here are wholly mine, the final product is immeasurably better because of the contribution of all these wonderful people.

CHAPTER 1
Introduction

Police coercion has long been a central focus among those who have studied the police. According to Friedrich, "[p]olice use of force is theoretically important because it involves the execution of perhaps the essential function of the state and practically important because it affects the public's attitudes and behaviors toward the police and government more generally" (1980: 82). To Bittner (1970), the defining aspect of the police role revolves around the capacity to use force. Not surprisingly, many studies pertaining to police use of force have been completed in the past few decades, and have enriched our understanding in this area (Westley, 1953; Reiss, 1968; Chevigny, 1969; Toch, 1969; Bittner, 1970; Friedrich, 1977; Muir, 1977; Black, 1980; Sykes and Brent, 1983; Fyfe, 1988; Bayley and Garofalo, 1989; Garner et al., 1995; Klinger, 1995; Worden, 1995). Despite this, there still exists a lack of reliable information on police use of force incidents – to such an extent that the United States Congress now requires the Attorney General to collect use of force data from police departments on an annual basis in accordance with Section 210402 of the Violent Crime Control and Law Enforcement Act of 1994.

Few issues are more critical to police-community relations than use of force, and in an era of community policing, the emphasis is even greater. Police administrators throughout the nation are continually in need of information that will lead to greater insight regarding how and why officers resort to force – information that provides clues about how to minimize the amount of violence in police encounters with the public.

Using data collected as part of an observational study of the police in Indianapolis, Indiana, and St. Petersburg, Florida, I examine police use of nonlethal force in an attempt to better understand *how* and *why* police resort to force. For purposes of this study, police force involves *acts that threaten or inflict physical harm on citizens.*[1] Additionally, force is measured according to the *severity of harm it imposes on a citizen.* Therefore, the range of police force is placed along a "continuum" ranging from least to most severe harm.[2] Verbal force involves commands and threats.[3] Physical force includes: restraint (e.g., pat down, handcuff, firm grip); pain compliance techniques and takedown maneuvers (e.g., wristlock, hammerlock, pushing and shoving, throw downs); and striking with any part of the body (e.g., hands, fists, arms, feet) or external mechanisms (e.g., flashlight, baton, use of chemical agents, stun gun).

   I do not explicitly attempt to either measure or explain excessive force behavior. Nonetheless, the analyses presented in Chapter Seven concerning the application of a force continuum does implicitly refer to possible excessive force behavior. I argue that the appropriateness of force cannot be determined without first identifying situations where officers resort to force when little to no citizen resistance is encountered.

   In the following chapters, I focus on five general areas of concern. Three involve *how* and two involve *why* officers use force. The first deals with how often officers resort to force. Evidence suggests police force is an infrequent event. Just how rare, however, is a matter of debate. For instance, in one study, force occurred in one percent of the cases analyzed, while in another it was used 22 percent of the time (McLaughlin, 1992; Garner et al., 1995).[4]

   The second area involves an examination of the various types of force used by the police. Police force comes in many varieties. A blow to the head with a baton is not the same as grabbing and restraining a citizen. Similarly, grabbing and restraining a citizen is not the same as issuing a threat, which is coercive but nonphysical. Thus, police force is measured along a continuum ranging from no force to maximum force (use of impact methods). While the use of police force appears to be relatively rare, less is known about variation in force, and even less about nonphysical (e.g., verbal commands and threats) coercive actions (Klinger, 1995). If much of policing consists of talking, as some have demonstrated (Sykes and Brent, 1983), then this aspect of police behavior requires further investigation.

Third, how force is applied within given encounters is examined. A police-citizen encounter is an interactional process in which both parties act and react to one another. As a result, multiple types of force may be used in any given encounter. How officers choose to apply these various types of force and in what combinations provides a better understanding of the manner in which police-citizen encounters are handled. Additionally, probing the dynamics of individual encounters allow one to learn how officers move up and down the force continuum (e.g., how often they start high as opposed to low and what impact this has on subsequent force behaviors).

What factors influence police decisions to apply various types of force is the fourth area investigated. Three primary theoretical explanations on the causes of police force have been advanced over the past 30 years. These include sociological, psychological, and organizational explanations. Thus, these three perspectives are used to guide analyses regarding why officers use force and the extent of their coerciveness.

Finally, an exploratory and innovative approach (the Resistance Force Comparative Scale) to examining the relationship between citizen resistance and police use of force is offered. Most police departments provide officers with a "force continuum" or "force escalation ladder" to guide use of force decisions based upon the level of resistance encountered by citizens.[5] This part of the study examines the extent to which officers actually apply a continuum of force in relation to citizen resistance. Moreover, it looks at what factors are associated with those instances when officers do and do not follow along a force continuum.[6] It is widely held by both law and police policy that the appropriate amount of police force is that which is reasonably necessary to achieve compliance. Since scholars, police administrators, lawyers, judges, and others have always struggled with what does and does not constitute excessive force, this type of analysis is invaluable to a better understanding of the level of force that *may* be labeled inappropriate.[7]

The data available in this study provide for the creation of a sequencing pattern, which measures the nature and extent of citizen resistance and corresponding officer use of force. In essence, for each police-citizen encounter, one can account for citizen resistance and subsequent police force. There is perhaps no stronger or more accurate means available for detailing how officers respond to a given level of citizen resistance.

Such an approach affords a view of those cases on the opposite end of the spectrum - instances when citizen resistance provides for, or warrants, an escalation of police force but fails to prompt such a response. These cases are particularly interesting in light of how much attention has been given to excessive force in the past. It provides an opportunity to learn more about what prompts officers to use "less" rather than more force.

The following chapter provides a review of the literature on police use of force. The operating perspective, theoretical framework, research questions, and hypotheses are then presented in Chapter Three. This is followed by the design and method of the study in Chapter Four. In Chapter Five, the first three research questions are examined, which consider the extent, nature, and application of force (as well as citizen resistance) within individual police-citizen encounters. Chapter Six investigates the causes of police force in relation to the highest level of force used, while Chapter Seven examines the application of the force continuum with respect to citizen resistance. Finally, the conclusions and implications are presented in the final chapter.

CHAPTER 2
Review of the Literature

Social evolution has many stages. One such stage entails determining and codifying those behaviors deemed to be unacceptable – criminal laws. This is a critical and highly complex process surrounded by intense debate and scrutiny. So too is the development of an institution designed to ensure that such laws are followed: police. Limitations or parameters must be set defining the extent of power granted to this institution to enforce laws. Perhaps Bittner (1970) provides the most eloquent contemporary description of the rise of policing as one of the last institutional structures of democratic governments and the struggle to limit power. Bittner argues that relinquishing to the police the right to use coercive actions goes against middle class values of achieving peace by peaceful means. However, there are instances when only a forceful police action can maintain or restore peace, so the police are given the right to use force. Thus, the police are faced with a paradox: to stop violence the police may sometimes need to resort to violence (Sherman, 1980a). Although coercive police tactics are viewed as an evil, they are a necessary evil nonetheless.

In 1931 the National Commission on Law Observance and Enforcement (Wickersham Commission) brought national attention to the issue of police violence in the form of brutality for the first time. The commission published the *Report on Lawlessness in Law Enforcement* that characterized "third degree" police tactics as a major institutional problem (National Commission on Law Observance and Enforcement, 1931). Over twenty years later, Westley (1953) was one of the first scholars to study the police and their views toward the application of force. He discovered that officers rely on force because they view it as an effective means to control those in need of control. Westley also found that force was used as a way to gain public and peer respect.

Despite Westley's early insight, it was not until the mid-1960s that the first wave of scholarly attention was given to police use of force. Much of this attention was directed at excessive force, most notably deadly force. In many cities throughout the country, riots ignited after claims of excessive police force. The President's Commission for Law Enforcement and Administration of Justice concluded that these allegations of police violence were legitimate. Shortly after, the Law Enforcement Assistance Administration (LEAA) was created with the aim of improving the criminal justice system. In an attempt to professionalize policing, the LEAA provided funds for police officers to attend college. The administration also allocated money for research on criminal justice issues, the first large scale federal effort toward such ends. As a result, most of what is known about police use of force has been acquired over the past 30 years, and a majority of this research has focused on deadly force. Less attention has been given to nonlethal force.

Data on police force have generally been derived from four sources: observational studies, officer use of force reports, citizen complaints, and surveys. Each of these mechanisms has strengths and weaknesses. For example, observational research while generally providing rich detail, is rarely used to collect force data as a result of the labor intensiveness of the technique. Conversely, almost all departments collect some type of citizen complaint data, but this mechanism only involves reported cases of excessive force. Nonetheless, police use of force inquiries most often attempt to determine one or more of the following: frequency and prevalence of police use/abuse, degree of variation in types of forceful actions and the application of force within individual encounters, and the causes of police force/abuse. The research presented here follows in this tradition. It examines the extent of police force using observational data, determining how force varies and is applied within individual encounters, and explores the causes of such variation. Accordingly, the following literature review is organized around these three themes. Following this review the limitations of prior work is discussed, which sets the stage for the proceeding inquiry.

2.1 EXTENT OF FORCE

Observational Studies

Reiss (1968) was one of the first researchers to systematically measure the extent of police force. In 1966 he conducted an observational study of police in Chicago, Boston, and Washington D.C. When examining the issue of police force, Reiss was primarily interested in measuring excessive force. He created an expert panel to review incidents where the "...policeman struck the citizens with his hands, fist, feet, or body, or where he used a weapon of some kind – such as a nightstick or a pistol" to determine if excessive force was used (1968: 3). Of 1,565 police-citizen encounters with suspected offenders, 44 involved instances where officers struck citizens in the manner Reiss outlined. Of these 44 encounters, 37 were judged by the review panel to have involved excessive force (2.4%) (1968). Friedrich (1977; 1980) re-examined Reiss' data. Unlike Reiss, Friedrich relied solely on the observers' classification of whether force was used at all, and if so, whether he or she believed force was excessive. Using this classification method and based on 1,565 police-suspect encounters, he found that reasonable physical force was applied in 51 cases (3.3%) and excessive force in 29 cases (1.8%).

In 1977, a larger scale observational study known as the Police Services Study (PSS) was carried out in 24 departments in three metropolitan areas (Rochester, New York; St. Louis, Missouri; and Tampa, Florida). Using data from this study, Worden (1995) analyzed 1,528 police-citizen encounters involving suspected offenders. He concluded that reasonable force was used 2.4 percent of the time and excessive force was applied 1.5 percent of the time. Another police observational study was done in the mid-1980s by Bayley and Garofalo (1989) in New York City. Of 467 police-citizen encounters classified as "potentially violent," they found some form of physical force was used about eight percent (37 cases) of the time.[1]

As part of a training evaluation regarding police use of force, Fyfe (1988) conducted observational research with the Metro-Dade Police department in Miami, Florida. Of approximately 2,000 potentially violent police-citizen situations, he found that force 'greater than firm voice commands' occurred about 12 percent of the time.[2] Klinger (1995) also examined the Metro-Dade data, but looked at a subset of cases classified as disputes. He found that in 241 dispute cases, some form of physical force was used 17 percent of the time. However, he also looked at voice commands and found this type of force was used most frequently (39%).

In summary, observational studies have examined the extent to which police use of force occurs. Several of these studies have also attempted to measure the extent of excessive force. From these efforts, it appears that both force in general, and excessive force, are rare events.[3]

Use of Force Reports
Officer use of force reports is another data collection method used to assess police force. Analyzing 123,500 arrest reports from Rochester, New York between 1973-1979, Croft (1985) found some form of physical force used in approximately two percent of these arrests. In a later study, Croft, along with Austin (1987), examined police use of force in Rochester and Syracuse. Examining data from 1984 and 1985, they found force was used in five percent of arrests in Rochester and in four percent of arrests in Syracuse.[4]

Using force reports from custody arrests over a 12-month period in St. Paul, Minnesota, Lundstrom and Mullan (1987) found force was used in 14 percent of the cases. No attempt was made to distinguish between reasonable and excessive force in the Croft (1985), Croft and Austin (1987), or Lundstrom and Mullan's studies. A few years later, McLaughlin (1992) also looked at use of force reports in approximately 11,000 arrests made by Savannah, Georgia officers. He found physical force was used only one percent of the time. One of the most recent studies to examine use of force reports was conducted by Garner and colleagues (1995) in Phoenix, Arizona. They found the highest rate of physical force to date; of 1,585 arrests over a two-week period, officers used some form of physical force 22 percent of the time.

What is particularly interesting in force studies that rely on use of force reports is the variation in rates of force found. As highlighted above, some of these studies (Croft, 1985; McLaughlin, 1992) have found reported force to be very low, similar to what has been found in observational research, while others (Lundstrom and Mullan, 1987; Garner et al., 1995) have found force to be relatively high. Since all these studies use arrests as a base to compute findings it cannot be a matter of differential comparison (e.g., comparison of arrests versus suspects). One interpretation with studies that found lower rates of force may be the result of officer bias in filling out report forms.[5] At the high end it could be the result of counting handcuffing as "use of force."

One benefit of using use of force reports is that they have become a more common data collection technique in recent years for both researchers and police administrators. Many departments now require officers to complete a use of force report whenever an officer uses any form of physical force. An additional benefit is that some reports also include questions pertaining to the level of citizen resistance. This element was often lacking previously, but it can provide a better understanding of the conditions in which force is used.

Citizen Complaints

Yet another method used to examine use of force is citizen complaints. In 1966 and 1967, Chevigny (1969) examined citizen complaints of the New York City Police department. Of 441 complaints filed, he found that 164 involved allegations of abusive police force. Dugan and Breda (1991) surveyed 165 police agencies in Washington state in 1987 and 1988; analyzing 691 complaints, they found that 123 involved physical force. Although many jurisdictions have recently streamlined the citizen complaint process (better and more accurate procedures), it still appears that measuring use of force through this mechanism is more limited than reliance on use of force reports because many incidents (where force is used) do not produce complaints. In the Reiss (1968) data set, of the 37 cases classified as excessive, only one resulted in a citizen complaint. In a more recent survey, only one out of every three persons who claimed to have been subjected to police physical abuse followed up by filing a complaint (Winick, 1987).

Surveys

Finally, surveys are also used to determine the extent of police force. In 1966 Bayley and Mendelsohn (1969) surveyed 806 Denver citizens about police brutality. Of these, fifteen percent of Hispanics, nine percent of Blacks, and four percent of Caucasians claimed that they had personally experienced police brutality. Campbell and Schuman (1968) conducted a national survey of citizens in 15 cities for the National Advisory Commission on Civil Disorders. When asked whether they had been "roughed up" by police officers, seven percent of the black respondents and two percent of white respondents claimed that they had. A 1991 Gallup poll found that five percent of citizens surveyed reported having ever been physically mistreated or abused by police, while 20 percent reported that they knew someone who had been physically mistreated or abused (Gallup, 1991).

2.2 VARIATION IN TYPE AND APPLICATION OF FORCE

In addition to examining the extent of police force, some researchers have also attempted to measure variation in types of force police use. In 1991, the Police Foundation (Pate and Fridell, 1993) conducted a national survey of police departments concerning the extent of force by officers, types of force used, number of citizen complaints, and force reporting procedures. Because of the diversity of agencies surveyed, they standardized incidents of force per 1,000 sworn officers. For city departments, they found handcuffing to be, by far, the most frequently used type of force (490 incidents per 1,000 sworn officers). The next most frequent type of force used was 'bodily force', with 272 incidents per 1,000 sworn officers. The McLaughlin (1992) study revealed only 133 reports of force out of 11,000 arrests, but further analyses were conducted to examine the type of force used. Forty-five of the 133 incidents involved instances where the officer punched or kicked citizens, 11 in which the officer struck the citizen with a baton, and two where the citizen was maced. The McLaughlin (1992) and Police Foundation (1993) studies highlighted the fact that "[n]onlethal force encompasses a wide variety of police actions" (Klinger, 1995: 171). According to Klinger, "[e]xplicit recognition of the diversity of force that is classified as nonlethal is important not only because it identifies differences in kinds of force but also because it points to differences in severity as well" (1995: 171). Klinger acknowledges that because there are different types of force police use, force can be ranked in terms of severity. Therefore, force can be measured along a continuum ranging from the least to the greatest amount of force. Garner and colleagues (1995) in their Phoenix study, and McEwen (1996) who reviewed police use of force data collection efforts at the national level, also refer to the importance of data collection and analysis in regard to a continuum of force.

Despite McLaughlin's contribution, Klinger (1995) went on to note two deficiencies in McLaughlin's work and those that came before it. First, prior attempts have failed to examine how various types of force are used within individual encounters. In other words, different types of forceful police actions can take place within single encounters (e.g., grabbing to restrain *and* striking to subdue). Second, such studies have been limited to classifying only force that is physical in nature. However, force can also be in the form of verbal coercion such as commands and threats. Klinger incorporated these two features into his analysis of the Metro-Dade data. He examined 241 police-citizen encounters involving disputes and found that officers used some form of physical or verbal coercion 164 times in 97 encounters. Clearly, multiple forms of force were used within single encounters.

Klinger also analyzed combinations of force within single encounters. Of the 97 cases in which some form of force was used, distinct combinations emerged. In 58 of these cases, officers only used one form of force (56 commands, 2 firm grip). In 22 cases a command and firm grip was used. Pain compliance, a firm grip, and a command were used in another 11 cases. The remaining six cases occurred in numerous combinations.

Examining force in this manner discloses several important findings. First, most of the force applied was verbal (58 of 97 cases). This type of force has generally been overlooked in the past, but is obviously a behavior that occurs with some frequency. Second, in 35 of the 41 cases in which physical force was used, it was in the form of either a firm grip or pain compliance hold, those physical behaviors at the lower end of the force continuum. Unless one distinguishes between types of force, all cases (in this study 41 cases) would be grouped together as if the level of force were similar or alike, which is misleading. As evidenced by Klinger, most force was of the lowest level. Third, when higher forms of force were used (e.g., firm hold) within a given encounter, lower forms were also applied (e.g., voice command). Of 97 cases that involved voice commands or some form of physical force, 98 percent of them involved voice commands. The implication is that officers did not increase or immediately apply a higher level of force without using lower forms as well, although Klinger did not employ temporal sequencing. Garner and colleagues (1995) also examined varying types of physical force. Like Klinger, they found that most of the physical force used was at the lower end of the continuum. Of 1,235 cases involving physical force, 918 were in the form of restraints.

It is somewhat difficult to discern the significance of the similarities and differences between these two studies. For one, Klinger's work was based on data collected through observational research and looked only at disputes. The Garner data was based on use of force reports as part of all arrests. Second, Klinger did not include handcuffing as part of physical restraint, while Garner and colleagues did. Nonetheless, several significant issues emerge from these studies. First, inclusion of verbal force is an important part of the nonlethal force picture. Second, force comes in many forms and to understand how officers use their coercive powers, one has to account for these varying types of force. In addition, Garner and colleagues incorporated varying levels of citizen resistance into their analysis, which is a focal point of the research presented here.

Besides counting how often the police use force and distinguishing between various types of force, some scholars have explored a slightly different angle regarding the application of force. This involves an attempt to model the micro-processes of how force is used within police-citizen encounters in order to control or manage the encounter. Sykes and Brent (1980, 1983) conducted an observational study in a mid-size city and analyzed approximately 3,000 police-citizen encounters, focusing more on the micro-process of the police-citizen encounter than previous observational studies. They sought to explore the interactional process between officers and citizens, and how officers regulate or control encounters. They proposed that officers are trained to "take charge," and conceptualized three means of control used to do so: definitional (questioning), imperative (commands), and coercive (the threat or actual use of physical coercion). They found that, for the most part, officers handled situations through definitional and imperative control. The use of coercive tactics were rarely used and usually only after lesser forms of nonphysical tactics failed.

Bayley (1986) also looked at how officers managed encounters with citizens and tactics they used to do so. Like Sykes and Brent, he examined the interactional process of police-citizen encounters. He proposed that police-citizen encounters move through three stages: contact, processing, and exit. Examining traffic stop and disturbance encounters, he found that officers use a wide variety of tactics at each of these three stages. Further, he found that decisions made early in an encounter can affect subsequent decisions to use force. For instance, beginning encounters with tactics such as listening, questioning, or seeking information usually led to a less coercive outcome such as a verbal warning or offering advice. Conversely, taking a more coercive approach at the start (e.g., verbal or physical restraint) had a greater likelihood of leading to a more coercive outcome. Another interesting finding was that mere police presence was often enough to quell citizen resistance, thus preventing subsequent use of physical force.

Finally, the aforementioned Metro-Dade study conducted by Fyfe (1988) examined actions taken by patrol officers to deal with potentially violent situations (PVs). As with the other research summarized in this section, this study highlights the actual behavior of officers within individual police-citizen encounters. In other words, what is going on in these encounters that help us to better understand how force is applied? However, Fyfe also looked at police actions prior to the point of mobilization. The purpose of Fyfe's study was to examine the effects of training on how officers handled potentially violent situations, so as to minimize the likelihood of police-citizen violence. Along the lines of Bayley (1986), Fyfe broke down a potentially violent situation into four stages: unassigned time (e.g., time before an officer is dispatched or aware that a PVs is about to unfold), approach (e.g., time between dispatch to PVs and face to face contact), contact (e.g., entry stage), and resolution (e.g., disposition). Among other findings, he found that actions taken prior to involvement in potentially violent situations (e.g., knowledge of the patrol beat, places, people) may reduce the potential for police force (or subsequent use of police force during the encounter). Interestingly, he also found that some officers in certain situations may not have been aggressive enough in handling potentially violent encounters. That is, they failed to take charge when "it was clearly appropriate to take charge" (1989: 22).

2.3 CAUSES OF POLICE FORCE

The study of police coercion has not been very theoretical. Rather, it has been examined in the context of a broader understanding of police behavior and discretionary decision making, which itself has not been grounded in a solid substantive theory of police behavior. This fact was first highlighted by Sherman in 1980 (1980b). More recently, Riksheim and Chermak, after reviewing previous studies on police behavior regarding the decision to use force, arrest, detect criminal activities, and engage in service behaviors, concluded, "[c]learly, theoretical development [of police behavior] is lagging far behind the quantitative attempts to estimate the relationships between variables" (1993: 377).[6] Nonetheless, the literature has introduced three primary explanatory perspectives that serve as theoretical guides to understanding police use of force: sociological, psychological, and organizational.

Sociological
Understanding police behavior within a sociological framework often involves examining the social dynamics of police-citizen encounters. This approach has most often been aligned with Donald Black's theory of law (1976).[7] Black posits that the application of law can be explained in terms of social space or distance. In the context of police force, Black's theory predicts that the police will be more coercive toward those perceived to have lower status, such as minorities and the poor. More directly, this area of explanation examines the structural or situational characteristics in which police and citizens interact. In general, researchers who have applied a sociological approach to police behavior posit that officers rely on, or look to, situational cues as a basis to judge how a particular incident should be handled. Perhaps Bittner's (1970) statement regarding officers' "intuitive grasp of situational exigencies" best illustrates this perspective.

Thus, applying a sociological approach, the following determinants have been hypothesized to affect the use of police force: citizen race, gender, class, age, demeanor, sobriety, mental state, and emotional state; number of officers present; number of citizens present; location of encounter; and type/seriousness of offense.

Reiss (1968) examined his data from a sociological viewpoint. He found that most victims of police force were young, lower-class, and classified as suspects. He also found that 78 percent of the time force occurred in police-controlled settings such as the patrol car, precinct, or public street, and that there were rarely any civilian witnesses. Those who defied the officers' authority were the most likely to be on the receiving end of undue force. Almost half (48%) of all excessive force victims had either challenged the officers' authority or physically resisted arrest, and 32 percent were considered deviant in some manner by officers (e.g., intoxicated, homosexual, drugs addicts) (1968).[8]

In 1966 and 1967 Chevigny (1969) analyzed citizen use of force complaints made to the New York Civil Liberties Union. Of those complaints that were sustained, in 71 percent of the cases police force was the result of citizen defiance to police authority. Further, defiance was primarily verbal rather than physical. Toch (1969) also examined police-citizen violence. He conducted interviews with both officers assaulted by citizens and citizens assaulted by officers in Oakland. He concluded that most of the violent interactions were the result of citizen disrespect. Toch was also able to analyze the interactional process between officer and citizen. He found that half of the cases that led to excessive force complaints began with a verbal request by an officer followed by a citizen's failure to abide by the request. At that point, the officer escalated to a command, which the citizen disobeyed and the cycle continued on to physical force. Toch's study was the first to empirically demonstrate the escalation of police-citizen violence within individual encounters.

Friedrich (1977) also used a sociological approach to examine why officers resort to force. Like Reiss, he found support for a sociological explanation. For instance, he found that use of force was more likely if a citizen was antagonistic, agitated, intoxicated, lower-class, suspected of a felony, and if there were bystanders present (e.g., another citizen or officer). Friedrich also looked at psychological and organizational explanations, which will be discussed below.

In 1995, Worden re-examined the Police Services Study (PSS) data gathered in 1977. Like Friedrich, he analyzed the determinants of force from several different theoretical frameworks. He too found similar results to Reiss and Friedrich; situational determinants bore the strongest relationship to the use of force. He found suspects that were antagonistic, lower-class, male, intoxicated, and black were more likely to be victims of force (1995).

Garner (1996) uncovered several significant predictors of police force toward citizens. Arrestees who were alleged to have been involved in a violent offense, were antagonistic, male, involved in a gang, intoxicated, or known to have a weapon or reputation of being resistant toward the police, were all more likely to be the recipients of forceful police actions. Other factors found to impact officer use of force included the increased presence of both police and bystanders, and officer contact and cover tactics.

Another area of explanation often overlooked but nicely illustrated by Sykes and Brent (1983), and to some extent Bayley and Garofalo (1989), involves officer success or failure to control through noncoercive means. As previously mentioned, Sykes and Brent (1983) found that officers rarely resort to force and when they do it is usually after other means of control have failed. In other words, officers resort to force because they are unable to exert control in other ways, thereby leaving force as the only option. This should not be confused with the way most researchers have applied situational variables. Reiss (1968), Friedrich (1977, 1980), Worden (1995), and others looked at situational factors but only in the form of those that are either present or not present in a police-citizen encounter. For example, was the citizen antagonistic, intoxicated, emotionally or mentally disturbed? The fact that these factors increase the likelihood of officers resorting to force does not tell us anything about the officers' efforts prior to making a decision to use force. It could be that officers "jump" right into applying force more readily with these citizens or it may be that officers have a more difficult time dealing with these people because of the behavior they are displaying, which then results in police force. The problem with looking at the encounter as a whole is that you cannot determine which of these two competing explanations are more accurate. Friedrich (1977) found that police officers treated intoxicated citizens more forcefully than non-intoxicated citizens while controlling for antagonistic behavior on the part of the citizen. This implies that the police treat intoxicated citizens more harshly simply because they are "drunk", not because of their actions, something that both Westley (1953) and Reiss (1968) alluded to in their research. However, this fails to answer the question of whether the police treated them harshly *only* because they were drunk or because officers were unable to deal with behavioral manifestations of their drunkenness. But the approach taken by Sykes and Brent distinguishes between the two.

Perhaps this issue is a matter of semantics, the primary issue being that officers end up having to use force on intoxicated citizens more readily on average. Therefore, it may not matter if it was a result of officers being unable to control them in ways that are not coercive. What may matter is the fact that the citizen was drunk, which caused the officer to respond with force. Perhaps the answer to this puzzle depends on how one frames the question. For instance, does it matter if the police respond more readily with force when certain factors are present in an encounter? Illustrating this view, one may say "a crazy person is a crazy person and reasoning with him or her usually does not work so there is no use trying it." Or, does it matter whether the police attempt to exhaust all noncoercive means before resorting to coercive means, regardless of whether certain factors are present? This view may be characterized as "a crazy is a crazy, but sometimes reasoning does work so it is worth trying before becoming forceful." According to one department's policy (St. Petersburg) on handling mentally impaired citizens, the latter seems to be the appropriate method.

Psychological

According to a psychological theoretical perspective, officer characteristics, experiences, views and outlooks are posited to have an effect on police behavior. Simply stated, is there something about particular officers that help explain why they use force and how much they use? This explanation rests on the assumption that officers with certain traits, experiences, or attitudes will respond differently in similar situations. Factors that have been hypothesized to matter include: officer race, gender, education, training, age, length of service, views toward citizenry, attitude toward role orientation (e.g., crime fighter versus service-oriented), workgroup, and patrol assignment.

Muir's (1977) theoretical orientation may best illustrate the role of the individual. Muir was primarily interested in characterizing "good" versus "bad" police officers. He constructed a four-fold typology into which officers could be grouped depending on two dimensions: their view of human nature and their attitude toward the use of coercive authority. Others have also constructed typologies of officers based on various dimensions to explain the use of force (White, 1972; Brown, 1981). However, minimal systematic evidence exists to document the impact of officer belief system in relation to use of force.

Brown's (1981) study of officers in three departments in southern California was based on observations and interviews with officers concerning how they went about various discretionary decisions. Based partly on Brown's study, Worden concludes "behavior is not a simple extension of attitudes, as organizational and other social forces can attenuate the impact of attitudes on behaviors" (1995: 35). In short, most explorations regarding the links between attitudes and police behavior have been impressionistic at best. However, as Worden (1995) notes, none of the previous psychological studies solely examined the use of force. As a result, Worden tested several officer attitudes and their relation to the use of force. He posited that officers, "who are most likely to use force could be expected to (a) conceive the police role in narrow terms, limited to crime-fighting and law enforcement, (b) believe that this role is more effectively carried out when officers may use force at their discretion, (c) regard the citizenry as unappreciative at best and hostile and abusive at worst" (1995: 34). He found that officers with negative views toward the citizenry (e.g., believed citizens were unappreciative) were more likely to use both reasonable and improper force. Officers with more favorable views toward force (e.g., believed discretion should be at the officer level) were significantly more likely to use improper force. Finally, he found that how officers conceive the police role did not have an effect.

Unlike research attempting to link attitudes with use of force behavior, there has been more of an accumulation of research pertaining to the impact of officer traits and experiences on use of force, but to a lesser extent than might be surmised. Cohen and Chaiken (1972) looked at the relationship between 33 officer background characteristics and various work performance indicators among 1,915 New York City police officers from 1957-1968. One of these measures examined use of force complaints against officers. They found that age, race, and education were all significantly related to citizen complaints. Officers who were white, older, and more educated received fewer complaints. In terms of education, Cascio (1977) also found that more educated officers received fewer complaints. Conversely, Worden (1995) found that officers with a four-year degree were significantly *more* likely to use physical force classified as "reasonable", but found no effect on force judged to be "excessive."

Unlike Cohen and Chaiken (1972), most research has not found officer race to be a predictor of force. Friedrich (1977), Croft (1985), Garner et al. (1995), and Worden (1995) all found no difference in terms of officer race. However, Friedrich (1977) did conclude that black officers patrol more aggressively and make more arrests, irrespective of citizen race. As per gender effects, Worden (1995) found none while Garner and colleagues (1995) found that male officers were more likely to use force on male arrestees. Not surprisingly, information regarding gender and race is sparse. Until the past decade or so, police departments were almost exclusively made up of white males. As a result, making valid comparisons has not been possible in many studies.

Research has shown that less experienced officers are more active; they patrol more aggressively (Friedrich, 1977), and make more officer-initiated stops (Worden, 1989) than their more experienced counterparts. However, officer experience appears to have little to no influence on officer use of force behavior. Worden (1995) found that officer length of service had no effect on either the use of reasonable or excessive force behavior, while Garner and colleagues (1996) found that officer experience was an "inconsistent" predictor of force.[9] Finally, the amount and type of training officers receive has been hypothesized to have an impact on use of force decisions (Fyfe, 1988). Nonetheless, this has been largely unexplored. Even the Garner (1996) study, one of the most recent inquires on use of force, failed to account for differences in officer training.[10] One reason this may be absent in most studies is the difficulty of obtaining training information that can be linked to individual officers. Another reason may be that researchers consider such variables as length of service and education to be adequate proxies for training.

Organizational

Organizational theory looks to the role organizations play in shaping officer behavior. Two predominant organizational theories have emerged in the past 30 years. In 1968, Wilson proposed an organizational theory that emphasized the formal structure of an organization and the political environment within which it operates. The theory presumes that through organizational rules, regulations, standard operating procedures, incentives and disincentives, combined with direction from top administrators, a style of policing develops. In other words, a common vision becomes part of each officer's mind set of how to handle the everyday aspects of police work. Thus, similar incidents that occur at the street-level will be handled similarly by different officers in that department. Wilson (1968) proposed that within a department, one of three styles of policing develops: legalistic, service, or watchman. For use of force purposes, this theory suggests that departments classified as watchman are the most likely to engage in forceful police actions.

Others have also emphasized the influence of organizational policies. Ground breaking work done by Fyfe in the 1970s demonstrated the impact of restrictive administrative policies on lethal police force. After the New York City police department adopted a restrictive firearm policy in 1972, police firearm discharges decreased by some 30 percent. Further, Sherman and Cohn (1986) examined police shootings in big city departments between 1970 and 1984 and found that the number of citizens killed by police shootings was cut in half.

A second organizational theory looks to the impact of the informal structure (police culture) rather than the formal structure (Brown, 1981). This theory presumes that the police culture serves to protect and isolate officers from internal and external scrutiny more than it does to forge a particular style of policing. Instead, operating through the protection of one another, officers are able to develop their own unique styles. For instance, in the three departments Brown (1981) studied, he found that individual, not departmental, styles of policing emerged within each of the three departments. Similar to Brown, Manning (1989) examined the role of the informal structure. Although Manning concedes that first-line supervisors may have some influence on officer behavior, he concludes that the formal aspects of a police organization have little impact on officer behavior.

Environmental criminologists like to point out that it is easier to alter or manipulate environmental features than to alter the behavior of criminals and their victims. In a similar fashion, researchers see promise in organizational theories because of the view that the organization is more readily manipulable (at least the formal aspect). The problem, however, is that it is difficult to test adequately many of the organizational theories that have been proposed because of the expense and difficulty of collecting information on multiple agencies.

The extant research on testing organizational hypotheses regarding use of force are limited to a few studies. Friedrich (1977), using the Wilson (1968) typology, found little support for a net organizational effect, although findings were in the predicted direction. Worden (1995) also examined Police Services Study (PSS) data from an organizational perspective. He examined three organizational characteristics: degree of bureaucratization, emphasis placed on crime-fighting activities by the chief, and a measure for informal culture. Of these, only the degree of bureaucratization was significantly related to the use of "reasonable" force. The more bureaucratized the department, the greater the likelihood force was used. According to Worden, it would appear that in smaller departments with fewer levels of hierarchy, the formal aspects of the organization may matter.

In summary, situational explanations seem to offer the most insight on why officers use force. Those factors that most consistently predict the use of force are characteristics of the citizens and their behavior (e.g., demeanor, antagonistic or aggressive behavior, intoxication, and gender). Both organizational and individual officer characteristics have failed to explain much in terms of police force.[11]

2.4 LIMITATIONS OF PRIOR WORK

There are several elements of these previous studies that have hindered our understanding of police use of force. The three highlighted here form much of the basis for how I originally set out to fill the existing gaps in the extant research. First, prior works have primarily examined the application of police force in the form of what has been termed excessive force, focusing on extreme police violence such as brutality. Second, they have tended to conceptualize police force dichotomously: excessive force/nonexcessive force, physical force/nonphysical force. Third, they often examine or view the application of police force in the context of a static rather than a dynamic process. The following describes these limitations in more depth.

Excessive Police Force versus All Police Force
"Excessive" force is not easily defined. Many scholars have struggled with a variety of terms to describe police violence. These include: excessive use of force, use of excessive force, brutality, unauthorized force, wrongful force, unjustified force, misuse of force, and unnecessary force. While these phrases are interchangeable to some, others note fine distinctions. For example, use of excessive force can be defined as more force than needed to gain compliance in any given incident, while excessive use of force may be defined as using force in too many incidents (Adams, 1995). Fyfe (1997) makes the distinction between brutality (a willful and knowingly wrongful use of force) and unnecessary force (force used by well-meaning officers ill-equipped to handle various incidents). Worden (1995) also distinguishes between different types of force. He defines excessive force as that which is more than required to subdue a citizen, and unnecessary force as that which precedes a citizen's resistance or continues after citizen resistance has ceased.

One reason for the recent attention placed on defining police violence in more finite terms may be the result of apparent progress made in the control of such behavior. Through a variety of control mechanisms (e.g., criminal laws, administrative policies, greater minority political empowerment, civil protections) it would seem that such extreme behavior is more infrequent today despite some highly publicized incidents to the contrary. Thus, several policing experts are beginning to further examine types of force that are not overtly egregious, but may be unnecessary (in the sense as defined by Fyfe).

Klockars (1995) argues most police agencies gauge officer use of force using minimum standards. That is, the criteria for the legitimate use of force is that which is not a criminal violation, prevents any civil liability, and is of a nature that will not bring embarrassment to the department. These standards are necessary, but are they sufficient? Several police experts believe they are not. Klockars states, "[we] would not find the behavior of a physician, lawyer, engineer, teacher, or any other professional acceptable merely because it was not criminal, civilly liable, or scandalous and it is preposterous that we continue to do so for police" (1995: 17). He calls for broadening the focus of excessive force to include, "...the use of any more force than a highly skilled police officer would find necessary to use in [a] particular situation" (1995: 18). Even dating back to Bittner there has been an awareness that "the skill of policing consists in finding ways to avoid its use" (1974: 40).

Thus, many scholars argue that further insight on police use of force requires examining all instances of police force, not just those "artificially" labeled excessive force. Even further, one must look not only at instances when some aspect of physical force was employed, but all instances when physical force might have been used but was not. Just as there are instances when force may be excessive, there are times when force may be needed but is not used.[12] So, failure to include all cases when physical force may be reasonably needed prevents one from uncovering important factors associated with the use or nonuse of physical force.[13]

Police Force as a Dichotomy

Another common deficiency in many studies to date involves conceptualization of the dependent variable: police force. Such research often seeks to distinguish between excessive and reasonable force in accordance with the law or police policy. Similarly, studies that attempt to explain the causes of police force often do so using a dichotomous dependent variable (force versus no force; reasonable force versus excessive force), or in some cases, a trichotomous dependent variable (no force, reasonable force, excessive force). There are two problems with this approach. First, these studies usually only measure physical force. However, force can also be nonphysical in the form of commands and threats. Second, they often fail to take into account the varying degrees of physical (restraint techniques, pain compliance holds, striking) and nonphysical (commands, threats) force. Future researchers are advised to broaden the scope of the dependent variable to include a continuum of force. This would include not only physical forms of police force, but nonphysical actions as well.

Although most police departments train officers to apply varying levels of force in accordance with the level of resistance encountered by citizens, researchers almost universally fail to take this into account in their analyses. In any given police-citizen encounter, officers can and do apply numerous forms of both physical and nonphysical force. We need to better understand how all forms of police force are applied, in what circumstances, and to what extent.

Static versus Dynamic Process

A final limitation regarding prior work on police use of force involves the process of how it is applied. Studies that seek to explain or predict use of force decisions too often look at the police-citizen encounter as if it were a single discrete event, without noting the developmental nature of interaction over time within that event. For instance, Worden (1995) in his analysis, found that antagonistic citizens were significantly more likely to be on the receiving end of some type of physical force. This is an important finding, but we still do not know the nature or extent of such antagonistic behavior, only that it occurred at some point during the encounter. Further, we do not know whether the citizen's antagonistic behavior preceded or followed an officer's coercive behavior. Examining police-citizen encounters statically also fails to account for the number of times the citizen and officer displayed such forms of behavior.

Unless one more closely probes the interactional process in which the encounter takes place, he or she will miss out on valuable cues as to what prompts use of force incidents. The weakness of the approach taken by most researchers is that it fails to account for "sequential" behaviors displayed by both the citizen and the officer throughout the entire encounter. Most analyses look solely at what factors are present or absent during an encounter and fail to capture the numerous behaviors of both citizens and officers occurring during the encounter. As stated by Fridell and Binder, the police-citizen encounter must be "seen to encompass a pattern of interaction between an officer and an opponent and multiple decisions by both" (1992: 386). That is, like transactions between nations, transactions between people have a history, and what one does at any point will be based on the nature of the history up to that point.

2.5 RELEVANCE OF RESEARCH

Section 210402 of the Violent Crime Control and Law Enforcement Act of 1994 calls for an uniform collection of police use of force data. The intent is to gain a better understanding of how and why officers resort to force. The United States Attorney General delegated responsibility of this directive to the National Institute of Justice (NIJ) and Bureau of Justice Statistics (BJS). These agencies have recently released their latest report concluding (National Institute of Justice, 1999, pgs. vii-x):

What we know with substantial confidence:
- Police use force infrequently.
- Police use of force typically occurs at the lower end of the force spectrum, involving grabbing, pushing, or shoving.
- Use of force typically occurs when police are trying to make an arrest and the suspect is resisting.

What we know with modest confidence:
- Use of force appears to be unrelated to an officer's personal characteristics. Such as age, gender, and ethnicity.
- Use of force is more likely to occur when police are dealing with persons under the influence of alcohol or drugs or with mentally ill individuals.
- A small proportion of officers are disproportionately involved in use of force incidents.

What we do not know:
- The incidence of wrongful use of force by police.
- The impact of differences in police organizations, including administrative policies, hiring, training, disciple, and use of technology on excessive and illegal force.
- Influences of situational characteristics on police use of force and the transactional nature of these events.

The report notes that force appears to be rare; more research is needed on what factors are related to force; we still know little about the transactional nature of the police-citizen encounter, and so on. Unfortunately, this report tends to mirror the previous two rather than breaking much new ground, rehashing the same state of affairs.

Admittedly, several studies highlighted in this latest report aim to improve our understanding of force, but we are still very much in the infancy of really pinpointing, in more precise terms, exactly how and why officers resort to force. Repeated citizen surveys, or analyses of citizen compliant records or use of force reports, simply cannot answer many of the questions that linger. For example, according to the report, previous research findings "...do not address the transactional, or step-by-step unfolding, of police-public encounters. Was suspect resistance the result of police use of force, or did police use force after experiencing suspect resistance?" (ix, 1999). This same conclusion was reached in the original report, which only serves to emphasize just how little we truly understand. We are not going to get any closer to the answer by conducting another survey, by allocating money for another researcher to look at use of force reports, or by doing yet another secondary analyses on citizen complaint data.

It is clear that the unfolding of citizen and police actions within an encounter is recognized as a crucial link to a better understanding, yet researchers continue to rely on means that in no way can disentangle such behaviors adequately. On one hand the research community says it recognizes the need to do so, but on the other it continues to attempt to answer this question using inadequate data and inappropriate methods that simply cannot break down the dynamic process of a police-citizen encounter. With the exception of Sykes and Brent's work of the early 1980s, few researchers have come close to considering the police-citizen encounter as a dynamic process and then breaking that process down into understandable and useful segments. Certainly, Bayley and Garofalo's work makes an effort in this direction, but falls short of providing the level of detail desired.

CHAPTER 3

Operating Perspective and Research Questions

To better understand the application of police force, I begin with three premises. *First, all potential acts of force need to be considered.* The sampling frame applied here was not restricted to only excessive force, or even physical force cases. Rather, all police-suspect encounters are examined.

Second, police force is best understood when conceived and measured along a continuum according to the severity of harm it imposes on citizens. Grouping all force together as if all acts are similar masks important variations. As a result, each instance of force was measured and coded into one of the following categories: commands, threats, pat downs, handcuffing, firm grips, pain compliance techniques, takedown maneuvers, striking with parts of the body, and striking with an external mechanism. Hence, an explicit threat is more forceful than a command; a firm grip is more forceful than a command or threat; a takedown maneuver is more forceful than a command, threat, or firm grip; and striking with an external mechanism is more forceful than a command, threat, physical restraint, or takedown maneuver.[1]

Third, the police-suspect encounter needs to be broken down into behavioral sequences and citizen resistance incorporated into these sequences. An encounter does not occur all at once, but evolves over time. Within each encounter, multiple behaviors, on both the police officer's and citizen's behalf, are possible. An officer may apply force numerous times within an encounter. In addition, as noted above, the type, and thus severity, can also vary with each use of force. Similarly, a citizen may resist, may do so numerous times, and may do so using various types of resistance. Therefore, like police force, citizen resistance is conceived and

29

measured along a continuum according to the severity of defiance presented to the officer. As a result, each instance of resistance was measured and coded into one of the following categories: passive, verbal, defensive, and active. It follows that verbal resistance is more resistant than passive resistance; defensive physical resistance is more resistant than passive or verbal resistance; and, active physical resistance is more resistant than passive, verbal, or defensive resistance.[2]

Examining citizen resistance along with police force is critical to adequately understanding the context in which force is used. Virtually any inquiry concerning how or why officers use force is augmented by the inclusion of citizen resistance. In sum, knowing an officer used force tells us very little without knowing the specific type of force used, how many times it was used, and what the citizen behavior was prior to each use. Within this basic operating structure the following research questions are addressed.

3.1 HOW OFTEN DO OFFICERS USE FORCE?

Based on scientific inquiry over the past thirty years it appears that the use of police force is an infrequent event. Despite this, there is still a substantial amount of variation found from one study to another [as low as one percent (McLaughlin, 1992) and as high as 22 percent (Garner et al., 1995)]. This study provides another examination of the extent of police force. This is particularly important for two additional reasons. First, measuring the extent of police force through observational inquiry offers a rare opportunity for looking at forceful behavior live, as it occurs at the street level. In much the same way that Uniform Crime Data (UCR), self-reports, and victimization surveys each offer a slightly different version of the crime picture, observational studies, use of force reports, citizen complaints, and surveys each offer a different picture of police force. In other words, observational research provides a picture that cannot be obtained by using other methodologies. Second, it has been almost twenty years since the most recent large scale observational study. Fyfe (1996) argues in a recent article that the nature of policing has undergone tremendous change since Reiss began collecting observational data in the

1960s.[3] Thus, a fresh look at the extent of police force is warranted, especially since many departments are in the process of implementing community policing.

3.2 HOW DOES FORCE VARY?

As discussed previously, police use of force has traditionally been measured in a dichotomous manner. Such an approach fails to capture the variation of different forms of police force by not incorporating nonphysical forms of force (e.g., commands, threats) nor distinguishing between varying levels of physical force (e.g., hand restraint, pain compliance, use of chemical agents, striking). As stated by Garner and colleagues, "[m]easures of the simple dichotomy between force and no force (or excessive and reasonable force) neither capture the full range of police or suspect behavior nor recognize the great variety of force-related behavior in law enforcement" (1996: 2). More appropriately, police force can be conceived and measured along a continuum ranging from minimal force to maximum force: from verbal, to physical restraint, to impact methods. With the exception of a few studies (Sykes and Brent, 1980, 1983; Klinger, 1995; Garner et al., 1996), the extent to which police use lower forms of coercion (both verbal and less coercive forms of physical force such as restraint) has not been readily documented.

3.3 HOW IS FORCE APPLIED IN INDIVIDUAL ENCOUNTERS?

The first two questions are broad in scope. They aim to measure the extent of police force and the different types of force used. Conversely, this question is directed at the micro-processes of police force in four ways.

Compared to physical force, we know much less about how often officers apply lower forms of coercive acts, and even less about the interaction between lesser and higher forms of force. There is a big difference between an encounter where the officer does nothing more than throw a citizen to the ground and one in which an officer questions, commands, threatens, and then throws a citizen to the ground. An encounter evolves over time with the potential for several police and citizen actions. Failure to account for varying types of force that occur during an encounter provides neither a complete nor accurate picture of how officers apply their coercive powers.

Second, just as important as examining varying types of force behaviors within individual encounters, detailing combinations of different forms of force within single encounters is also crucial. Klinger (1995) discovered that when higher forms of force are applied, officers tend to use lower forms of force during the encounter as well. By tracking an encounter temporally, one can investigate how often officers use a form of physical force without first using any type of verbal force. Using immediate physical force without any attempt at verbal force should certainly raise concern, especially if citizen resistance is not present.

Third, it is also important to measure how often officers' use of force modulates within individual encounters (e.g., how officers move about the force continuum). How often do officers start low on the force continuum as opposed to high, and visa versa? How often do they move up, down, then back up the continuum? The degree of fluctuation provides for a better sense of how police go about handling encounters with the public. Training protocols on the use of force call for officers to start as low on the continuum as possible and then apply coercive actions according to the dictates of the situation. However, we have very little systematic information on how this is actually accomplished in the everyday world of the patrol officer. Such probing into the dynamics of individual police-citizen encounters is critical to a better understanding of how officers use their coercive powers.

Finally, some believe that an officer must take charge at the outset of an encounter in order to control the situation (e.g., the idea of setting a tone early on) and establish his or her authority. Conversely, exerting too much control at the outset may increase the probability that the encounter will escalate to the point where officers end up having to use even more force. Numerous scholars have hypothesized that officer behaviors early in an encounter can lead to more forceful behaviors later in encounters (Binder and Scharf, 1980; Bayley, 1986; Worden, 1995). According to Worden, "[o]fficers not only respond to situations but also help to create them; sometimes, officers' choices early in police-citizen encounters can contribute to the emergence of circumstances that require the use of force." (1995: 39). The outcome of an encounter may differ depending on how the officer chooses to begin the encounter. Officers who begin encounters with verbal coercion as opposed to a non-coercive tactic may be more likely to have to use some form of force later in the encounter.

3.4 CAUSES OF POLICE FORCE?

The final two questions address the "causes" of force, or what accounts for the way police exercise discretion in use of force decisions? Assuming that police force can and should be measured along a continuum, the determinants of the highest level of force used (as per the force continuum) are examined using the following theoretical framework.

Theoretical Framework
Examining *how* officers use force is a fairly straightforward endeavor. How often do officers use force? What types of force do officers tend to use more than others? How often do officers use multiple forms of force within individual encounters? How does force fluctuate within encounters? These questions are not particularly theoretically oriented. Answers to such questions speak more to a descriptive understanding of the application of force than to a theoretical explanation. However, examining *why* officers resort to force requires more theoretical grounding.

As illustrated in Chapter Two, numerous theoretical orientations have been offered to explain police force. One perspective looks at situational characteristics of the encounter, another focuses on the individual officer, and a third emphasizes organizational features. This leaves future researchers interested in studying police force with two options: use one or more of these perspectives to guide future analyses, or posit new theories. I rely primarily on the former, but also attempt the latter to a limited degree.

Since the examination of police force has traditionally been advanced in terms of situational, psychological, and organizational explanations, the initial inquiry takes this approach. First, it allows the reader to easily grasp the general areas under examination. The audience does not have to search or try to immediately digest a new way of looking at "why" officers use force. Conceptualization of force in terms of "levels" and a "continuum" is sufficiently challenging in its own right. The strength of this research is found in such conceptualization, as opposed to theoretical advancement. It should be made vividly clear that this research is primarily about new ways to *conceive and measure* the application of force as opposed to new ways to *explain* force.

Second, applying these three general areas provides a new opportunity to look at what factors emerge as key determinants. Not since Worden's (1995) analysis of Police Services Study data has such an extensive examination of police force been undertaken. This study allows for a comparison of what factors affect use of force decisions. The objective is not so much to contrast one general area (e.g., situational) against another (e.g., psychological) in an attempt to determine which is a more powerful explanation, but rather to determine which factors *within* each area are found to have an affect on force decisions. For example, citizen race has been found to be a significant factor is some studies (Cohen and Chaiken, 1972), but not others (Friedrich, 1977; Croft, 1985; Worden, 1995). Similarly, officer experience has generally been posited to affect use of force decisions, yet it has not emerged in prior studies as a significant factor. Does this still hold today, at least within the two departments observed in this study? The only way to know is to test it. In effect, a holistic approach is applied in reference to asking "why" do officers use force, much like Friedrich did with the Reiss/Black data of the 1960s and much like Worden did with the Police Services Study of the 1970s. This is an opportunity to apply the same approach with data collected some 20 years later in the context of two different departments.

Having made the argument that it is advantageous to look at possible explanations of force in such a broad and encompassing manner, it must also be recognized that this approach is somewhat generic and to some extent limiting. First, it may be considered a "kitchen sink" approach whereby a multitude of various possible explanations are posited, mixed all together, and thrown into a model. The result can be a lack of theoretical direction. Second, looking at the same three general areas of explanation and various factors within each presupposes that each operates in isolation of one another, which does little to advance theoretical development beyond its current state. In a sense, continuing to rely or fall back on situational, psychological, and organizational explanations of police use of force fails to recognize how various factors interact with one another. So while it is important, and even beneficial, to organize the determinants of police force within these areas, there is also the need to stretch the boundaries somewhat by looking across areas as well to see how they interact. Individual views toward legal guidelines within the context of varying organizational contexts is emphasized here, although one could test a number of different relationships with these data. In the following paragraphs, the three general areas of theoretical explanation are briefly reviewed. This is followed by a brief synopsis of how officer views toward legal guidelines may be interwoven within different organizational influences.

Situational

Worden (1995) found that situational factors offered the most explanatory power in determining use of force decisions. In summarizing his findings, he notes that it is not surprising that officers are more likely to use force on resistant citizens. In other words, intuitively one would expect that police resort to force when faced with resistance. In use of force language, citizen resistance is comparable to evidence in arrest decisions. Both are a legal justification for subsequent police action. Before publication of the American Bar Foundation (ABF) study in the 1950s, common wisdom dictated that officers made an arrest when evidence of a crime was present. After this study was released there was an explosion in research examining how extra-legal factors influence the decision to arrest. Research on the use of force must also make a distinction between legal and extra-legal determinants. However, researchers have not adequately accounted for legal factors in use of force inquires, mainly citizen resistance. Therefore, to understand the role that extra-legal factors play in use of force decisions, more precise measures of legal factors must be incorporated. Although I commence with a focus on legal justifications for using force (e.g., citizen resistance, officer safety, citizen safety, arrest) it should be understood that my primary focus is on the role that extra-legal factors play. I begin by emphasizing the legal justifications for using force solely as a means (as control) to ensure or bolster confidence in potential subsequent findings of extra-legal factors.

First, how do sociological or situational factors influence officer behavior to use force? Upon closer examination, there are actually two separate explanations within this perspective. Black (1976) posits that the application of law can be explained in terms of social space or distance. That is, officers will be more coercive toward minorities, lower class citizens, and juveniles. The principal prediction is that force varies by "who" the citizen is.

Others (Sykes and Brent, 1980; 1983), have taken an interactionist approach and posit that it is not who the citizen is that matters, but "what the citizen does." This can be broken down into yet another dimension according to legal and extra-legal determinants - for example, using force in response to citizen resistance as opposed to using force to punish a citizen because he or she fails to show deference to police authority. The distinction between who a citizen is as opposed to what a citizen does in terms of police forceful behavior should not be understated. Legally, officers are expected and required to respond to citizen "actions" rather than "traits." Even further, they are required to respond to legal behaviors (e.g., resistance) as opposed to extra-legal behaviors (e.g, disrespect).

Justification for the use of force is most notably found when citizens are resistant, when there is a threat to citizen or officer safety, and in the course of making an arrest. Each of these determinants are tested and are expected to be highly significant. In addition, a number of other citizen behavioral manifestations (e.g., intoxication, mental impairment, emotional distress, disrespect) as well as characteristics (e.g., race, age, class, gender) are tested to determine which play a role. The purpose is to determine which factors within this area of explanation influence police force, rather than comparing these factors against psychological or organizational determinants.

Individual

A second perspective, individual explanations, can also be broken down into two areas: one based on officer attitudes and another on officer characteristics and background experiences. The first of these, social psychological theory, is based on officer attitudes and views. In the context of police force, such a theory presumes that officers with certain views will behave differently than those with dissimilar views. Within this framework, three different outlooks are tested - one based on an internal projection and the other two on external projections. The first looks at how the officer views *oneself* (e.g., role). A second examines how the officer views the *citizenry*. And a third analyzes how the officer views the *law*. Each are laid out in further detail.

First, how one views their role is arguably a potentially strong determinant for how we behave. A factory floor machinist who views preventive maintenance as more important than corrective maintenance is probably going to utilize scanning probes more often than rectification devices. Similarly, a cop who views law enforcement as his primary responsibility as opposed to service-oriented activities is probably going to resort to force more readily rather than relying on other means to resolve an incident. As part of the officer survey, officers were asked how strongly they believed enforcing the law was their top priority. It is hypothesized that officers with an enforcement orientation will be more coercive than those who do not.

Second, officer behavior may be modified not only by how he or she views one-self, but in how he or she view the citizenry. Muir's theory on police behavior and the use of force provides guidance in this area. Muir (1977) posited that officers differ in their view toward the application of force in terms of their ability to reconcile the need to use force as well as their ability to understand the nature of human suffering. According to Muir, a "good" officer is one who is able to do both. Officers must be comfortable with the fact that force is sometimes required to accomplish a desired, and preferably just, outcome. This may be in the form of breaking up a fight and subduing a suspect. It may be in the form of taking someone into custody to make an arrest. Ultimately, there are times when force is called for and an officer has to be comfortable with using force in such situations. Second, an officer needs to empathize with the citizen he or she is dealing with. A good officer has the ability to place him or herself in the role of the citizen. The ability to recognize the many differing factors surrounding the citizens' situation.

A full scale test of Muir's theory is beyond the data capabilities of this study. However, one measure from the officer survey is used as a proxy for capturing one of the two components Muir refers to: the ability to understand human suffering or empathize with citizens. Officers were asked how "trustworthy" citizens are. While this falls short of directly capturing the outlook Muir tries to explicate, it does provide some indirect insight on officers' view toward the citizenry. As such, officers who view citizens negatively (e.g., being distrustful) are hypothesized to be more likely to use force than those who view the citizenry in a positive light. Entering situations with the preconceived notion that citizens are untrustworthy may prompt such officers to be more coercive than if they begin with the assumption that citizens are trustworthy.

The third hypothesis involves officer attitudes toward the law. It is presumed that one's view toward the law and its constraints would have an affect on how willing one is to adhere to it. If one believes the law is legitimate, it is reasonable to believe that one would be more likely to abide by it as opposed to those who do not. Officers were questioned about the importance of legal guidelines and whether they overlook such guidelines in the course of their duties. Officers viewing the law as a hindrance and stating that they overlook such guidelines were hypothesized to be more coercive than those who do not.

Besides the psychological dimensions of officer beliefs and behavior, others have emphasized officer characteristics and background experiences (Fyfe, 1988; Worden, 1995). For example, Fyfe (1988) has hypothesized that officer training can influence officer behavior. Officers with training in verbal tactics to defuse situations, for instance, may be less coercive than their counterparts who have received less or no training. Similarly, experienced officers or those with higher educational levels are hypothesized to be less coercive. Many police departments have implemented educational requirements as a condition of employment. The belief is that education matters. While it is rare that such policies explicitly state that educated officers are deemed better equipped to handle contentious situations in a less forceful manner, it is certainly reasonable to assume that this is one area of behavior subsumed within this line of reasoning.

Again, the intent of testing these various individual hypotheses is to determine which of these play a role in officer behavior, not in whether individual explanations explain more than situational or organizational explanations. Is force a function of who the officer is, in terms of views and beliefs (e.g., role perception, attitude toward the citizenry, view toward legal constraints) or is it more a function of his characteristics and experiences (e.g., training, education, experience)?

Organizational

Various organizational influences may impact use of force decision making. Four specific types are emphasized. The first of these emphasizes the formal aspect of the organization at the department level. According to Wilson's theory, officers working in a department that stresses aggressive police tactics should resort to force more often and with greater severity than those working in a department that is service-oriented. Indianapolis and St. Petersburg serve as useful departments to test such a theory. Indianapolis policy was designed around an aggressive get tough approach, while St. Petersburg adopted more of a problem-solving model.[4] Relying on Wilson's theory, it is predicted that Indianapolis officers will be more coercive than St. Petersburg officers.

While Indianapolis officers may rely on force more often than St. Petersburg officers, it is also plausible to presume that officer behavior may be less a function of what is being promulgated at the department level and more a function of immediate supervision. That is, an officers' first-line supervisor may have more of an affect on a subordinate's behavior than what is being stressed at the top of the organization. Line-level officers are often far removed from the policies and emphasis coming from the top of the organization. As part of the officer survey, officers were asked how often first-line supervisors criticize or attempt to modify their actions. This item is used as a proxy to gauge how free officers feel to go about their duties, one of which is to use force. It is posited that the less constraint the officer feels, the more inclined he or she may be to use force. Ideally, a measure asking how often supervisors monitor and review use of force cases would be available, but this item was not included in the survey.

Department and first-line supervision are formal aspects of control. Others (Brown, 1981; Manning, 1989) have emphasized the informal aspects of organizations such as the work group. Perhaps force is influenced more by how officers perceive the attitudes of fellow officers as opposed to what is being emphasized by management. In effect, officers may be guided more by peer influence rather than by managerial influence. Officers working with other officers who view legal guidelines as a constraint that should be disregarded may be more forceful than those working with officers they perceive as falling in line with legal guidelines. Officers may feel either less pressure to conform to such guidelines if they believe their fellow officers disregard these guidelines, or may even feel some pressure to abandon guidelines if they feel their partners are doing so. If the perception is that many of an officer's peers are failing to adhere to legal guidelines, then the need to refrain from using force may be less of a concern than if he or she worked with a group that was more tightly bound by such constraints.

Finally, a contemporary adaptation of organizational impact, in the context of community policing, may involve the role in which organizations place officers. Officers who function as community policing officers may be expected to be less coercive than those with traditional call-oriented 911 assignments. After all, 911 officers by the very nature of their job are oriented more toward law enforcement duties as opposed to community policing officers who are primarily service-oriented.

Hybrid
The impact of force decisions may be better determined by looking across levels of explanation. In other words, officers with certain proclivities may be more inclined to act on these when placed in a context that promotes such behavior. For instance, Mastrofski and Ritti (1996), in examining the influence of police training on DUI enforcement practices, found that the effects of training are contingent on organizational context. Similar interactive effects may be present concerning police use of force behavior.[5] Three particular interactions are tested here, each involving officer perceptions concerning the importance of legal guidelines. Officer

views toward legal guidelines are combined with each of the first three organizational influences posited earlier. It is hypothesized that Indianapolis officers with a proclivity to overlook legal guidelines will be more coercive than their St. Petersburg counterparts. Similarly, it is hypothesized that officers with a proclivity to overlook legal guidelines who work for a supervisor that rarely intervenes or attempts to modify their behavior will be more coercive than those who work for a first-line supervisor that more closely monitors officer behavior. Third, it is posited that officers with a proclivity to overlook legal guidelines and work with a group of officers with the same beliefs will be more coercive. Each assumes that officers with an inclination toward viewing legal guidelines negatively may be further influenced by the organizational context in which they find themselves, which may more readily permit them to resort to forceful ways.[6] Each of the hypotheses outlined in this section are explicitly stated in the following section.

Hypotheses [7]

In accordance with the theoretical framework outlined above, the following hypotheses are tested:

Citizen
Officers are more coercive toward:
- male citizens
- nonwhite citizens
- younger citizens
- poorer citizens
- citizens displaying signs of anger or fear
- citizens displaying signs of alcohol or drug use
- citizens displaying signs of mental impairment
- citizens displaying disrespectful behavior

Officer

Officers who are more coercive are:
- male
- white
- less experienced
- less educated

Officers who are more coercive:
- have less training in verbal mediation
- view their role as one of crime fighter
- view the citizenry as distrustful
- believe overlooking legal guidelines is necessary to do their job

Organizational
- Indianapolis officers (law enforcement-oriented) are more coercive than St. Petersburg officers (service-oriented)
- Officers who work for a supervisor who is supportive of their decisions are more coercive
- Officers who work with peers (work unit) who believe overlooking legal guidelines is necessary to do their job are more coercive
- 911 officers are more coercive than community policing officers

Hybrid
- Officers who believe overlooking legal guidelines is necessary to do their job and who work for Indianapolis are more coercive
- Officers who believe overlooking legal guidelines is necessary to do their job and work for a supervisor who is usually supportive of their decisions are more coercive.
- Officers who believe overlooking legal guidelines is necessary to do their job and work in a unit whose members also believe overlooking legal guidelines is necessary to do their job are more coercive.

3.5 WHAT FACTORS ACCOUNT FOR HOW OFFICERS MOVE ABOUT THE FORCE CONTINUUM?

Another way to examine how officers apply a continuum of force in relation to the level of citizen resistance is to code the occurrences of each instance of force and resistance within single encounters, and then to determine whether the officer: a) refrained from moving up the continuum despite resistance, b) moved up and down the continuum incrementally based on resistance, c) or applied higher forms of force given the level of resistance. Doing so, requires establishing criteria for what constitutes the level of corresponding force for each coding category. The objective is to develop an analytic scheme that allows one to examine police-citizen encounters and determine if the officer applied or followed along the force continuum based on the level of resistance he or she faced. This scheme, the Resistance Force Comparative Scale (RFCS), is presented in the following chapter. Such an approach determines what factors (drawn from the same theoretical orientation used in the prior research question) are associated with those instances when officers either follow or do not follow along the force continuum.

CHAPTER 4
Methodology

Data for this study were drawn from the Project on Policing Neighborhoods (POPN). The intent of the POPN was to provide a comprehensive picture of everyday policing in the 1990s by studying police-citizen street-level behavior through systematic social observation.[1] The POPN was a follow-up to the Police Services Study (PSS) of the 1970s and the Black-Reiss observational study of the 1960s.[2] Indianapolis, Indiana and St. Petersburg, Florida served as the two research sites. Indianapolis field work was conducted in 1996, and St. Petersburg field work was conducted in 1997.

4.1 CITIES AND DEPARTMENTS

Indianapolis and St. Petersburg were selected as study sites because both were engaged in implementing community policing, both were diverse in social, economic, and demographic terms, and both were receptive to hosting a large research project for approximately one year each. Table 4-1 shows some of the features of each community and police department.

Both cities had similar forms of government, a strong-mayor system. Indianapolis was the larger of the two cities, but also experienced greater levels of social and economic distress (e.g., % minority, % unemployed, % poverty, % female-headed households). Both had a similar level of crime, although St. Petersburg had a greater per-officer crime workload. Minority representation was similar across the two departments while Indianapolis had a greater percentage of female and college educated officers.

Table 4-1: Characteristics of Indianapolis and St. Petersburg

	Indy	St. Pete
Pop. of service area (1995 estimated)	377,723	240,318
% of pop. minority (1990)	39	24
% of pop. unemployed (1990)	8	5
% of pop. 50% below poverty (1990)	9	6
% of female-headed house (1990)	17	10
UCR Index/1,000 residents (1996)	100	99
UCR Index crime rate/officer (1996)	37	47
Form of city government	Strong mayor	Strong mayor
# of full-time sworn officers (1996)	1,013	505
# of full-time sworn officers in patrol (1996/1997)	416	246
% of patrol officers who are minority (1996/1997)	21	22
% of patrol officers who are female (1996/1997)	17	13
% of patrol officers with 4-year college degrees (1996/1997)	36	26
# recruit training hours (1993)	1,392	1,280
Year community policing initiated	1992	1990
# community policing specialists	25	60
# patrol districts/beats	4/50	3/48

Many features were similar across the two departments including attempts to civilianize numerous positions, upgrading technological capabilities, an emphasis on attending community meetings, and soliciting consumer input through citizen surveys. Both also decentralized operations. Indianapolis had four districts physically scattered throughout the city. St. Petersburg had three separate districts, each contained within the same physical location.[3]

Improving community relations was listed as a top priority in both cities. Chiefs in both cities had a strong community policing background. In Indianapolis, Donald Christ was heralded for instituting a successful community policing program while deputy chief of the south district prior to becoming chief. In St. Petersburg, Darrel Stephens had received national recognition for his community policing work in Newport News, Virginia and as director of the Police Executive Research Forum (PERF). Stephens' replacement, Goliath Davis, was a lifelong resident of the city and longtime advocate of improving police-citizen relations.[4]

Officials in each city had a slightly different vision of how to go about carrying out community policing. Indianapolis officials emphasized a "get tough" approach. Under Christ's tenure as chief, the organizational philosophy on community policing became more defined and was broadly characterized by two mandates: first, give broad decision making power to individual districts. Second, emphasize staying "tough" on crime. According to departmental leadership, community policing must involve directed and aggressive patrol as well as the more common "soft" elements (e.g., greeting and meeting).

About a half year prior to field work, Indianapolis implemented a program called "safe streets" that highlighted the aggressive enforcement side of community policing. Safe streets was "launched as an enforcement program designed to get officers involved in stopping crime in targeted areas by an increased uniform presence" (Indianapolis Police Department Interdepartmental Memo, 1995). The goal was to "begin a more aggressive approach to community policing" (Indianapolis Police Department Interdepartmental Memo, 1995). Two high crime neighborhoods in each district were selected for this intensive enforcement operation. For a five week period these eight beats received 24-hour attention by officers assigned to the beats during non-normal working hours. The officers working these beats were paid with overtime money and were not subject to having to answer any dispatched calls for service. The regularly assigned on-duty patrol officers to these beats handled all calls for service. After this initial five week period, each district chief was given control and responsibility for molding and shaping the safe streets program to fit the needs of the district.

Indianapolis also committed less resources to community policing. As seen in Table 4-1, although there were 416 sworn officers assigned to the patrol division only 25 were community policing officers. In contrast, St. Petersburg had 246 sworn personnel assigned to patrol duties, 60 of which were community policing officers.[5] Indianapolis assigned its 25 officers to three of the four districts. These officers worked in teams. How the teams operated depended on the district. In one district they operated much like a street-level narcotics unit. In another, officers focused mainly on community relations (e.g, stopping in businesses, talking with residents, etc.). In the third, officers took more of a problem-solving approach, consistent with that prescribed by Goldstein (1980).

Rather than working with other community policing officers in teams, St. Petersburg deployed its community policing officers throughout the city under an approach termed geographic deployment.[6] The overarching concept of geographic deployment was perceived by police administrators as a fundamental change in how officers were assigned, as well as supervised, to provide service delivery to citizens. Under the old system, officers were time based (e.g., shift) as opposed to geographically based. Their focus was bound by what occurred on their shift. They worked with fellow officers on the same shift handling problems in their area of responsibility. Geographic deployment sought to make geographic responsibility the main ingredient of service delivery. Under this system, officers were encouraged to look at the problems that occur in their community policing area beyond one's shift. The community policing officer in each community policing area served as a facilitator with other members of the team.[7] Community policing officers were encouraged to work with patrol officers across all three shifts to combat problems in that area. Although patrol officers were still time bound by a specific shift, the intent was for them to work more with fellow team members on recurring problems in the community policing area rather than other patrol officers assigned on the same shift throughout the district.

Finally, the issue of race and police force is particularly relevant in the context of this research. About a year prior to field work each city experienced a civil disturbance as the result of perceived excessive force incidents. In Indianapolis, a small disturbance (contained to a few block faces) occurred when a few dozen people descended upon the north district police station to complain of excessive force and racial slurs used in the arrest of an African-American male a day earlier. When the crowd did not get the attention it thought it should have by district officials, one member of the crowd threw a rock through a police vehicle window and a disturbance ensued. There were few injuries and the department quickly quelled the violence within a few hours.

In St. Petersburg, a disturbance occurred after a white officer shot and killed an African-American male during a traffic stop. When the officer approached the driver of the vehicle the suspect would not respond to his commands. The officer subsequently positioned himself in front of the vehicle and instructed the suspect to exit the vehicle. Accounts of what occurred next are conflicting, but the officer ended up drawing his weapon and firing into the vehicle three times, striking and killing the suspect, which resulted in a subsequent disturbance. Although most of the disturbances were contained within one district and subsided by the next morning, sporadic episodes of violence occurred for the next three days.

4.2 DESIGN AND METHOD

A cross-sectional design with two methods of data collection: *field observation* and *interviews* are used here. Although experimental and quasi-experimental designs are often the preferred method for uncovering causation, they are mainly the result of built-in control the researcher enjoys from the outset, and such designs are not always possible (Cook and Campbell, 1979; Babbie, 1995). As noted above, the data used here have been collected cross-sectionally as part of a larger study. This left no choice in design considerations.

According to Babbie, the primary strength of observational study "lies in the depth of understanding it may permit" (1995: 300). This is particularly evident for the purpose of examining the interactional nature of police-citizen encounters. Further, field observation allows for "a direct, detailed account of what happens on patrol by someone whose sole job is to provide a *disinterested* account. Such detail, thoroughness, and accuracy are not available through popular social science methods of surveys (of the police or public) and official records" (Mastrofski et al., 1995: 20).

The other data collection method, survey research, is one of the most popular data collection methods used in social science. This method is particularly suited for studying individuals' perceptions and attitudes. Thus, officer interviews provide measures that capture several of the concepts under study.

Observations

The mode of observation used is best classified as observer-participant. According to Babbie, "[t]he observer-participant is one who identifies him or herself as a researcher and interacts with the participants in the social process but makes no pretense of actually being a participant" (1995: 284). Prior to beginning field work, a team of observers (field researchers) underwent an intensive four month training program that consisted of how to conduct their observations as observer-participants. Observers also completed on-site training rides before beginning actual rides.

Field researchers accompanied patrol officers throughout a matched sample of work shifts in each of the selected beats of a city (shift and beat selection described below). While on patrol, observers took brief field notes describing when various activities and encounters with the public occurred, who was involved, and what happened.[8] According to POPN protocol, an *encounter* involved a face-to-face communication between officers and citizens that took over one minute, involved more than three verbal exchanges between officer and citizen, or involved significant physical contact between the officer and citizen. The day following the ridealong, observers transcribed their field notes into detailed narrative accounts and coded them according to a pre-defined protocol.

Beat Selection

In Indianapolis, 12 of the city's 50 patrol beats were selected for observation. Similarly, 12 of 48 patrol beats were selected in St. Petersburg. Beat selection was biased toward beats where POPN researchers expected to observe higher levels of police activity than the average in the city: areas that had higher levels of social and economic distress than characteristic of the entire city. This bias was intentional. Project directors wished to observe large numbers of encounters between police and citizens. The bias is consistent with neighborhood selection in the earlier Police Services Study (1977) and by Reiss (1966). This explicit selection bias means that findings from Indianapolis and St. Petersburg are not intended, nor likely, to be typical of what occurs in all parts of these cities or of activity by all of their patrol officers. However, because the two samples of beats selected were similar in the two sites, it is possible to make cross-department comparisons within the range of beats selected – that is, among those areas with higher social and economic distress.

Beats were selected in clusters defined by socioeconomic conditions. The socioeconomic conditions used to cluster neighborhoods were: percent of families with children that are headed by a female, percent of the adult population that is unemployed, and percent of the population that is below 50 percent of the poverty level. An index of socioeconomic distress was constructed by adding together scores on each of the three variables. The index ranged in Indianapolis patrol beats from a low of 4 to a high of 76, with a median of 36. In St. Petersburg the index ranged from 4 to 103, with a median of 15. Study beats were selected in clusters in the second, third, and fourth quartiles of the Indianapolis distribution, maximizing variation possible across Indianapolis districts in each cluster.[9] St. Petersburg beats were selected to match those chosen in Indianapolis, and were also distributed across St. Petersburg's districts.[10]

Ride Sampling

In Indianapolis 194 different patrol officers and 48 different supervisors were observed covering almost 2,800 hours of observations and consisting of 6,485 police-citizen interactions. In St. Petersburg, 128 different patrol officers and 37 supervisors were observed, covering almost 2,900 hours of observation and consisting of 5,500 police-citizen interactions.[11] Both general patrol officers and community policing officers were observed in rough proportion to their representation in the personnel allocation to the study beats. In total, 336 and 360 shifts were observed in study beats in Indianapolis and St. Petersburg respectively.

The goal was to reach a quota sample that: (1) covered all work shifts for each beat, (2) included the diversity of patrol units that worked the study beats and larger areas that covered those beats, and (3) included both slow and busy days of the week. The study did not seek a strictly representative sample of patrol shifts because it needed a sufficient number of observations of certain patrol units and encounters with the public (more likely to occur during some shifts). Consequently, busy days (Thursday through Saturday) were oversampled, as were shifts and units where problem-oriented activity was more likely.

Field researchers were instructed to ride with the officer assigned to a study beat on a given shift. Because some officers in some districts cover zones that include other beats in addition to the study beat, some rides were conducted with these officers too. If no officer was assigned to a study beat on a given ride, then the observer was assigned to ride with the officer responsible for covering that beat or the officer whom the supervisor considered most likely to receive assignments in that beat.

Sometimes field observers switched from one officer to another during an observation session. This occurred if the original officer checked off work early (for personal time off) or was engaged in an assignment to court or some other administrative duty that had no direct bearing on service to the assigned beat (e.g., training) and that was scheduled to take more than two hours. If the originally assigned officer resumed patrol in the study beat later during that shift, the field researcher switched back to the originally assigned officer. If an assigned officer ended the shift with less than two hours remaining, the field researcher ended observation also. Shift supervisors were instructed not to alter officer assignments to beats due to the presence of a field researcher. A careful check of supervisor assignment practices was conducted to ensure officer assignments were not being artificially changed as a result of the observer's presence.

Sampling Frame

The project was designed to collect information on a wide array of police topics. However, the subject here concerns police use of force only. Therefore, cases for study were narrowed from the total number of police-citizen interactions to those that offer the greatest potential for use of force. Previous observational studies on use of force have most often narrowed the pool of cases to those most relevant to the use of force. Bayley and Garofalo (1989) referred to such cases as "potentially violent mobilizations." These involved disputes, interventions by the police to apply the law against specific individuals, and attempts to question suspicious persons. Fyfe (1988) identified such cases as "potentially violent situations," which included routine traffic stops, high-risk traffic stops, crimes in progress, and disputes. Reiss (1968) and Worden (1995) classified potential force instances somewhat differently. They defined such cases as any that involved a suspect. This study follows their lead by examining all cases that involve suspected offenders. In addition, citizens classified as disputants were also included. POPN protocol called for each citizen involved in a police-citizen encounter to be classified according the their role (e.g., suspect, victim, witness, etc.). Citizens were classified as disputants when it was unclear to the observer whether the citizen was a suspect, victim, or both. Thus, erring on the side of inclusiveness, disputants are also included. In total, 3544 suspect-disputant encounters were observed, 1,994 in Indianapolis and 1,550 in St. Petersburg.

Interviews

In addition to observation of patrol officers and their supervisors, in-person structured interviews with officers and supervisors assigned patrol duties were completed in each city. Survey items included questions pertaining to officers' views, perceptions, and experiences on the beats they served, the work of police, the department, and community policing. In Indianapolis, interviews were completed with 398 officers (over 95% of all patrol officers) and with 69 of 74 patrol supervisors. In St. Petersburg, 240 patrol officer interviews were completed (over 97% of all patrol officers) and with all patrol supervisors. Researchers administering these interviews were hired and trained for this sole purpose. Interviews were conducted in a private room and took approximately 25 minutes each.

4.3 VALIDITY, RELIABILITY, AND GENERALIZABILITY

Project managers took several steps to manage issues of validity and reliability.[12] I went to each site five months prior to the beginning of data collection to prepare managers and officers for the upcoming study. I conducted numerous rides with officers to get them acclimated to the project. Observers underwent intensive training before collecting data on site. This included at least five practice observation sessions during training at the home university and one or two orientation rides on site.

Validity

In comparison to alternative methods, field research ranks favorably in regard to validity. Field research is rarely superficial. It offers the ability to tap into measures difficult to gather through official records, survey, or experimental research. Uncovering the patterns of police force and citizen resistance within individual encounters, for instance, is extremely difficult when using official records. Having an observer witness potential force situations first-hand is critical to fully understanding the context in which force is or is not used. Officer use of force reports and citizen reports of alleged police force are important indicators, but in both instances the party responsible for detailing the circumstances has a stake in the reporting. Field research relies on a disinterested third-party, specifically trained to be removed from the target of observation. Nonetheless, there are several validity concerns.

One concern using POPN data is that it was not specifically designed to study use of force. Second, one must be fully cognizant of the degree of subjectivity inherent in the coding of narrative reports. While all of the relevant behaviors under study are defined and listed at the outset, *a certain degree of interpretation is still required.* Although first-hand reports are used, these come in the form of written accounts. The written accounts were the basis from which descriptive variables were coded. On rare occasions researchers did not make clear the exact sequence of behaviors. Further, it is also sometimes difficult to discern certain actions (e.g., whether the instruction by an officer is actually a command or request). As a result, it is certainly possible, and almost definite, that another person reading the narrative accounts would come up with instances where my coding and their coding do not match. This is simply unavoidable.

Finally, reactivity to the presence of observers is a concern. To decrease reactivity, field researchers were trained in ways to make officers as comfortable as possible with their presence. Officers were allowed to examine observer field notes if they so desired. Researchers guaranteed that officers' identity would be protected.[13] Only about one half of one percent of the officers' encounters with the public did observers detect evidence suggesting that officers had changed their behavior due to the researcher's presence. Further, observers characteristically reported cordial relations with officers during ridealongs. Observers reported that only 12 percent of their observation sessions began with the officer having a negative attitude about the observer's presence, and this dropped to only two percent of the officers demonstrating that view by the end of the observation session. Finally, field observers noted many instances of police behavior that could have been cause for disciplinary action, a phenomenon noted in previous field studies of patrol officers (Reiss 1971). If officers had altered their behavior in response to being observed, they would not have taken these actions. The following passages require no additional commentary:[14]

Encounter 1 (peeping Tom)
O1 arrived at the scene. This was a trailer park, the home of lower class blacks. The trailer park, however, had few trailers. Most of the dwellings were small, one-room, shacks rented on a weekly basis. Since the call had been placed from a pay phone in front of the complex's laundry facility, O1 and O2 went there first. In front of the phone, O1 and O2 met a 29 year old black male, lower class based on lack of a home phone, extensive criminal record, and unemployment.

O1 asked C1 what the problem was. C1 said that his neighbor was peeking through his bedroom window and that this had been going on for several days. C1 added that he had asked the man to stop it but he was not able to understand, due to being high on crack cocaine. O1 asked C1 where the neighbor was now. C1 said that he should be sitting on his front porch. So O1, O2, and

C1 walked over to speak with the suspect. Once there, we saw a 40 year old black male, sitting on the steps to a small trailer, rocking back and forth with blood-shot eyes. C2, the 40 year old black man, was lower class based on a crack cocaine addiction, residence in a run-down trailer, extensive criminal record, and worn out clothing.

C2 was clutching a baseball bat in one hand and a broken fishing pole in the other hand. Once C2 saw us he stood up and brandished the bat, threatening to hit one of the officers (and perhaps my self as well). O2 yelled for him to put down the bat, but C2 refused. C2 said that he was going to hit one of us on the head, although it was not clear which one of his he intended to hit. O2 pulled out his mace, preparing to spray C2.

However, C2 dropped the bat and approached us. O1 asked C2 what the problem was. C2 moved very close to me and hit his open hand with a clenched fist. C2 accused C1 of being a pimp. C2 believed that C1 had his prostitute's underneath his trailer late at night. C2 claimed that he could hear their moans, as they (allegedly) had sexual intercourse.

O1 shown his flash light around C2's trailer and noticed that it was surrounded by boards, all the way around. O1 commented that there was no room even for a mouse to get underneath the trailer. C2 cursed at this and replied that "[he] could hear them fuckin all night long."

C1 then broke in and said that this had nothing to do with why he had called the police. C1 wanted O1 to deal with his allegations that C2 was peeping through his window late at night. O1 asked C2 if he had been doing that and C2 denied it. C1 accused C2 of lying to the police.

O1 and O2 then spoke together privately and came to a decision. O1 told the two men that they were going to leave. O1 added that if the two men did not stay away from each other, they both would be arrested. C1 replied that they both were on parole and that would mean long prison sentences. O1 told them that "this was all the more reason they should leave each other alone." As the officers were leaving, C1 told them that as soon as they left, he would "beat the shit out of C2." C1 said that he was sure that C2 would come after him again with the baseball bat and that he had a right to defend himself. O2 agreed that C1 had a right to defend himself.

At this point, both officers left the scene, but did not leave the trailer park. O1 and O2 hid behind one of the trailers, waiting for the two men to fight each other. O2 told me how he planned to solve the situation. O2 said that as soon as they started fighting, he would break up the fight and spay them both with mace. O2 said that they (including O1) would give each of the men a long burst of mace directly in the eyes.

O1 and O2 removed their mace cans and stood by, waiting for a fight to develop. After about ten minutes, it appeared that the fight was about to begin. O1 and O2 approached the men, but C2 quickly backed down and went inside his trailer. O2 yelled in that if he came out again, he would not like what would happen. O2 then picked up the baseball bat and threw it about 200 feet away from the home of C2. O1 and O2 then left the scene for good.

Debriefing O1. O1 said that the problem they faced in this encounter is that they did not have enough evidence to arrest either one of the men until a fight developed. They could not leave the scene, because this might result in the fatal injury of one of both of the men. O1 felt that if the men had "been maced," this would have taken the fight out of them. *I asked O1 if he would have arrested the men after macing them. O1 said that he probably would have arrested them at that point.*

Encounter 2 (suspect who has fled from police and was caught by the county sheriff)
O1 exits his car and runs toward C1 (B/M, 20, middle class) who is lying on the ground and is handcuffed by the county sheriff. *Asshole, O1 yells at C1, and kicks C1 once on his left side body.* At the same time, O2 (W/M, 26) is helping the other county sheriff to control the second suspect. O1 runs to the second suspect and the county sheriff tells O1 that the suspect's car hit the other car and asks O1 to check out the situation of the second car. O1 agrees.

Encounter 3 (dispatch trouble with a person)
En route to drug store for trouble with a person. When we arrived, O2 and O3 were talking to C1, a low-income b/m, age 30, who was standing on the sidewalk. O3 informed O1 that C1 had been placed on the trespass list the previous night for making threats to the manager. *O1 grabbed C1, who was very drunk, and slammed him into the wall, face first. C1 tried to turn around and O2 again slammed him into the wall and held him while O1 handcuffed him.* O3 said he would do the report since he had done the trespass order.

Encounter 4 (police custody)
O1 arrives at the main entrance to the projects. There are about 20 officers, 2 Lt, 1 Sgt, 2 officers from another dept, a Detective, and the wagon there. O1 walks into the mass off officers. *There are eight BM's handcuffed and sitting on the ground. O2 (WF 26) was walking up to each BM handcuffed and spraying them in the face with mace.* There were black people everywhere surrounding the circle of police.

Reliability

While field research scores high on validity, it often suffers in terms of reliability. The primary threat is reliability of observers' recorded observations. To ensure coding reliability, reliability checks where completed prior to going into the field as well as during the data collection phase. Observers were provided with detailed instructions on what and how to record observations. Additionally, three quality control persons were assigned to specifically guide field researchers and review their work.

Generalizability

According to Babbie, "[o]ne of the chief goals of science is generalization" (1995: 302). Clearly, findings produced from this study are most valuable if they are generalizable to other departments and the officers in those departments. To some extent generalizability is limited in this study. As a result of the beat selection there is a limitation on the degree of generalizability to both officers working non-study beats and officers in other departments. This is not to say that there is no generalizability, however. In particular, the benefits of this research, in respect to generalizability, can be seen in two ways.

First, both departments are of mid-size. A great deal of past research has focused on large departments, or what the Police Foundation has called the "Big Six" (New York, Los Angeles, Chicago, Houston, Philadelphia, and Detroit) (Walker, 1992: 42). The New York City Police Department, for example, has nearly 40,000 police officers and a maze of bureaucratic structures. Moreover, the sheer size and diversity of the city makes it not comparable to virtually any other city in the country. In short, research findings from such a large city makes generalizing extremely difficult. By contrast, there are more cities across the nation similar in many respects to Indianapolis and St. Petersburg than there are to the big six.

Second, as are many mid-size departments, both cities were in the process of implementing community policing, but in different ways. Indianapolis focused on a get tough approach, while St. Petersburg emphasized a problem-solving approach. How and why force is used in the context of these differing styles can be illustrative to other mid-size departments either implementing or considering an approach to implement community policing.

4.4 DATA CONSTRUCTION

The database developed for this research is an adaptation of the original POPN observational database. Many of the items used here were taken directly from this original database (e.g., citizen gender, age, wealth, race, number of bystanders on scene, number of officers on scene, etc.). Others were taken from the interview data (e.g., officer training, view toward crimefighting, years on the job, etc.) and merged with the observational data at the citizen level. The remaining variables were coded directly from the narrative reports. Each of the 3,544 encounters were read and sequenced out (e.g., placed in a time-ordered manner to identify what actions occurred prior to others) to identify citizen resistance and police force.[15] In addition to sequencing instances of citizen resistance and police force, several other variables were also sequenced. These include: arrest, disrespect, officer safety, and citizen safety. This was done to determine "when" during the course of an encounter these particular actions took place. It is important, for instance, to know whether there was an officer safety issue (e.g., a gun present) prior to the use of force or after. These variables were then added to the final database, which was used in this research.

4.5 VARIABLE DESCRIPTION

Force
Force is defined as acts that threaten or inflict physical harm on citizens. Police attempts to question, advise, persuade, or suggest did not qualify as force and were not included as such. For example, officers inquiring about the location of someone, suggesting the citizen take out a warrant, or advising how a restraining order can be obtained did not count as force. Force is measured according to severity of harm it imposes on a citizen, and is placed along a "continuum" ranging from least to most severe harm. Force is ranked in the following manner: none, commands, threats, pat downs, handcuffing, firm grips, pain compliance techniques, takedown maneuvers, strikes with the body, and strikes with external mechanisms.

A command is defined as a statement by an officer that is in the form of an order (e.g., wait right here, drop the knife, leave now, etc.). Threats involve a command followed by an explicit or implicit intended consequence for not complying (e.g., drop the knife or you are going to get maced, if I have to tell you again you are going in, etc.). For some analyses, commands and threats are placed into one category and designated "verbal force."

Pat downs are defined as instances when an officer physically touches a citizen as part of a cursory search. Handcuffing involves placing restraints on a citizen's wrists, while a firm grip includes an officer grabbing a citizen in a forceful manner with a tight grip. For some analyses, pat downs, handcuffing, and firm grips are grouped together into one category and designated "physical restraint."

Pain compliance techniques are defined as holds that cause pain to a specific body part (e.g., hammerlock, wristlock, finger grip, carotid control, and bar arm control). Takedown maneuvers include instances when citizens were thrown, pushed, or shoved to the ground, against a wall, against a car or any other surface (leg sweeps also included). For some analyses, pain compliance techniques and takedown moves are placed into one category and designated "pain-takedown."

Finally, strikes with the body include hitting a citizen with the hands, fists, feet, legs, or any other part of the body (e.g., slapping, punching, kicking). Strikes with an external weapon include the use of any item that was not part of the body (e.g., flashlights, batons, police radios, stun guns, macing). For some analyses, these two forms of force are grouped together and designated "impact force." For yet other analyses, these two forms, in addition to pain-takedowns, are combined together and also designated as impact force.

In Chapter Five, when analyzing how force is used, the continuum is broken down into these nine separate levels or categories of force. This level of specificity is used so as to allow for the greatest degree of description. In Chapter Six, when predicting the highest level of force, four categories are used (none, verbal, restraint, impact). This allows for a more intuitive interpretation when presenting results from the ordered probit model, as well as providing a sufficient number of cases within each category, specifically impact force. In Chapter Seven, when examining what factors affect whether officers follow a continuum of force, six categories are used (none, commands, threats, restraint, pain-takedowns, impact). This conceptualization allows for the greatest ease in linking potential force types with citizen resistance.[16]

Resistance

Citizen resistance is defined as acts that thwart, obstruct, or impede an officer's attempt to elicit information; failure to respond or responding negatively to an officer's commands or threats; and any physical act, proactive or reactive, against an officer's attempt to control the citizen. Citizen behavior that was cooperative and responsive to police direction was considered and coded as no resistance. For example, the citizen did not: a) ignore or verbally reject police verbal communication, direction, or control; b) evade or flee from police; or c) strike an officer (actual or attempted).[17] Resistance is measured according to the severity of defiance it poses to police, and is placed along a "continuum" ranging from least to most severe harm. Resistance is ranked in the following manner: none, passive, verbal, defensive, active.

Passive resistance is defined as citizen behaviors that are unresponsive to police verbal communication or direction. Citizen behaviors in this category must not be verbalized or involve physical movements in a defensive or aggressive mode, but rather are demonstrated through inactivity (e.g., citizen ignores or disregards police attempts at verbal communication or control, goes limp, fails to physically respond or move). Verbal resistance includes a citizen verbally rejecting police verbal communication or direction. Citizen behaviors in this category must be verbal in nature and not physical (e.g., a citizen telling the officer he or she will not comply with police direction, to leave alone, or go bother someone else).

Defensive resistance is defined as citizen attempts to evade police attempts at control. Citizen behaviors in this category must involve some type of physical behavior in a defensive mode (e.g., attempts to leave the scene, flee, hide from detection, pull away from officer's grasp). Active resistance includes citizens either attempting or actually attacking or striking an officer. Citizen behaviors in this category must involve some type of physical behavior in an aggressive mode (e.g., citizens lunging toward the police; striking police with hands, fists, kicks or any instrument that may perceived as a weapon such as a knife, stick, frying pan).

Predictors

Table 4-2 provides a description of the variables used in the models run in Chapter Six and Chapter Seven, along with how they were measured. In Chapter Six, the highest level of force is predicted. Force is broken down into an ordinal measure with four categories: none, verbal, physical restraint, and impact. In Chapter Seven, whether officers followed a continuum of force is examined. Here, force is broken down into a dichotomous measure: followed continuum and used more force; as well as a multi-categorical measure: used less force, followed continuum, used more force. While many of the variables are self-explanatory, several require additional explanation to clarify how and why they were conceived in the manner defined in Table 4-2.

Within the citizen characteristics section, wealth was determined by the citizen's appearance and dress, property and possessions, as well as information provided by the citizen about his or her possessions (e.g., job, home, other resources). Chronic poverty was defined as the condition of someone who appeared not to have a domicile that could shelter from the elements. Low wealth was defined as someone who has regular food, shelter, and clothing, but can provide these things only at a very modest level or only slightly above subsistence. Middle wealth was defined as someone with a job above minimum wage or otherwise able to support themselves and their families. Above middle was defined as someone whose appearance and possessions suggest the capacity to afford many luxury items. In cases where the observer was presented with conflicting information (e.g., shabby appearance but an occupation or home suggesting greater wealth), they were instructed to take the "totality of cues" into account and select the category that best seemed to fit overall.

Citizens who were in a heightened state of emotion, as manifested in terms of fear or anger, were coded yes for the emotional state measure. The drug/alcohol use measure was coded yes if there was any indication of alcohol or drug use, including the smell of alcohol on the breath, slurred speech, impaired motor skills, or unconsciousness.

Table 4-2: Variable Description

Outcome Variables:

Description:

Force1 (Highest Level)
Chapter 6

Ordinal variable, 0 = none, 1 = verbal, 2 = restraint, 3 = impact
Level of police force.

Force2 (Follow, More)
Chapter 7

Dummy variable, 0 = follow continuum, 1 = more force.
(See Section 4.6 for further description).

Force3 (Less, Follow, More)
Chapter 7

Multi-categorical variable, 0 = follow continuum, 1 = less force, 2 = more force.
(See Section 4.6 for further description).

Citizen:

Gender

Dummy variable, 1 = male, 0 = female.

Race

Dummy variable, 1 = nonwhite, 0 = white.

Age

Ordinal variable, 1 = 0-5 years, 2 = 6-12 years, 3 = 13-17 years, 4 = 18-20 years, 5 = 21-29 years, 6 = 30-44 years, 7 = 45-59 years, 8 = 60+ years.

Table 4-2: Variable Description (cont.)

Wealth

Ordinal variable, 1 = chronic poverty, 2 = low, 3 = middle, 4 above middle. Determined by the citizen's appearance and dress, property and possessions, as well as information provided by the citizen about his or her possessions (e.g., job, home, other resources).

Emotional State

Dummy variable, 1 = yes, 0 = no. Citizen in a heightened state of emotion, as manifested in terms of fear or anger.

Drug/Alcohol

Dummy variable, 1 = yes, 0 = no. Citizen displays indication of alcohol or drug use, including the smell of alcohol on the breath, slurred speech, impaired motor skills, or unconsciousness.

Mental State

Dummy variable, 1 = yes, 0 = no. Citizen unable to perceive situations as a reasonable person would or to control one's emotions and actions.

Table 4-2: Variable Description (cont.)

Disrespect

Dummy variable, 1 = yes, 0 = no.
Citizen displays disrespect to the individual or authority of the police officer.

Resistance

Ordinal variable, 1 = none, 2 = passive, 3 = verbal, 4 = defensive, 5 = active
Level of citizen resistance.

Officer:
Gender

Dummy variable, 1 = male, 0 = female.

Race

Dummy variable, 1 = nonwhite, 0 = white.

Experience

Interval variable, years on the job.

Education

Ordinal variable, 1 = less than high school, 2 = high school graduate/GED, 3 = some college/no degree, 4 = Associate Degree, 5 = >2 years college no B.S., 6 = Bachelors Degree, 7 = some graduate work/no degree, 8 = Graduate Degree.

Table 4-2: Variable Description (cont.)

Verbal Training	Ordinal variable, 1 = none, 2 = <1 day, 3 = 1-2 days, 4 = 3-5 days, 5 = >5 days. "How much training did you receive in mediation in the past three years?"
Crimefighter	Ordinal variable, 1 = agree strongly, 2 = agree somewhat, 3 = disagree somewhat, 4 = disagree strongly. "Enforcing the law is by far a patrol officer's most important responsibility."
Distrust	Ordinal variable, 1 = agree strongly, 2 = agree somewhat, 3 = disagree somewhat, 4 = disagree strongly. "Police officers have reason to be distrustful of most citizens."
Individual Legal Guidelines	Ordinal variable, 1 = agree strongly, 2 = agree somewhat, 3 = disagree somewhat, 4 = disagree strongly. "In order to do their jobs, patrol officers must sometimes overlook search and seizure laws and other legal guidelines."

Table 4-2: Variable Description (cont.)

Organizational:

Site
Dummy variable, 1 = Indianapolis, 0 = St. Petersburg.

Assignment
Dummy variable, 1 = 911 officer, 0 = Community officer.

Supervisor Criticism
Ordinal variable, 1 = agree strongly, 2 = agree somewhat, 3 = disagree somewhat, 4 = disagree strongly.
"The decisions or judgements I make are seldom criticized or modified by my supervisor."

Workgroup Legal Guidelines
Ordinal variable, 1 = all or most, 2 = about half, 3 = a few, 4 = none.
"How many officers in your unit would say that in order to do their jobs, they must sometimes overlook legal guidelines?"

Control:

Number of Officers
Interval variable, number of officers on scene.

Table 4-2: Variable Description (cont.)

Variable	Description
Number of Bystanders	Interval variable, number of bystanders on scene.
Anticipate Violence	Dummy variable, 1 = yes, 0 =no. Was there any indication of anticipated violence before the encounter began?
Proactive	Dummy variable, 1 = yes, 0 = no. Was this encounter proactive?
Problem	Dummy variable, 1 = yes, 0 = no. Was the problem pre-defined as a potentially violent situation?
Arrest	Dummy variable, 1 = yes, 0 = no. Taking a citizen into custody for the purpose of charging him or her with a criminal offense.
Officer Safety	Dummy variable, 1 = yes, 0 =no. Did citizen have any sort of weapon on his or her person or within "jump and reach?"

Table 4-2: Variable Description (cont.)

Citizen Conflict	Ordinal variable, 1 = none, 2 = calm verbal, 3 = agitated verbal, 4 = threatened assault, 5 = assault. Level of conflict between disputing parties.
Pattern1 through Pattern3 Chapter 7 - Logistic Regression	Dummy variables, 1 = yes, 0 = no. Series of dummy variables that identify what actions occurred prior to any break in the continuum. Pattern1 (Officer Initially Applies Force - verbal), Pattern2 (Officer Initially Applies Force - physical), Pattern3 (No Force is Used).
Pattern1 through Pattern4 Chapter 7 - Multinomial Logit	Dummy variables, 1 = yes, 0 = no. Series of dummy variables that identify what actions occurred prior to any break in the continuum. Pattern1 (Officer Initially Applies Force - verbal), Pattern2 (Officer Initially Applies Force - physical), Pattern3 (Citizen Initially Resists - defensive or active), Pattern4 (Citizen Initially Resists - passively or verbally).

Table 4-2: Variable Description (cont.)

Missing

Chapter 7 - Logistic Regression

Chapter 7 - Multinomial Logit

Dummy Variables, 1 = yes, 0 = no.

Series of dummy variables that identify officer variables with missing cases. Missing1 (Officer Experience), Missing2 (Officer Education), Missing3 (Training), Missing4 (Crimefighter), Missing5 (Distrust), Missing6 (Individual Legal Guidelines), Missing7 (Supervisor Criticism), Missing8 (Workgroup Legal Guidelines), Missing9 (Individual Legal Guidelines/Supervisor Criticism Interaction), Missing10 (Individual Legal Guidelines/Workgroup Legal Guidelines Interaction).

Hybrid:

ISite1 through ISite4

Four dummy interaction variables, LSite1 = Indianapolis officers who believe overlooking legal guidelines is necessary, LSite2 St. Petersburg officers who believe overlooking legal guidelines is necessary, LSite3 = Indianapolis officers who do not believe overlooking legal guidelines is necessary, LSite4 = St. Petersburg officers who do not believe overlooking legal guidelines is necessary.

Table 4-2: Variable Description (cont.)

ISuper1 through ISuper4

Four dummy variables, LSuper1 = Officers who believe overlooking legal guidelines is necessary and work for a supervisor who rarely modifies his or her decisions, LSuper2 = Officers who believe overlooking legal guidelines is necessary and work for a supervisor who usually modifies his or her decisions, LSuper3 = Officers who do not believe overlooking legal guidelines is necessary and work for a supervisor who rarely modifies his or her decisions, LSuper4 = Officers who do not believe overlooking legal guidelines is necessary and work for a supervisor who usually modifies his or her decisions.

IWork1 through IWork4

Four dummy interaction variables, LWork1 = Officers who believe overlooking legal guidelines is necessary and work with officers who believe overlooking legal guidelines is necessary, LWork2 = Officers who believe overlooking legal guidelines is necessary and work with officers who do not believe overlooking legal guidelines is necessary, LWork3 = Officers who do not believe overlooking legal guidelines is necessary and work with officers who believe overlooking legal guidelines is necessary, LWork4 = Officers who do not believe overlooking legal guidelines is necessary and work with officers who do not believe overlooking legal guidelines is necessary.

Citizen mental impairment was defined as the inability to perceive situations as a reasonable person would or to control one's emotions and actions. There must have been some indication that it was a chronic condition, not arising solely from the immediate circumstances.

The crimefighter measure was based on the following statement to officers, "[e]nforcing the law is by far a patrol officer's most important responsibility." It was hypothesized that the greater an officer agreed with this statement the more inclined he or she would be to self-define him or herself as a crimefighter as opposed to service-oriented; and the greater the perceived crimefighter role, the greater the likelihood of using force. To form the distrust measure, officer's were asked if, "[p]olice officers have reason to be distrustful of most citizens." Again, it was hypothesized that the more officers agreed with this statement, the more likely they would be to use force. Finally, for the legal guideline measure, the statement read, "[i]n order to do their jobs, patrol officers must sometimes overlook search and seizure laws and other legal guidelines." It was hypothesized that the more an officer agreed with this statement, the more forceful he or she would be.

In the control characteristics section, observers were asked to identify whether there was any indication of anticipated violence before an encounter began. The indication could have come from the dispatcher, other officers, or from the observed officers' own knowledge (revealed by comments). For the problem measure, observers were provided with a detailed list of possible "problem codes." A problem code resembled what an officer might be given by the dispatcher when he or she is dispatched to the location of a problem or what the officer considered as the problem before making a proactive stop. This was an exhaustive list containing several hundred potential problems such as neighbor trouble, gang trouble, shots fired, bomb threat, fight, robbery, and so on. Observers coded the nature of the problem for each encounter. For example, if an officer decided to pull a car over for an expired tag, the observer would list "missing or improper license" as the problem code. A variety of problem types were originally considered for inclusion into the model as predictors. However, there is little theoretical direction for what types of problems would predict an increased level of force. Possibly, one could posit that serious problems types (e.g., robbery) would lead to more force (as opposed to shoplifting for example). Therefore, cases could be split between felony and misdemeanors.

Five of the factors in the model (disrespect, citizen resistance, arrest, officer safety, and citizen safety) are what can be referred to as "timing" variables, meaning that they needed to be coded according to *when* they occurred during the encounter. Citizen resistance was defined in the previous section, while the other four are defined and described below. Unlike a static variable (e.g., citizen gender), which cannot change during the course of the encounter, timing variables can. If a citizen is a male at the beginning of the encounter, he is going to be a male at the end. If a citizen is resistant at the beginning of an encounter, he may or may not be resistant at the end. His behavior, and thus this measure of his behavior, varies within the encounter. To ensure that a cause and effect relationship can be discerned, these five timing variables had to have occurred before observing the highest level of force (Chapter Six) or application of the force continuum (Chapter Seven). For example, if physical restraint is the highest level of force in a given encounter, then only the actions that occurred before that are considered. If a citizen is passively resistant prior to restraint but active after, passive is used as the predictor, not active.

Disrespect involved a citizen doing something, or failing to do something, showing disrespect to the individual or authority of the police officer. This included a variety of verbal statements: calling the officer names, making derogatory statements about the officer or his family, making disparaging or belittling remarks, and slurs (racial, sexual, lifestyle). Ignoring the officer's commands or questions did *NOT* constitute disrespect, but rather was classified as passive resistance. In addition, certain gestures and actions were coded as disrespect. These included: "flipping the bird" (displaying the middle finger in the direction of the police), obscene gestures, or spitting in the presence of an officer (even if not in the direction of the officer).

In the officer characteristics section, several of the measures were taken from the officer survey. For the verbal training measure officers were asked, "how much training did you receive in mediation in the past three years?" Mediation was clarified by the interviewer as the type of training where officers are provided skills on how to diffuse a potentially difficult or violent situation through use of language. This type of training is commonly referred to as verbal judo.

Another approach would be to split cases into five or six categories such as disputes, public disorder, traffic, person crimes, property crimes, and so forth. A third approach, and the one applied, was to identify problem codes that could be considered potentially violent. This approach is similar to what other researchers have done when selecting cases for study (Fyfe, 1988; Bayley and Garofalo, 1989). These researchers hypothesized that certain types of cases (e.g., disputes, traffic stops, attempts to question suspicious persons) are more likely to lead to force than others (e.g., shoplifting). Therefore, they use these crime or problem types as the inclusion criteria. By using "potentially violent" problem types as a predictor in the model, it is hypothesized that such cases will predict force.[18]

An officer safety issue arose whenever a citizen had any sort of weapon on his or her person or within "jump and reach." A citizen safety issue occurred whenever the citizen involved in the encounter was in conflict with another citizen on scene. This measure was coded into five ordinally ranked levels of conflict ranging from calm verbal to physical assault. To be coded as a citizen safety issue, the conflict must have been immediate in the sense that the conflicting disputants must have been in the same general area. A citizen who was in conflict with a neighbor across the street in a house and out of any possible contact with this citizen was not coded as a citizen safety issue because there was none. Two citizens in the front of a house yelling at each other was coded as citizen conflict.

For the continuum analyses presented in Chapter Seven, once all sequences were coded a new variable (pattern) was created. This variable captures the combination of resistance and force actions prior to any break (use of less or more force) in the continuum. For example, imagine an encounter with four sequences. If the officer jumped the continuum (using more force) in the third sequence, the pattern would involve the citizen and officer actions in the first three sequences only. Hence, if in sequence one the citizen offered no resistance and the officer gave a command, then in sequence two the citizen passively resisted and the officer made a threat, then in sequence three the citizen offered no resistance and the officer used physical restraint, the pattern would be coded as: no resistance-command, passive resistance-threat, and no resistance, or numerically (see the Resistance Force Comparative Scale section 4.6 below) as 12231. If the continuum was followed throughout the entire encounter, the pattern was coded in such a way as to capture all resistance-force behaviors that occurred in the encounter.

The purpose of accounting for the pattern of resistance and force is to determine the extent to which actions early in an encounter help explain actions later in the encounter, specifically a break in the continuum. For example, do citizens who are initially resistant stand a better chance of officers using higher forms of force? Are officers who apply force early in an encounter more likely to end up using higher or lower forms of force later in the encounter? In Chapter Five, data are presented on how citizen resistance and force affect subsequent behaviors. In Chapter Seven, this concept is taken a step further by applying it in relation to whether these subsequent behaviors are in the form of a break in the continuum.[19]

From the original pattern variable two sets of dummy variables were constructed: one set for the logistic model and one set for the multinomial model (see Data Analysis section 4.7 below for necessity of two separate models) run in Chapter Seven. For the logistic model, encounters that followed a pattern where the officer initially used some form of verbal force were coded as pattern1.[20] Encounters where the officer initially used physical force were coded as pattern2. Encounters where no force was used prior to any break in the continuum were coded as pattern3. For the multinomial model, the encounters were divided into four distinct patterns. Pattern1 involved encounters where the officer initially used verbal force. Pattern2 were those where the officer initially used physical force. Pattern3 involved those where the citizen was initially resistant in the form of defensive or active resistance. Pattern4 contained those encounters where citizens were initially resistant in the form of passive or verbal resistance. Two sets of patterns had to be used, as opposed to just one involving the same behaviors, because cases contained in the logistic model involved citizens that never displayed any resistance (see Data Analysis section 4.7 below for necessity of two separate models). Therefore, encounters only unfolded in the form of force. Thus it was not possible to use citizen resistance as a determinant of police force.[21]

The missing case variables are used to avoid losing entire cases as a result of missing data on a few variables. The most common approach to dealing with missing data on any variable of interest is to employ listwise deletion, effectively eliminating the entire case. For instance, if data are available on 29 of 30 variables, the entire case is deleted despite available information on all but one variable. An alternative to listwise deletion is to include a missing case variable in the model to account for missing data on select variables. The missing case variable indicates if the case was missing on a particular variable. Once the missing case variables were created, all missing values were then coded as zero. This technique has been effectively applied elsewhere (see DeJong, 1997, 1998).

Of the hybrid variables, with the exception of site, which was already a dichotomous measure, each of the variables were recoded into a dichotomous measure using the top and bottom two responses.[22] For example, officers who agreed (strongly or somewhat) with the individual legal guidelines statement were classified as those who believed legal guidelines served as a constraint; officers who disagreed with the statement (strongly or somewhat) were classified as those who did not. The same approach was used with the supervisor criticism and workgroup legal guideline measures.

4.6 RESISTANCE FORCE COMPARATIVE SCALE (RFCS)

The final research question addresses the application of force in relation to citizen resistance. This relationship is examined through use of what is often referred to as the "force continuum"(see Desmedt, 1984; Connor, 1991; McLaughlin, 1992; Garner et al 1995; Alpert and Dunham, 1997). The force continuum typically involves matching various levels of citizen resistance to various levels of police force. The concept of a force continuum offers guidance as to what options appear most appropriate for a given level of resistance. Police departments often present and use the continuum as a guideline that promotes police escalation of force in "small increments" that are just beyond the level of resistance encountered. Thus, to achieve citizen compliance (with respect to a force continuum) officers are encouraged to use a level of force that is just beyond the level of citizen resistance encountered.

The continuum is used here in two ways. First, it is used as a standard against which to *measure, not judge* police behavior. No judgement is made as to whether an officer acted properly or improperly. Second, by using the continuum as a measuring standard in this way, the extent to which police behavior adheres to an "incrementalist" approach of escalating and de-escalating force emerges. The continuum is simply a way to characterize and examine how officers apply force in relation to the resistance they encounter. Before one can begin to *judge* the appropriateness of police force, one must measure the extent to which force has been applied in an incrementalist manner. It should also be clear that this is not an attempt to ascertain whether officers are following a particular policy concerning the force continuum. Only one of the two departments had a specific policy regarding the force continuum and this only detailed the police force side of the continuum, with citizen resistance referred to only in vague terms and not categorized into specific levels.

In reality, the continuum is actually two continua - one for police behavior and one for citizen behavior. Descriptions of each are arranged along an ordinal scale in terms of the severity of harm each presents to the other. The Resistance Force Comparative Scale was developed to account for successive citizen and police behaviors throughout each encounter. Development of this analytic scheme (displayed in Table 4-3) is roughly based on corresponding force categories previously developed in relation to the force continuum.

The intent here is simply to determine the extent to which officers actually respond to various levels of resistance with similar levels of police force, which is designed to help determine whether an incrementalist approach to applying force is typical. The objective is to see if officers: a) refrain from moving up the continuum despite resistance, b) move up and down the continuum incrementally based on resistance, c) move up the continuum without an equivalent level of resistance. This then allows for the examination of what factors are associated with those instances when officers either follow or do not follow along the force continuum (drawn from the same set of predictors used in examining the highest level of force).

Table 4-3: Resistance Force Comparative Scale (RFCS)

Levels of Citizen Resistance	Levels of Police Force
1-No Resistance	1-No Force
2-Passive	2-Command
3-Verbal	3-Threat
4-Defensive	4-Restraint and Control
5-Active	5-Pain Compliance/Takedown
	6-Impact

Citizen Resistance	Less Force	Equivalent Force	More Force
1	--------	1,2	3,4,5,6
2	1	2,3	4,5,6
3	1,2	3,4	5,6
4	1,2,3	4,5	6
5	1,2,3,4	5,6	--------

Measuring and ranking police force in relation to citizen resistance is a technique similar to Alpert and Dunham's (1997) "Force Factor," since it provides a means or analytic tool for measuring and examining police use of force relative to citizen resistance.[23] However, it differs in one key way. Alpert and Dunham only measured the "highest" level of police force and citizen resistance, while this study examines the entire encounter and measures multiple uses of both police force and citizen resistance. Each instance of resistance and force were coded into sequences within each encounter so as to link resistance behaviors with force behaviors. A sequence was defined *as any occurrence of either citizen resistance, police force, or both.* A sequence is always characterized by the citizen action followed by the police action. In essence, a sequence pairs the citizen behavior with that of the officer. For a sequence to occur, there must have been some form of resistance or force. There were two exceptions to this. First, encounters where there was neither citizen resistance nor police force were coded in one sequence of "no resistance-no force" to signify that neither behavior was present at any time during the encounter. Second, in instances when another officer was on the scene and used force, when the observed officer did not, a sequence was coded to signify that force had occurred, but distinguished that the sequence was a result of another officer using force as opposed to the observed officer.

Based on this analytic scheme (Table 4-3), a determination was made as to whether the continuum was followed *for each sequence*. Once each sequence was coded, then the entire string of sequences were examined and a determination was made as to whether the continuum was followed *as a whole* - this is the dependent measure used in the logistic regression and multinomial logit models in Chapter Seven. If the outcome for each sequence was the same for the entire string of sequences, then the final outcome also remained the same. For example, if there were three sequences and in each one the continuum was followed, then the final outcome was that the officer followed the continuum (e.g., met the level of citizen resistance with only incrementally more force).

If the outcome in some sequences was that the officer used less force, while in others the officer followed the continuum, then the final outcome recorded was that the officer used less force. For example, if there were three sequences and in two the officer used less force and in one followed the continuum, then the final outcome was that the officer used less force. In other words, as long as "less force" was used in at least one of the sequences and there was never the application of "more force," the case was coded as less force.

If the outcome in some sequences was that the officer used more force, while in others followed the continuum, then the final outcome was that the officer used more force. In other words, as long as "more force" was used in at least one of the sequences and there was never the application of "less force," the case was coded as more force.

If the outcome in some sequences was that the officer used less force, while in others used more force, the encounter was excluded from the quantitative analyses.[24] For example, if there were three sequences and in two the officer used less force and in one used more. Cases where officers refrained from applying a given level of force as well as used more force given the level of resistance did not present an acceptable choice on which to try to predict or explain. Arbitrarily selecting one over the other was deemed unacceptable. These cases are examined qualitatively, for the most part, after presentation of the other cases.

It is important to note that a *sliding* scale is applied (as per the basic analytic coding scheme) as the encounter moves from one sequence to another when *repeated* citizen resistance or force is applied. For instance, if a resistant citizen continues the same level of resistance in consecutive sequences, equivalent officer force is coded at the next highest level of force. For example, if in sequence one a citizen passively resists and the officer issues a threat, and in sequence two the citizen again passively resists the officer is no longer restricted to the use of a command or threat, which is what the basic coding structure calls for without considering a sliding scale. In this case, the officer is permitted to use restraining force as equivalent force.

Further, if an officer chooses to use less force after any level of citizen resistance, given the basic coding structure, and the citizen repeats the same level of resistance in the following sequence, the officer is restricted to the basic coding structure options. For example, if in sequence one the citizen offers passive resistance and the officer chooses to not use force (rather, tries persuasion, suggestion, etc.), and in sequence two the citizen again passively resists, for the force to be coded as equivalent the officer is restricted to a verbal command or threat. Going right to a higher form of force such as restraint is coded as more force since the officer failed or skipped any attempt at verbal force.

The basic coding structure is nothing more than a means to help identify instances when it appears officer force is not congruent - according to the criteria of the continuum - with citizen resistance (whether less than or more force). According to the coding structure, an officer is always given at least two levels of force in which to apply equivalent force. The intent is to provide adequate leeway without being overly restrictive of real world circumstances. The aim is to identify only those cases where citizen resistance is *substantially* different than the level of force applied by the officer.

Applying this analytic scheme does not mean any one approach by an officer was proper or improper. It is possible that police experts or administrators may classify several different approaches as justifiable. However, this does allow for the examination of the differences in how police use their coercive powers, and more specifically the extent to which officers follow an incrementalist approach to escalating and de-escalating force. Thus, it is imperative to view this classification scheme as simply a way in which to better understand how coercive officers are in relation to citizen resistance and what factors account for this. A most important aspect of classifying force using this analytic scheme is that it highlights factors associated with those instances in which officers are able to resolve incidents with less rather than more force, something that is rarely undertaken in studies on police use of force. If, as McEwen states, "the aim of progressive police departments is to reduce the amount of force needed to resolve conflicts, not just to identify and deal with excessive force," then this type of analysis is crucial to a better understanding of police use of force (1996: 7). Furthermore, as Sykes and Brent have stated, "[o]ne comes to understand violence, not nonviolence, by studying violence." (1983: 25). Thus, if we want to learn about what factors are related to less force, rather than more force, we need to examine those factors related to less force in particular.

Additionally, one of the benefits of examining police force as I have laid out is that you control at the outset citizen resistance. From a legal and policy perspective the nature or degree of citizen resistance is presumably a crucial factor in what legitimizes or makes force justifiable in the first place. According to Klinger, "[t]he laws that govern the use of force by police officers across the U.S. dictate that officers use no more force than is necessary to overcome the resistance offered by citizens" (1995: 171). If officers apply additional force that is not in accordance with citizen resistance, there is certainly cause for concern and a possible basis for labeling such force as inappropriate, especially once other legal determinants are controlled for (e.g., threat to officer and citizen safety). Further, if such behavior is biased toward certain citizens (minorities, lower class, etc.) there is cause for even greater concern. The same can be said if certain officers (either by individual characteristics or attitudinal dispositions) engage in such behavior.

A few final notes involve the control of arrest, officer safety, and citizen safety within the coding scheme. These factors do not need to be statistically controlled in the model since they were controlled for in the coding of the sequences. An arrest usually, although not always, involves some form of physical restraint as the person is taken into custody. As such, the coding of arrest cases allowed for an officer to use up to level four force - restraint and control even when the citizen is not resistant.

Officer and citizen safety is also taken into account in the coding. Whenever an officer safety issue was raised (when a weapon is present or within "jump and reach") officer force was coded as equivalent regardless of the level of force. When a citizen was in conflict with another citizen on the scene, and this conflict involved calm verbal or agitated verbal conflict between parties, equivalent force was increased to include up to restraint and control regardless of the citizen resistance level. If citizen conflict involved a threat to harm or an actual assault, equivalent force included all levels of force.

4.7 DATA ANALYSES

Data are analyzed using a variety of methods in the following chapters. The first three research questions involving *how* force is used by officers require the use of simple frequency counts, percentages, and cross-tabulations. The primary intent is to show how often officers resort to force and how force varies. These results are presented in Chapter Five.

To examine the final two research questions pertaining to *why* officers use force, three multivariate statistical models are used: ordered probit, logistic regression, and multinomial logit. Research question four asks, "why do officers use force?" The dependent variable, highest level of force, is measured ordinally: no force, verbal force, restraining force, and impact force. As such, the ordered probit model is the appropriate estimation technique given a polytomous dependent variable with ordinal response categories (McKelvey and Zavoina, 1975; Liao, 1994; Long, 1997).[25] Researchers have often treated ordinally ranked dependent variables as if they were interval and applied ordinary least square (OLS) regression. Doing so, however, can provide misleading results. More specifically, coefficients derived from OLS can significantly underestimate the effects of regressors on ordinal dependent variables (McKelvey and Zavoina, 1975; Winship and Mare, 1984). Results from this analysis are presented in Chapter Six.

The final research question examines whether officers apply force in relation to citizen resistance, apply less force given citizen resistance, or apply more force given resistance. This requires two analyses. Since only two of these three options (followed the continuum or used more force) are possible in encounters where a citizen is nonresistant throughout, a logistic regression model is first estimated. In effect, an officer cannot de-escalate a situation where a citizen never resists, thereby only providing for one of two choices - stay within the continuum framework or go above the framework.[26] The logistic regression model is the appropriate method for use with a dichotomous outcome variable (Liao, 1994).

For those encounters where a citizen does display resistance, an officer has one of three options, which becomes the dependent variable. Because this variable takes on more than two discrete values that cannot be naturally ordered, a multinomial logit model is employed (Aldrich and Nelson, 1984; Long, 1997). According to Long, "[t]he multinomial logit model (MNLM) can be thought of as simultaneously estimating binary logits for all possible comparisons among the outcome categories. Indeed, estimates from binary logits provide consistent estimates of the parameters of the MNLM" (1997: 149). In other words, the multinomial logit is nothing more than a simple extension of the binary logit. The model determines the odds of an observation falling into one category as compared to another (omitted) category. LIMDEP (Limited Dependent variable) software was used for running both the ordered probit and multinomial logit models. SPSS software was used for running the logistic regression model.

Finally, it is important to recognize that this work measures the effects of independent variables at different levels of analysis: citizens, officers, and departments. Recent statistical models (e.g., hierarchical linear modeling, HLM) are alleged to provide more reliable estimates of the standard error of coefficients, resulting in a better estimate of statistical significance of coefficients. Hence, logistic regression and ordered probit estimates artificially deflate the standard error of organizational and officer characteristic coefficients, which make it easier to find statistically significant effects on the officer and organizational level variables. However, recent HLM techniques require high order assumptions that often cannot be met outside of a controlled setting. HLM was originally conceived for education research, which involved schools at one level of analysis and students at another level. Such research almost always provides an adequate number of students as well as schools. In the current research such control was not present. Further, perhaps the strongest reason for not utilizing HLM was the fact that a substantial number of officers were observed in too few suspect encounters, which would therefore provide biased estimates. Of the 305 officers observed across the 3,544 suspect encounters, 74 (or nearly 25%) were observed in less than five encounters.

## CHAPTER 5

The Nature of Force
Extent, Variation, and Application

I begin by examining the extent of force, including analyses and discussion of the variation in force types officers use. Following this, the extent of, and variation in, citizen resistance is analyzed. Finally, the micro-process of the police-citizen encounter is examined in regard to the application of force, with particular emphasis given to citizen resistance. There are two primary objectives: first, to provide a general accounting of force and compare findings, where applicable, with those from previous studies; and second, to set the stage for the analyses concerning the link between citizen resistance and police force, to be presented in Chapter Seven.

5.1 FORCE

Until recently, according to conventional wisdom, the use of police force was believed to be a fairly rare phenomenon, usually occurring less than five percent of the time and certainly less than 10 percent of the time. In 1995, Garner and colleagues, in analyzing police use of force reports in Phoenix, reported that some form of physical force was used in 22 percent of all arrests. By far, this was the highest reported use of force uncovered to date. However, the difficulty with comparing findings on the frequency of police force is twofold. First, different researchers use different data collection methods when computing force, which can affect the rate of reported force. For instance, Garner and colleagues (1995) looked at police use of force reports involving only arrests. Worden (1995), conversely, examined observational data involving all suspected offenders and found force was used in only 2.4 percent of the encounters studied. Second, how a researcher defines force can dramatically alter a frequency rate. In the Garner study (1995) handcuffing was counted as force, while in the Worden study (1995) handcuffing was not counted. It is imperative, therefore, that the statistical results be understood both in terms of the context in which the data were collected as well as the manner in which they were defined.

In comparison to previous works, the most distinctive feature about the definition of force presented here is that it includes verbal as well as physical force. In recent years, several researchers have come to recognize the importance of including verbal commands and threats in a definition of force. Scholars such as Garner (1995) and Klinger (1995) have called on researchers to consider commands and threats in the universe of behaviors considered force because of the coercive nature of these acts. As a result, verbal commands and threats are included here. Table 5-1 presents the frequency of force uncovered. For comparative purposes, three additional definitions of force are also offered with their corresponding frequencies.

Table 5-1: Extent of Force
Encounters Involving at Least One Use of Force*

Type Force	Number of Encounters	Percent of Encounters
Any Force (verbal or physical)	2068	58.4
Physical	744	21.0
Physical (excluding handcuffs)	555	15.7
Physical (excluding handcuffs and patdowns)	167	4.7

*of total number of encounters (N=3,544)

Using the most inclusive definition of force (verbal and physical), 2,068 (58.4%) of the 3,544 observed encounters involved some form of force being used at least once. If verbal force is removed from the equation and only physical force is included, the percentage of encounters involving force drops to 21.0 percent. This finding is similar to what was reported in the Garner study (1995) from Phoenix. One of the suspected reasons force was found to be so high in that study was the inclusion of handcuffing in the counting of force incidents.

To determine the impact of handcuffing here, Table 5-1 also shows the frequency of force by excluding handcuffing. When this is done the frequency of physical force drops to 15.7 percent. This figure is still substantially higher than what has generally been found in the past. This may be the result of including pat downs as part of physical force. The threshold for physical force in many of the earlier studies involved at least a firm grip type action, whereby the citizen was being handled more forcefully than for just a pat down. Table 5-1 clearly demonstrates just how much the extent of force can vary simply by how inclusively it is defined. In addition, incorporating verbal commands and threats into the mix dramatically increases the occurrence of force, to over half of all observed encounters.

While Table 5-1 demonstrates how the frequency of force can vary simply by adjusting the definition of force, it only provides a broad perspective on how often force is applied. What it does not show is the significant amount of variation in the types or forms of both verbal and physical force. As part of this research, a great deal of emphasis is placed on type or level of force, and thus the *severity* of force. Police force is conceived and measured along a continuum ranging from minimal force (verbal commands) to maximum force (use of external weapons). This allows for a fuller description and understanding of the variety of force used. Table 5-2 illustrates the varying types of force applied in order of severity.

I begin by looking at both verbal and physical force combined into one category. I then separate these two forms of force. From there, I break out specific types of force subsumed within the verbal and physical categories.

Table 5-2: Extent of Force by Type
*Encounters Involving at Least One Use of Force**

Force Type	Number of Encounters	Percent of Encounters
Verbal and Physical	2068	58.4
Verbal	1782	50.3
Physical	744	21.0
Command	1616	45.6
Threat	403	11.4
Pat Down	424	12.0
Handcuff	370	10.4
Firm Grip	118	3.3
Pain Compliance	14	0.4
Push/Throw	45	1.3
Strike with Body	24	0.7

*of total number of encounters (N=3,544)

By breaking down force into various forms, a clearer picture develops of the types that are used often and the types that are rarely applied. As Table 5-2 demonstrates, verbal force accounts for a majority of all force (50.3%), while physical force is used in about one in five encounters (21%). Breaking it down further, Table 5-2 shows the types of both verbal and physical force that are used most often. Almost half (45.6%) of all encounters involved a verbal command. In some respects this is surprising given prior accounts, such as Sykes and Brent's work (1983) in the early 1980s, that emphasized the "talking" aspect of police work and a strong reliance on officers' ability to persuade, suggest, and advise. Conversely, given the command nature of police and the fact they are dealing with suspected offenders, such a high rate of issuing commands may not be all that surprising.

Since few studies have examined verbal commands as part of force, it is hard to know just what the norm is. There is little with which to compare this finding (Klinger, 1995; Garner et al., 1996). The use of threats occurred in 403 (11.4%) of the 3,544 encounters, substantially lower than commands. Again, however, it is difficult to determine the norm, given a scarcity of research.

Looking at the extent of physical force, pat downs and handcuffing account for the majority of force used. Pat downs were used in 12 percent of all observed encounters (n=424), while handcuffing resulted in 10.4 percent (n=370) of encounters. Following this was use of a firm grip at 3.3 percent (n=118) and then takedown maneuvers at 1.3 percent (n=45). Pain compliance techniques (e.g., wristlock) and any sort of impact method (striking with the body or external mechanism) all occurred in less than one percent of all encounters. Clearly, the majority of physical force is found in restraint rather than in forms such as striking, hitting, macing, and the like.

In addition to exploring the extent of force across encounters, it is just as important that one examine the frequency of force *within* encounters. Table 5-3 shows how often force is applied multiple times within individual encounters. Looking at physical and verbal force taken together, 2,068 of the 3,544 observed encounters involved some form of force. However, 1,041 (50.3%) of the 2,068 actually involved more than one use of force. These multiple force encounters account for an additional 3,152 acts of force for a total of 4,179 acts, producing a number higher than the number of observed encounters.

Table 5-3 further breaks down force into physical and verbal force separately. Of the 1,782 encounters involving verbal force, 755 involved more than one use of force accounting for an additional 2088 acts. In total, while verbal force was used in 1,782 encounters, 3,115 acts of force actually resulted. In terms of physical force, 222 of the 744 force encounters had multiple uses of force resulting in another 542 acts. In total, while physical force was used in 744 encounters, 1,064 acts of force actually resulted. We begin to clearly see how only counting the number of encounters involving some use of force produces a much underestimated figure on the total number of forceful acts. It is only when multiple uses of force are counted do we begin to get a more accurate picture.

Table 5-3: Extent of Force by Type
Encounters Involving Multiple Uses of Force*

Force Type	Total # Encs.	# Encs. with 1 Force Act	# Encs. with 1+ Force Act	Add'l Acts of Force	Total # Force Acts
Verbal and Physical	2068	1027	1041	3152	4179
Verbal	1782	1027	755	2088	3115
Physical	744	522	222	542	1064
Commands	1616	1002	614	1634	2636
Threats	403	343	60	136	479
Pat Downs	424	412	12	24	436
Handcuff	370	366	4	8	374
Firm Grip	118	103	15	33	136
Pain	14	13	1	2	15
Push/ Throw	45	35	10	22	57
Strike with Body	24	17	7	16	3

*of total number of encounters (N=3,544)

Table 5-3 also provides multiple breakdowns for each particular type of verbal and physical force. Some force types, such as commands (n=1,616), are applied multiple times in a fairly high number of encounters. Others (e.g., firm grip, pain compliance techniques) have a fairly low number of multiple uses within individual encounters. As Table 5-3 illustrates, failure to examine multiple uses of force within encounters can alter the perception of just how much or often the police use force in their daily interactions with suspected offenders. Reliance only on the number of encounters involving force distorts, and in this case underestimates, how much force actually is applied.

Table 5-4: Extent of Force Within Individual Encounters

Number of Forceful Acts	Number of Encounters	Percent of Encounters
0	1476	41.6
1	1027	29.0
2	547	15.4
3	226	6.4
4	121	3.4
5	68	1.9
6	38	1.1
7	20	0.6
8	13	0.4
9	3	0.1
10	1	0.1
11	2	0.1
12	1	0.1
13	1	0.1
Total	3544	100.0

Given the considerable number of encounters with multiple uses of force, attention focuses on the number of times force is used in each encounter, as displayed in Table 5-4. In the 1,041 encounters involving multiple uses of force, slightly over half (n=547) involved force being used twice. In 226 encounters, force was used three times within the same encounter; in 121 encounters force was used four times; and in 68 encounters force was used five times. Officers used force six or more times in the remaining 79 cases.

As the number of times force is used within an encounter increases, there is a steady decline in the number of encounters, with the exception of eleven forceful tactics. Still, in 14.0 percent (n=494) of the observed encounters, force is being applied three or more times per encounter. This is no small matter as the extent of force, as previously noted, is traditionally measured simply by counting the number of encounters in which force is used at least once. One cannot discount the role of multiple uses of force within single encounters if a more accurate count or depiction of force is to be gleaned.

To determine what forms of force are most prevalent in what combinations, Table 5-5 provides the top 15 combinations of force (including one time and multi-force encounters).[1] In 689 encounters, officers relied simply on a single command, while in 232 encounters officers used two successive commands. Physical restraint (n=201) and threats (n=124) were the next most frequently used types of force within single encounters. A command followed by physical restraint (n=89) rounded out the top five. Of the top 15 combinations, eight involve only verbal force, while the remaining seven involve physical force either singularly or in combination.

While a vast array of combinations (n=201) were used over the 2,068 encounters involving force, the top 15 account for 82.2 percent (n=1,700) of the 2,068. Of these 1,700 encounters, verbal force was used either solely or in combination in 72.3 percent (n=1,229). While a substantial number of encounters involve at least one form of force and many others involve multiple uses of force, we see that much of this force is in the form of verbal as opposed to physical force. Thus, regardless of whether force is examined as a whole (e.g., not counting multiple uses) or in segments (e.g., counting multiple uses), verbal force accounts for a majority of behavior.

Table 5-5: Top 15 Combinations of Force
Within Individual Encounters

Force Combination*	Number of Encounters	Percent of Encounters
Com	689	19.4
Com/Com	232	6.5
Rest	207	5.8
Threat	124	3.5
Com/Rest	89	2.5
Com/Threat	67	1.9
Com/Com/Com	57	1.6
Rest/Com	53	1.5
Rest/Rest	53	1.5
Com/Rest/Comm	28	0.8
Com/Rest/Rest	23	0.6
Com/Com/Threat	22	0.6
Com/Com/Com/Com	21	0.5
Com/Com/Rest	18	0.5
Threat/Com	17	0.5
Other	368	10.3
No Force	1476	41.6
Total	3544	100.0

*Com=Command, Rest=Restraint

Further evidence concerning the added role of verbal force in relation to physical force is found in Table 5-6. Here we see that verbal fore is used by itself in 1,324 encounters while physical force is used on its own in only 286 encounters. Both verbal and physical were used in 458 encounters.

Table 5-6: Verbal/Physical Force Combinations

Force Type	Number of Encounters	Percent of Encounters
No Force	1476	41.6
Verbal Only	1324	37.4
Physical Only	286	8.1
Verbal and Physical	458	12.9
Total	3544	100.0

Yet another way to look at how force is applied within individual encounters is to determine how force fluctuates as an encounter plays out. The concept of a force continuum calls for an officer to begin an encounter with as little force as possible and then move up or down in severity according to the dictates of the situation, most notably the level or severity of citizen resistance. Table 5-7 illustrates the flow or fluctuation of force, when more than one use of force is applied, as an encounter proceeds.

There were 13 different combinations of fluctuation across 1,041 encounters involving more than one use of force. Of these 1,041, in 408 the officer remained at the same level, neither increasing nor decreasing the level of force. In 457 encounters, the officer increased the level of force, and sometimes went on to fluctuate between increases and decreases, after initially starting with a lower form. Conversely, in 149 of the encounters, the officer decreased the level of force after initially starting with a higher form. This sort of breakdown suggests that officers come into an encounter using lower levels of force and increase force as the encounter plays out.

Table 5-7: Degree of Force Fluctuation
Within Individual Encounters
Encounters with More than One Forceful Act

Degree of Force Fluctuation*	Number of Encounters	Percent of Encounters
Even	408	39.2
Inc	282	27.1
Dec	129	12.4
Inc/Dec	123	11.8
Dec/Inc	30	2.9
Inc/Dec/Inc	37	3.5
Dec/Inc/Dec	10	1.0
Inc/Dec/Inc/Dec	12	1.1
Dec/Inc/Dec/Inc	5	0.5
Inc/Dec/Inc/Dec/Inc	2	0.2
Dec/Inc/Dec/Inc/Dec	1	0.1
Inc/Dec/Inc/Dec/ Inc/Dec/Inc	1	0.1
Dec/Inc/Dec/Inc/ Dec/Inc/Dec/Inc	1	0.1
Total 13	1041	100.0

*Inc=Increase, Dec=Decrease

5.2 RESISTENCE

In Chapter Three the importance of citizen resistance in relation to police force was discussed. By examining citizen resistance, we get a better understanding regarding the use of force. Accordingly, citizen resistance was broken down into five different levels: no resistance, passive, verbal, defensive, and active. The extent of citizen resistance is presented in Table 5-8.

Table 5-8: Extent of Resistance by Type
Encounters Involving at Least One Resistant Act*

Type Resistance	Number of Encounters	Percent of Encounters
Any Resistance	446	12.6
Passive	230	6.5
Verbal	213	6.0
Defensive	89	2.5
Active	19	0.5

*of total number of encounters (N=3,544)

Some form of citizen resistance was used in 446 of the 3,544 encounters. Much like police force, as the level of resistance increases, the number of encounters decrease. Further, most resistance is in the form of passive (n=230) or verbal (n=213) resistance as opposed to the more severe forms of defensive (n=89) or active (n=19). In fact, these higher forms of resistance are found in less than 3 percent of all encounters.

Also similar to police force, acts of citizen resistance can occur more than one time within individual encounters. Table 5-9 shows how often citizens are resistant multiple times within individual encounters. While 446 of the 3,544 encounters involved some form of resistance, 200 of the 446 involved more than one resistant act. These 200 accounted for an additional 695 resistant acts on top of the 246 that occurred one time, for a total of 941 across the 3,544 encounters. Table 5-9 also shows that within each level of resistance, there are encounters where multiple forms of resistance occur. Verbal resistance, when multiple resistant acts are included, is the category with the highest number of resistant acts (n=383).

Table 5-9: Extent of Resistance
*Encounters Involving Multiple Uses of Resistance**

Resistance Type	Total # Encs.	# Encs. with 1 Resist. Act	# Encs. with 1+ Resist. Act	Add'l Acts of Resist.	Total # Resist. Acts
Any Resistance	446	246	200	695	941
Passive	230	163	67	205	368
Verbal	213	124	89	259	383
Defensive	89	51	38	113	164
Active	19	13	6	13	26

*of total number of encounters (N=3,544)

Table 5-10 shows the extent of resistance by the number of times multiple resistance is present within individual encounters. Citizens engaged in no resistance in 3098 encounters, while resisting only one time in another 246 or 6.9 percent. As was found with police force, as the number of resistant acts per encounter increases, the number of encounters decreases. In only 3.3 percent (n=114) of the encounters do citizens engage in three or more resistant acts. This is a substantially different picture than that of police force. Recall that with police force, it was found that in 494 (14%) of the 3,544 encounters, police used three or more forceful tactics. Judging from these preliminary analyses on citizen resistance, it is evident that police force is occurring more often than citizen resistance.

Table 5-10: Extent of Resistance Within Individual Encounters

Number of Resistant Acts	Number of Encounters	Percent of Encounters
0	3098	87.4
1	246	6.9
2	86	2.4
3	45	1.2
4	26	0.7
5	17	0.5
6	6	0.2
7	11	0.3
8	4	0.1
9	1	0.0
10	2	0.1
12	1	0.0
13	1	0.0
Total	3544	100.0

To determine what forms of resistance are most prevalent in what combinations, Table 5-11 provides the top 10 combinations of resistance (including one time and multi-resistant encounters).[2] While 84 different combinations were used over the 446 encounters involving resistance, the top 10 account for 77.6 percent (n=336) of the 446. Of these 336 encounters, passive or verbal resistance was used either solely or in combination in 88.2 percent (n=305). Hence, we see that whether one or multiple forms of resistance are present, most take the form of lower level resistance (passive or verbal).

**Table 5-11: Top 10 Combinations of Resistance
Within Individual Encounters**

Resistance Combination	Number of Encounters	Percent of Encounters
Passive	120	3.4
Verbal	95	2.7
Verbal/Verbal	30	0.8
Defensive	30	0.8
Passive/Passive	21	0.6
Verbal/Verbal/Verbal	14	0.4
Defensive/Defensive	11	0.3
Passive/Passive/Passive	9	0.3
Passive/Verbal	9	0.3
Passive/Passive/ Passive/Passive	7	0.2
Other	100	2.8
No Resistance	3098	87.4
Total	3544	100.0

As with police force, it is also important to look at the degree of fluctuation within encounters with respect to citizen resistance. Table 5-12 illustrates the flow or fluctuation of resistance, when more than one resistant act is present, as an encounter proceeds. There were 10 different combinations of fluctuation across the 200 encounters involving more than one use of force. Of these 200, in 113 resistance remained at the same level, neither increasing or decreasing. In 40 encounters the officer only increased force, while in 24 there was only a decrease in the level of force.

Table 5-12: Degree of Resistance Fluctuation
Within Individual Encounters
Encounters with More than One Resistant Act

Degree of Resistance Fluctuation	Number of Encounters	Percent of Encounters
Even	113	56.5
Inc	40	20.0
Dec	24	12.0
Inc/Dec	6	3.0
Dec/Inc	10	5.0
Inc/Dec/Inc	1	0.5
Dec/Inc/Dec	1	0.5
Inc/Dec/Inc/Dec	2	1.0
Dec/Inc/Dec/Inc	1	0.5
Dec/Inc/Dec/Inc/Dec	2	1.0
Total 10	200	100.0

*Inc=Increase, Dec=Decrease

In 49 encounters, the citizen increased the level of resistance, and sometimes went on to fluctuate between increasing and decreasing, after initially starting with a lower form. Conversely, in 38 of the encounters, the citizen decreased the level of resistance after initially starting with a higher form. For police force, in the majority of the encounters where an officer used more than one level of force, he or she increased force after initially starting with a lower form suggesting that officers begin with lower forms of force and increase the level as the situation dictates.

Since citizens tend to increase (n=49) resistance as the encounter plays out, as opposed to decreasing it (n=38), this suggests that officers may be adapting to increased levels of resistance offered from citizens.

However, considering that in 151 of the 200 multi-resistant encounters citizens either remained at the same level of resistance or decreased it, such a high number of encounters where police increase force (n=457) is interesting. Officers are clearly increasing force in a substantial number of encounters where there is no increase in citizen resistance.

As will be more thoroughly investigated in Chapter Seven, a number of the increases in force may be the result of taking a citizen into custody, which almost always involves physical restraint (e.g., handcuffing). As a result, such a simple comparison as presented here would be misleading because arrest is not being controlled. The intent here is simply to begin to lay out the basic patterns of force and resistance. Controlling for possible extenuating circumstances is done in the following chapters.

5.3 RESISTANCE/FORCE

Until this point, police force and citizen resistance have been presented separately. However, each instance of resistance and force were coded into sequences within each encounter so as to link resistance behaviors with force behaviors (as described in Chapter Four). Citizen behaviors were coded into one of the five levels of resistance discussed above according to severity: none, passive, verbal, defensive, or active. Police force was coded into one of six levels according to severity: none, command, threat, physical restraint (includes pat downs, handcuffing, and firm grips), take down/pain compliance (includes throw downs, leg sweeps, wristlocks, hammerlocks, carotid hold), and impact methods (includes striking with the body or external mechanism). Thus, there were thirty different combinations of resistance and force that could occur for each sequence. Again, force must be considered within the context of resistance. Failure to consider the presence, as well as extent (e.g., level and multiple acts), of citizen resistance provides an inadequate picture and ultimately tells us very little about force. Table 5-13 presents each of the 30 possible sequence combinations and lists the number of sequences observed in each.

Table 5-13: Resistance/Force Sequence Combinations[3]

Resistance/Force Combination	Number of Sequences	Percent of Sequences
No Resistance/No Force	2019 (772)	30.9
No Resistance/Command	2316 (351)	35.4
No Resistance/Threat	400 (68)	6.1
No Resistance/Restraint	839 (343)	12.8
No Resistance/Takedown	21 (8)	0.3
No Resistance/Impact	7 (2)	0.1
Passive/No Force	154 (42)	2.4
Passive/Command	143 (27)	2.1
Passive/Threat	20 (2)	0.3
Passive/Restraint	9 (10)	0.4
Passive/Takedown	11 (2)	0.1
Passive/Impact	11 (1)	0.1
Verbal/No Force	146 (40)	2.2
Verbal/Command	148 (19)	2.3
Verbal/Threat	50 (12)	0.7
Verbal/Restraint	26 (7)	0.4
Verbal/Takedown	7 (2)	0.1
Verbal/Impact	6 (0)	0.1
Defensive/No Force	33 (29)	0.5
Defensive/Command	28 (4)	0.1

Table 5-13: Resistance/Force Sequence Combinations (cont.)

Resistance/Force Combination	Number of Sequences	Percent of Sequences
Defensive/Threat	9 (3)	0.1
Defensive/Restraint	48 (8)	0.7
Defensive/Takedown	27 (7)	0.4
Defensive/Impact	19 (7)	0.2
Active/No Force	12 (6)	0.1
Active/Command	1 (2)	0.1
Active/Threat	0 (1)	0.0
Active/Restraint	4 (2)	0.1
Active/Takedown	6 (0)	0.1
Active/Impact	3 (1)	0.1
Total	6543	100.0

In total, there were 6,543 sequences across the 3,544 encounters or 1.8 sequences per encounter on average. This table provides a glimpse of how officers responded to each of the type of resistance that citizens presented to them within individual sequences. For instance, officers issued a command to a nonresistant citizen 2,316 times, which accounts for the most prevalent combination. Again, this is not necessarily surprising given the command nature of the police, especially given the fact they are dealing with suspected offenders. Where one becomes concerned, however, is when citizens are nonresistant or offering low level resistance and the officer applies a higher form of force. For example, in 50 of the sequences, the citizen is either nonresistant or passively resistant and the officer responds with some type of impact method or takedown/pain compliance tactic.

Conversely, there are a number of cases where the citizen is displaying higher forms of resistance and the officer chooses to respond with little to no force. In 74 cases the suspect displayed some form of physical resistance, either defensive or active, and the officer responded with no force or a command. In the former case it appears that the officer *may* be using inappropriate force on the excessive side, while in the latter it appears that the officer may be holding back from using force even though he or she may be authorized to use more. What is unknown is any of the extenuating circumstances. Does the citizen have a weapon? Is the citizen already handcuffed? Is the citizen threatening another citizen? What occurred in any of the prior sequences? In Chapter Seven each of these individual sequences are strung together and contributing factors are controlled for in an attempt to gauge whether officers are applying, or failing to apply, force that is not consistent with the resistance they are faced with. Prior to this investigation, a review of the number of sequences per encounter is warranted to understand the variation in the lengths of sequences across the 3,544 encounters.

Table 5-14 provides a description of the number of sequences that occurred by the total number of encounters. As this table shows, most encounters involved only one (n=2,258) or two sequences (n=588), and 96.1 percent (n=3,406) of all encounters involved five or less sequences. Yet another way to look at the relationship between force and resistance is to examine the impact each has on the other as the encounter proceeds. Several scholars have posited that what occurs early in an encounter can set the *tone* for the remainder of the encounter. For instance, some have hypothesized that officers need to take charge at the outset in order to maintain control throughout. However, taking charge right away may pose the risk of prompting a citizen to be resistant. Conversely, a citizen who is initially resistant may be more likely to encounter some form of force during the encounter as opposed to a nonresistant citizen. If a citizen is immediately resistant, officers may be less inclined to sit back and let things play out or give the citizen the benefit of the doubt. Whether it be police dealing with citizens, a store clerk dealing with a customer, or a boss dealing with an employee, starting off in a combative mode may lead to a more combative outcome.

**Table 5-14: Sequence Length Breakdown
by Number of Encounters**

Sequences Length	Number of Encounters	Percent of Encounters
1	2258	63.7
2	588	16.6
3	297	8.4
4	159	4.5
5	104	2.9
6	53	1.5
7	27	0.8
8	25	0.7
9	11	0.3
10	3	0.1
11	11	0.3
12	3	0.1
13	4	0.1
17	1	0.1
Total	3544	100.0

To examine what effect behaviors exhibited early in an encounter have on subsequent behaviors, the following three questions are posed. First, how does the initial police action affect subsequent suspect resistance throughout the remainder of the encounter? Second, how does the initial suspect action affect subsequent police force throughout the remainder of the encounter? And third, how does the initial police action affect subsequent uses of police force throughout the remainder of the encounter? Table 5-15 presents the results from the first of these three questions.

Table 5-15: How Officer Begins Encounter
According to Subsequent Citizen Resistance

		Police Force (N=3,544)			
		None N (%)	Verbal N (%)	Restraint N (%)	Impact N (%)
Citizen Resistance	None	1542 (94.9)	1312 (85.5)	329 (89.9)	13 (68.4)
	Passive	27 (1.7)	75 (4.9)	12 (3.3)	0 (0.0)
	Verbal	36 (2.2)	118 (7.7)	9 (2.4)	1 (5.3)
	Defensive	14 (.9)	20 (1.3)	12 (3.3)	5 (26.3)
	Active	6 (0.3)	9 (0.6)	4 (1.1)	0 (0.0)
	Totals	1625 (100)	1534 (100)	366 (100)	19 (100)

An interesting pattern is found when looking at the effect of police force on citizen resistance. There were 1,625 encounters when officers began with no force. Of these, 1,542 (94.9%) resulted in no subsequent resistance. Passive or verbal resistance was offered in 63 (3.9%) and some form of physical resistance was encountered in 20 (1.2%). In total, citizens resisted in 5.1 percent of the encounters. When officers began with verbal force, which occurred in 1,534 encounters, citizens ended up resisting in 122 (14.5%). Although there were a similar number of encounters that began with both no force and verbal force (1,625 versus 1,534 respectively), there was almost a 10 percent increase in citizen resistance when officers began with verbal force. When officers began with physical restraint (n=366), some form of subsequent resistance occurred in 10.1 percent (n=37). Only 19 encounters began with impact force. Of these, citizens ended up physically resisting in five and verbally once.

As this table illustrates, beginning an encounter with force leads to a greater frequency of citizen resistance. This is most notable for impact force, where in 31.6 percent of the encounters citizens responded at some subsequent point in the encounter with resistance. This is also true for verbal force. By starting off an encounter with verbal force, the officer is attempting to take charge, but there is an increased consequence - subsequent resistance. It could be that citizens falling into this category may have been resistant anyway. Officers may argue that they are attuned to identifying potential problem citizens and failure to crack down right away would lead to even greater resistance. A similar argument can be made of the nonresistant citizens. These citizens may not have been resistant regardless of what the officer did right away. This is something we cannot know for certain. Regardless, there is at least some increase in the number of citizens that become resistant subsequent to initial police force.

Results from the second question, ("how does the initial citizen action affect subsequent police force?"), are presented in Table 5-16. In 3,397 of the 3,544 encounters, citizens began by offering no resistance to the officer. When the encounter began this way, officers ended up using some form of force 57.5 percent (n=1,954) of the time. They applied verbal force in 1,260 (37.1%), restraint in 634 (18.6%), and impact in 60 (1.8%). If citizens began the encounter by displaying passive resistance, which occurred in 63 cases, officers used some type of force 68.3 percent (n=43) of the time, with the majority being verbal force (52.4%) followed by physical restraint (11.1%). As the level of initial resistance increased to verbal resistance (n=43), officers responded with force 74.4 percent of the time (n=32), with verbal force being the most frequent (n=23). When citizens began with defensive resistance (n=39), officers countered with force in 94.1 percent (n=37) of the cases. In only two cases did the citizen begin by actively resisting, which resulted in verbal force in one case and restraint in another.

Table 5-16: How Citizen Begins Encounter
According to Subsequent Police Force

		Citizen Resistance (N=3,544)				
		None N (%)	Passive N (%)	Verbal N (%)	Defense N (%)	Active N (%)
Police Force	None	1443 (42.5)	20 (31.7)	11 (25.6)	2 (5.1)	0 (0.0)
	Verbal	1260 (37.1)	33 (52.4)	23 (53.5)	8 (20.5)	1 (50.0)
	Restraint	634 (18.6)	7 (11.1)	7 (16.3)	20 (51.3)	1 (50.0)
	Impact	60 (1.8)	3 (4.8)	2 (4.6)	9 (23.1)	0 (0.0)
	Totals	3397 (100)	63 (100)	43 (100)	39 (100.0)	2 (100)

Again a distinct pattern emerges here. As the level of citizen resistance increases, as per the initial citizen action, the level of force increases. It appears that when citizens raise the stakes at the outset, officers resort to force more readily. When citizens begin with non-physical resistance (passive or verbal), officers rely more heavily on lower forms of force, most notably verbal and restraint. When citizens up the ante to defensive resistance, officers respond in kind by resorting to higher levels of force, particularly impact. It is important to note, though, that in only 147 of 3,544 cases did the citizen pose any resistance at all at the outset.

Besides looking at how officer behaviors affect citizens and visa versa, another way to examine the effect of police force early in an encounter is to look at subsequent uses of force as well. If the theory is that officers who use force at the outset do so to take charge, then it is reasonable to believe that no more force will be needed as the encounter progresses because the situation will be contained or under control.

However, we have already seen that when officers begin an encounter with force, there are a number of cases where the citizen responded with some form of resistance. Table 5-17 shows the results of examining initial police force along with subsequent uses of force.

**Table 5-17: How Officer Begins Encounter
According to Subsequent Police Force**

		Police Force (N=3,544)			
		None N (%)	Verbal N (%)	Restraint N (%)	Impact N (%)
Force Subsequent Sequences	None	1476 (90.8)	757 (49.3)	191 (52.2)	4 (21.0)
	Verbal	85 (5.2)	482 (31.4)	87 (23.8)	1 (5.3)
	Restraint	46 (2.8)	265 (17.3)	80 (21.9)	9 (47.4)
	Impact	18 (1.2)	30 (2.0)	8 (2.1)	5 (26.3)
	Totals	1625 (100)	1534 (100)	366 (100)	19 (100)

There were 1,625 cases where the officer began the encounter with no force. In 90.8 percent of these (n=1,476), no force was used at any time during the remainder of the encounter. Officers used verbal force in 85 (5.2%) and physical force in 64 (4.0%). When officers began with verbal force (n=1,534), some form of force was used again in 50.7 percent of the cases (n=777). They ended up using verbal again in 482 cases (31.4%) and physical force in 295 (19.3%). In the 366 encounters that began with physical restraint, verbal force was subsequently used in 87 cases (23.8%), restraint in 80 (21.9%), and impact force in eight (2.1%). Of the 19 cases where the officer initially used impact force, four (21.0%)

resulted in no additional force, one (5.3%) in verbal force, nine (47.4%) in restraint, and five in impact (26.3%).

As Table 5-17 illustrates, applying force at the outset is no assurance that additional force will not be used. It may be that the initial police force prompted the citizen to resist, thereby requiring additional force on the officers part. It may also be the case that the officer simply continued to use force in an attempt to maintain control of the situation. Nonetheless, it is evident that at least some measure of force at the outset eventually does lead to force again being used, at least in a fair percentage of the cases.

5.4 SUMMARY

A number of interesting findings emerged from this descriptive inquiry. First, in terms of police force, the percentage of encounters involving force changes dramatically depending on how it is defined . When verbal force is included in the mix, some form of force occurred in nearly 60 percent of the cases. When the most restrictive definition is applied (physical excluding pat downs and handcuffs), the percentage drops to around 5 percent. Second, regardless of how inclusive or restrictive force is defined, a number of encounters involve multiple uses of force, which account for a substantial increase in the number of times citizens are subjected to forceful tactics. Third, most force occurs at the bottom of the continuum in the form of verbal force, followed by physical restraint. This holds whether force is used once or more than one time during an encounter. Fourth, while there is moderate variation in the amount of force fluctuation (increase and decrease in force as an encounter unfolds) within encounters, in nearly 80 percent of the total number of encounters the degree of fluctuation is in the form of either remaining at the same level or involving just one increase or decrease. In other words, in only about 20 percent of the encounters do officers tend to go back and forth between increases and decreases in force (or visa versa).

Looking at citizen behavior, citizens displayed some form of resistance in about 12 percent of the observed encounters. Similar to the severity found with police force, as the severity of resistance increased, the number of encounters decreased. Second, a number of multiple resistant encounters were uncovered. Forty-five percent of the encounters involving at least one act of resistance involved multiple resistant acts. Therefore, for both police force and citizen resistance, a great deal of these behaviors are missed unless one counts multiple behaviors within encounters. Third, in encounters where citizens displayed more than one resistant act, the degree of fluctuation between increasing and deceasing resistance was relatively rare, found in about 10 percent of the 200 cases.

Finally, several patterns emerged when examining initial citizen resistance and police force within an encounter. First, officers who begin an encounter with force are more likely to encounter a resistant citizen at some subsequent point during the encounter. This is most pronounced when officers start with verbal force. Second, citizens rarely begin an encounter demonstrating some form of resistance. However, in those instances when they do, as the level of resistance increases so too does the level or severity of force. Third, the use of initial police force is no assurance that the officer will not apply additional force at some later point during the encounter. In other words, taking charge at the outset often results in further force at a later time. The interplay between initial citizen resistance and police force is further examined in Chapter Seven.

Overall, police use coercion frequently with citizens, but mostly at lower (verbal) levels. Most physical force is accounted for by handcuffing and patdowns – both of which are instrumental acts. We expect the police to resort to higher levels of force less frequently – and they *do* follow this expectation.

CHAPTER 6
Causes of Police Force

This chapter examines the causes of force. While it has been shown that force can be used numerous times within an individual encounter, only the highest level of force within a specific encounter is examined here. The issue of multiple uses of force is taken up in the following chapter. For purposes of this analysis, the ordinal measure of force consists of four categories: no force, verbal, physical restraint, and impact methods.[1] Careful attention has been given to the *timing* of citizen actions (e.g., resistance, disrespect, officer safety, citizen conflict, and arrest) within each encounter to ensure these actions occurred "prior" to the highest level of force. This is crucial to establishing a causal relationship. Studies based on other data collection methods are sometimes, if not often, lacking in this regard since reconstruction of *when* during the encounter various citizen actions occur cannot be determined. Researchers are left to speculate or assume that certain actions occurred prior to the use of police force.

I begin by providing descriptive statistics for each of the variables under study. In Table 6-1, the hypothesized relationships between each of the independent variables and force, along with the range, mean, and standard deviation are presented. I then examine bivariate relationships between the independent variables of interest and each level of force. Following this, an ordered probit analysis is presented. This involves a main effects model as well as one examining the hypothesized interactive effects. In addition, an analysis of predicted probabilities is presented, which provides a more intuitive interpretation of the findings.

6.1 BIVARIATE RELATIONSHIPS

Table 6-1: Descriptive Statistics

Variables	Hypoth. Impact	Range	Mean	S.D.
Outcome:				
Force	------	0-3	.81	.80
(None=0; n=1476)				
(Verbal=1; n=1324)				
(Restraint=2; n=669)				
(Impact=3; n=75)				
Citizen:				
Gender	+	0-1	.72	.44
Race	+	0-1	.62	.48
Age	-	1-8	5.21	1.36
Wealth	-	1-4	2.36	.56
Emotional State	+	0-1	.31	.46
Drug/Alcohol Impaired	+	0-1	.21	.40
Mentally Impaired	+	0-1	.03	.17
Disrespect	+	0-1	.09	.29
Citizen Resistance	+	1-5	1.21	.65
Officer:				
Gender	+	0-1	.84	.35
Race	+/-	0-1	.19	.39
Experience	-	1-32	7.32	6.05
Education	-	1-8	4.29	1.90
Verbal Training	-	1-4	1.69	1.17
Crimefighter	-	1-4	3.66	1.53
Distrust	+	1-4	2.69	1.14
Individual Legal Guidelines	-	1-4	3.16	1.21

Table 6-1: Descriptive Statistics (cont.)

Variables	Hypoth. Impact	Range	Mean	S.D.
Organization:				
Site	+	0-1	.56	.49
Assignment	+	0-1	.87	.33
Supervisor Criticism	+	1-4	1.29	.75
Workgroup Legal Guidelines	-	1-4	2.74	1.14
Control:				
Number of Officers	+/-	1-26	2.20	1.61
Number of Bystanders	+/-	1-99	4.18	5.55
Anticipate Violence	+	0-1	.08	.28
Proactive Encounter	+	0-1	.45	.49
Problem	+	0-1	.47	.49
Arrest	+	0-1	.11	.31
Officer Safety	+	0-1	.01	.12
Citizen Conflict	+	1-5	.04	.20
Hybrid:				
LSite1	+	0-1	.12	.33
LSite2	+/-	0-1	.05	.22
LSite3	+/-	0-1	.39	.48
LSite4	-	0-1	.35	.47
LSuper1	+	0-1	.16	.37
LSuper2	+/-	0-1	.01	.10
LSuper3	+/-	0-1	.67	.46
LSuper4	-	0-1	.06	.25
LWork1	+	0-1	.12	.32
LWork2	+/-	0-1	.05	.23
LWork3	+/-	0-1	.07	.26
LWork4	-	0-1	.66	.47

Results from the bivariate analysis are presented in Table 6-2.[2] Begin by examining the relationship between citizen characteristics and force. Eight of the nine variables within this section are significantly related to force at the p<.01 level, all in the hypothesized direction. The only factor not related to force is mental impairment. For two of these variables there is a difference between verbal and physical force within the independent variable. For example, 24.7 percent of the males encountered were subjected to either physical restraint or impact force compared to only 11.1 percent of females; while officers used verbal force on 38.7 percent of females compared to 36.8 percent of males. A similar pattern is found with citizens who displayed signs of drug/alcohol use. Physical force was applied to 34.4 percent of those displaying signs of drug/alcohol use, while such force was applied to only 17.3 percent of those not displaying signs of drug/alcohol use.

Officers used both verbal and physical force more often on nonwhite citizens than on white citizens. Thirty-eight percent of nonwhites were on the receiving end of verbal force compared to 35.9 percent of whites. Similarly, officers used physical force on 23.3 percent of nonwhites and on 16.7 percent of whites. This pattern tended to hold for citizen age, wealth, and emotional state as well. The younger the citizens, the more likely they were to be recipients of some form of force (pre-school aged children notwithstanding physical force); citizens classified as chronic poverty or lower class had force used on them more often than those in the middle or above middle class (with the exception of verbal force); and citizens who were fearful or angry were more likely to be recipients of force than those who were not.

The relationship between citizen resistance and force shows that the type of force most often applied is generally similar to the type of resistance encountered. Citizens who are passively or verbally resistant are most often met with verbal force (57.7% and 58.8% respectively). Citizens who display some form of physical resistance (defensive or active) are more likely to be subjected to either physical restraint or impact force. Citizen disrespect is particularly interesting in the bivariate sense as a result of the percentage of disrespectful citizens who received impact force. While only 1.4% of those who were not disrespectful to the officer had impact force used on them, 8.1% of those who were disrespectful did.

Table 6-2: Bivariate Relationships by Highest Level Force[3]

	No Force	Verbal	Restraint	Impact
Citizen:				
Gender				
Male (2552)	979 (38.3)	940 (36.8)	563 (22.0)	70 (2.7)
Female (992)	497 (50.1)	384 (38.7)	106 (10.6)	5 (0.5)
Chi Sq.=90.19, d.f.=3, p=.000				
Race				
White (1329)	627 (47.1)	478 (35.9)	202 (15.1)	22 (1.6)
NonWhite (2215)	849 (38.3)	846 (38.1)	467 (21.0)	53 (2.3)
Chi Sq.=34.08, d.f.=3, p=.000				
Age				
Pre-School,				
0-5 years (6)	2 (33.3)	4 (66.6)	--	--
Child,				
6-12 years (91)	32 (35.1)	51 (56.0)	7 (7.6)	1 (1.0)
Young Adult,				
13-17 years (445)	149 (33.4)	174 (39.1)	113 (25.3)	9 (2.0)
Older Teen,				
18-20 years (373)	123 (32.9)	134 (35.9)	104 (27.8)	12 (3.2)
Young Adult,				
21-29 years (862)	370 (42.9)	308 (35.7)	168 (19.4)	16 (1.8)
Adult,				
30-44 years (1318)	580 (44.0)	482 (36.5)	226 (17.1)	30 (2.2)
Middle-Aged,				
45-59 years (339)	178 (52.5)	113 (33.3)	42 (12.3)	6 (1.7)
Senior,				
60+ years (110)	42 (38.1)	58 (52.7)	9 (8.1)	1 (0.9)
Chi Sq.=100.38, d.f.=21, p=.000				
Wealth				
Chronic (130)	34 (26.1)	59 (45.3)	30 (23.0)	7 (5.3)
Low (2018)	799 (39.5)	736 (36.4)	431 (21.3)	52 (2.5)

Table 6-2: Bivariate Relationships by Highest Level Force (cont.)

	No Force	Verbal	Restraint	Impact
Wealth				
Middle (1377)	631 (45.8)	522 (37.9)	208 (15.1)	16 (1.1)
Above Middle (19)	12 (63.1)	7 (36.8)	--	--
Chi Sq.=56.86, d.f.=9, p=.000				
Emotional State				
Fear/Anger (1132)	424 (37.4)	431 (38.0)	228 (20.1)	49 (4.3)
No (2412)	1052 (43.6)	893 (37.0)	441 (18.2)	26 (1.0)
Chi Sq.=47.12, d.f.=3, p=.000				
Drug/Alcohol Use				
Yes (745)	213 (28.5)	275 (36.9)	219 (29.3)	38 (5.1)
No (2799)	1263 (45.1)	1049 (37.4)	450 (16.0)	37 (1.3)
Chi Sq.=133.65, d.f.=3, p=.000				
Mentally Impaired				
Yes (112)	47 (41.9)	44 (39.2)	16 (14.2)	5 (4.4)
No (3432)	1429 (41.6)	1280 (37.2)	653 (19.0)	70 (2.0)
Chi Sq.=4.42, d.f.=3, p=.219				
Disrespectful				
Yes (343)	105 (30.6)	136 (39.6)	74 (21.5)	28 (8.1)
No (3201)	1371 (42.8)	1188 (37.1)	595 (18.5)	47 (1.4)
Chi Sq.=78.71, d.f.=3, p=.000				
Citizen Resistance				
None (3146)	1427 (45.3)	1128 (35.8)	579 (18.4)	12 (0.3)
Passive (149)	24 (16.1)	86 (57.7)	26 (17.4)	13 (8.7)
Verbal (163)	22 (13.4)	96 (58.8)	34 (20.8)	11 (6.7)
Defensive (70)	3 (4.2)	12 (17.1)	26 (37.1)	29 (41.4)
Active (16)	--	2 (12.5)	4 (25.0)	10 (62.5)
Chi Sq.=453.47, d.f.=12, p=.000				

Table 6-2: Bivariate Relationships by Highest Level Force (cont.)

	No Force	Verbal	Restraint	Impact
Officer:				
Gender				
Male (3007)	1244 (41.3)	1115 (37.0)	579 (19.2)	69 (2.2)
Female (537)	232 (43.2)	209 (38.9)	90 (16.7)	6 (1.1)
Chi Sq.=5.26, d.f.=3, p=.153				
Race				
White (2838)	1207 (42.5)	1027 (36.1)	541 (19.0)	63 (2.2)
NonWhite (706)	269 (38.1)	297 (42.0)	128 (18.1)	12 (1.6)
Chi Sq.=8.87, d.f.=3, p=.031				
Experience (Years on Job)				
One (183)	86 (47.0)	64 (35.0)	31 (16.9)	2 (1.1)
Five (243)	80 (32.9)	87 (35.8)	70 (28.8)	6 (2.5)
Ten (167)	68 (40.7)	57 (34.1)	37 (22.2)	5 (3.0)
Chi Sq.=157.18, d.f.=93, p=.000				
Education				
< than High School (59)	17 (28.8)	35 (59.3)	7 (11.8)	--
High School Grad/ GED (428)	140 (32.7)	192 (44.8)	82 (19.1)	14 (3.2)
Some College, no degree (740)	343 (46.3)	263 (35.5)	121 (16.3)	13 (1.7)
Assoc. Degree (154)	64 (41.5)	62 (40.2)	25 (16.2)	3 (1.9)
>2 years college, no B.S. (565)	237 (41.9)	195 (34.5)	121 (21.4)	12 (2.1)
B.S./B.A. (1224)	543 (44.3)	431 (35.2)	229 (18.7)	21 (1.7)
Some Graduate, no degree (178)	63 (35.3)	65 (36.5)	42 (23.5)	8 (4.4)
Graduate Degree (8)	4 (50.0)	3 (37.5)	1 (12.5)	--
Chi Sq.=59.38, d.f.=24, p=.000				

Table 6-2: Bivariate Relationships by Highest Level Force (cont.)

	No Force	Verbal	Restraint	Impact
Verbal Training				
None (1926)	875 (45.4)	694 (36.0)	323 (16.7)	34 (1.7)
<1 day (596)	231 (38.7)	219 (36.7)	131 (21.9)	15 (2.5)
1-2 days (468)	171 (36.5)	185 (39.5)	97 (20.7)	15 (3.2)
3-5 days (210)	74 (35.2)	88 (41.9)	45 (21.4)	3 (1.4)
>5 days (128)	45 (35.1)	53 (41.4)	26 (20.3)	4 (3.1)

Chi Sq.=34.30, d.f.=15, p=.003

	No Force	Verbal	Restraint	Impact
Crimefighter				
Agree Strongly (1099)	462 (42.0)	414 (37.7)	204 (18.6)	19 (1.7)
Agree Somewhat (1746)	725 (41.5)	633 (36.3)	350 (20.0)	38 (2.2)
Disagree Somewhat (406)	166 (40.9)	166 (40.9)	61 (15.0)	13 (3.2)
Disagree Strongly (100)	53 (53.0)	32 (32.0)	14 (14.0)	1 (1.0)

Chi Sq.=17.70, d.f.=12, p=.000

	No Force	Verbal	Restraint	Impact
Distrust				
Agree Strongly (74)	23 (31.1)	35 (47.3)	14 (18.9)	2 (2.7)
Agree Somewhat (833)	348 (41.8)	300 (36.0)	59 (19.1)	26 (3.1)
Disagree Somewhat (1422)	599 (42.1)	553 (38.9)	241 (16.9)	29 (2.0)
Disagree Strongly (883)	362 (41.0)	310 (35.1)	198 (22.4)	13 (1.5)

Chi Sq.=22.54, d.f.=12, p=.032

Table 6-2: Bivariate Relationships by Highest Level Force (cont.)

	No Force	Verbal	Restraint	Impact
Individual Legal Guidelines				
Agree Strongly (105)	36 (34.2)	35 (33.3)	32 (30.4)	2 (1.9)
Agree Somewhat (531)	226 (42.5)	207 (38.9)	88 (16.5)	10 (1.8)
Disagree Somewhat (564)	226 (40.0)	215 (38.1)	108 (19.1)	15 (2.6)
Disagree Strongly (2091)	904 (43.2)	759 (36.3)	386 (18.5)	42 (2.0)

Chi Sq.=22.30, d.f.=12, p=.000

Organization:

Site				
Indianapolis (1994)	732 (36.7)	799 (40.0)	411 (20.6)	52 (2.6)
St. Pete (1550)	744 (48.0)	525 (33.8)	258 (16.6)	23 (1.4)

Chi Sq.=48.13, d.f.=3, p=.000

Assignment				
911 (3087)	1275 (41.3)	1157 (37.4)	589 (19.0)	66 (2.1)
CPO (457)	201 (43.9)	167 (36.5)	80 (17.5)	9 (1.9)

Chi Sq.=1.35, d.f.=3, p=.716

Supervisor Criticism				
Agree Strongly (2421)	1041 (42.9)	878 (36.2)	454 (18.7)	48 (1.9)
Agree Somewhat (612)	250 (40.8)	237 (38.7)	111 (18.1)	14 (2.2)
Disagree Somewhat (233)	81 (34.7)	90 (38.6)	54 (23.1)	8 (3.4)
Disagree Strongly (61)	32 (52.4)	22 (36.0)	6 (9.8)	1 (1.6)

Chi Sq.=21.27, d.f.=12, p=.046

Table 6-2: Bivariate Relationships by Highest Level Force (cont.)

	No Force	Verbal	Restraint	Impact
Workgroup Legal Guidelines				
All of most (352)	127 (36.0)	134 (38.0)	81 (23.0)	10 (2.8)
About half (374)	152 (40.6)	153 (40.9)	60 (16.0)	9 (2.4)
A few (1669)	720 (43.1)	613 (36.7)	305 (18.2)	31 (1.8)
None (908)	397 (43.7)	325 (35.7)	167 (18.3)	19 (2.0)
Chi Sq.=21.03, d.f.=12, p=.050				
Control:				
Number of Officers				
One (1212)	551 (45.9)	562 (46.4)	96 (7.9)	3 (0.2)
Two (1433)	599 (41.8)	530 (37.0)	279 (19.5)	25 (1.7)
Three (479)	175 (36.5)	149 (31.1)	141 (29.4)	14 (2.9)
Chi Sq.=502.25, d.f.=45, p=.000				
Number of Bystanders				
One (746)	339 (45.4)	274 (36.7)	120 (16.1)	13 (1.7)
Two (928)	390 (42.0)	368 (39.7)	154 (16.6)	16 (1.7)
Three (577)	243 (42.1)	209 (36.2)	112 (19.4)	13 (2.3)
Chi Sq.=275.89, d.f.=99, p=.000				
Anticipate Violence				
Yes (312)	120 (38.4)	96 (30.7)	80 (25.6)	16 (5.1)
No (3232)	1356 (41.9)	1228 (37.9)	589 (18.2)	59 (1.8)
Chi Sq.=27.76, d.f.=3, p=.000				
Proactive Encounter				
Yes(1604)	607 (37.8)	654 (40.7)	316 (19.7)	27 (1.6)
No (1940)	869 (44.7)	670 (34.5)	353 (18.1)	48 (2.4)
Chi Sq.=22.97, d.f.=3, p=.000				

Table 6-2: Bivariate Relationships by Highest Level Force (cont.)

	No Force	Verbal	Restraint	Impact
Potentially Violent Problem				
Yes (1677)	674 (40.1)	665 (39.6)	302 (18.0)	36 (2.1)
No (1867)	802 (42.9)	659 (35.2)	367 (19.6)	39 (2.0)
Chi Sq.=7.39, d.f.=3, p=.060				
Arrest				
Yes (391)	63 (16.1)	17 (4.3)	269 (68.7)	42(10.7)
No (3153)	1413 (44.8)	1307 (41.4)	400 (12.6)	33(1.0)
Chi Sq.=931.71, d.f.=3, p=.000				
Officer Safety				
Yes (54)	8 (14.8)	19 (35.1)	26 (48.1)	1 (1.8)
No (3490)	1468 (42.0)	1305 (37.3)	643 (18.4)	74 (2.1)
Chi Sq.=34.45, d.f.=3, p=.000				
Citizen Conflict				
No Conflict (3337)	1428 (42.7)	1202 (36.0)	641 (19.2)	66 (1.9)
Calm Verbal (35)	15 (42.8)	18 (51.4)	2 (5.7)	--
Agit. Verbal (114)	27 (23.6)	75 (65.7)	10 (8.7)	2 (1.7)
Threatened (38)	5 (13.1)	19 (50.0)	11 (28.9)	3 (7.8)
Assaulted (20)	1 (5.0)	10 (50.0)	5 (25.0)	4(20.0)
Chi Sq.=103.70, d.f.=12, p=.000				
Hybrid:				
LSite1				
Yes (455)	183 (40.2)	177 (38.9)	86 (18.9)	9 (2.0)
No (3089)	1293 (41.9)	1147 (37.1)	583 (18.9)	66 (2.1)
Chi Sq.=.63, d.f.=3, p=.88				
LSite2				
Yes (181)	79 (43.6)	65 (35.9)	34 (18.8)	3 (1.7)

Table 6-2: Bivariate Relationships by Highest Level Force (cont.)

	No Force	Verbal	Restraint	Impact
LSite2				
No (3363)	1397 (41.5)	1259 (37.4)	635 (18.9)	72 (2.1)
Chi Sq.=.48, d.f.=3, p=.923				
LSite3				
Yes (1387)	509 (36.7)	556 (40.1)	284 (20.5)	38 (2.7)
No (2157)	967 (44.8)	768 (35.6)	385 (17.8)	37 (1.7)
Chi Sq.=25.21, d.f.=3, p=.000				
LSite4				
Yes (1268)	621 (49.0)	418 (33.0)	210 (16.6)	19 (1.5)
No (2276)	855 (37.6)	906 (39.8)	459 (20.2)	56 (2.5)
Chi Sq.=44.82, d.f.=3, p=.000				
LSuper1				
Yes (590)	249 (42.2)	224 (38.0)	106 (18.0)	11 (1.9)
No (2954)	1227 (41.5)	1100 (37.2)	563 (19.1)	64 (2.2)
Chi Sq.=.64, d.f.=3, p=.886				
LSuper2				
Yes (41)	13 (31.7)	14 (34.1)	13 (31.7)	1 (2.4)
No (3503)	1463 (41.8)	1310 (37.4)	656 (18.7)	74 (2.1)
Chi Sq.=4.73, d.f.=3, p=.192				
LSuper3				
Yes (2393)	1028 (43.0)	869 (36.3)	447 (18.7)	49 (2.0)
No (1151)	448 (38.9)	455 (39.5)	222 (19.3)	26 (2.3)
Chi Sq.=5.50, d.f.=3, p=.138				
LSuper4				
Yes (243)	100 (41.2)	91 (37.4)	44 (18.1)	8 (3.3)
No (3301)	1376 (41.7)	1233 (37.4)	625 (18.9)	67 (2.0)
Chi Sq.=1.80, d.f.=3, p=.614				

Table 6-2: Bivariate Relationships by Highest Level Force (cont.)

	No Force	Verbal	Restraint	Impact
LWork1				
Yes (433)	173 (40.0)	167 (38.6)	84 (19.4)	9 (2.1)
No (3111)	1303 (41.9)	1157 (37.2)	585 (18.8)	66 (2.1)

Chi Sq.=.60, d.f.=3, p=.895

LWork2				
Yes (203)	89 (43.8)	75 (36.9)	36 (17.7)	2 (1.5)
No (3341)	1387 (41.5)	1249 (37.4)	633 (18.9)	72 (2.2)

Chi Sq.=.82, d.f.=3, p=.844

LWork3				
Yes (277)	99 (35.7)	111 (40.1)	57 (20.6)	10 (3.6)
No (3267)	1377 (42.1)	1213 (37.1)	612 (18.7)	65 (2.0)

Chi Sq.=6.73, d.f.=3, p=.081

LWork4				
Yes (2374)	1028 (43.3)	863 (36.4)	436 (18.4)	47 (2.0)
No (1170)	448 (38.3)	461 (39.4)	233 (19.9)	28 (2.4)

Chi Sq.=8.30, d.f.=3, p=.040

Of the eight officer characteristic variables, several were significantly related to force. Officer experience, education, and training were related at the p<.01 level. Officer race, views toward the citizenry, and views towards legal constraints were significant at the p<.05 level. Each were significant in the predicted direction with the exception of officer race and training.

Interestingly, of the encounters involving white officers, 57.5 percent involved some form of force being applied. Conversely, of the encounters involving nonwhite officers, 61.9 percent involved some form of force. Further, as officer verbal training increased there was a greater likelihood of force. For both verbal and physical force, encounters involving officers who had received the most verbal training (greater than five days) were more likely to involve force than those encounters involving officers who had received no training.

Both educated and experienced officers were less likely to be involved in encounters where force was used. For instance, those with a high school education resorted to force in 67.3 percent of the encounters while those with a Bachelor's degree used force in 55.7 percent. Encounters involving officers who perceived citizens as non-trustworthy (agree strongly) were more likely to involve force than those that did not (68.9% versus 59.0%). Further, encounters involving officers who perceived legal guidelines as a constraint were more likely to involve force than those that did not. Thirty percent of the encounters where physical restraint was applied involved officers who felt (agreed strongly) that legal guidelines acted as a constraint, while physical restraint was used in only 18.5 percent of the encounters where officers strongly disagreed with this assessment.

Three of the four organizational variables were significantly related to force in the predicted direction at the p<.05 level. As shown in Table 6-2, Indianapolis officers were likely to use all forms of force more often than St. Petersburg officers. Second, officers who felt that their supervisor rarely criticized or modified their actions (agree strongly) were more likely to apply some form of force compared to those who did not. Officer perceptions of how other officers within their workgroup view legal guidelines was the third organizational factor related to force. Officers who perceived that all or most of their co-workers felt constrained by legal guidelines were involved in forceful encounters more often than those who believed that none of their co-workers felt this way (64% versus 56.3% respectively)

As expected, all but one (type of problem) of the control variables were significantly related to force (all at the p<.01 level). Again, as predicted, some of these variables have quite strong effects. For instance, 79.4 percent of the citizens arrested were subjected to physical force while only 13.6 percent of those who were not received physical force. Other factors varied by the type of force most often applied. When officers anticipate violence, for example, they are more likely to use physical force than when they do not anticipate violence (30.7% versus 20.0% respectively). Conversely, during proactive stops as opposed to dispatched or citizen initiated encounters, officers rely more readily on verbal force (40.7% versus 34.5% respectively).

Turning to the hybrid variables, only two were significantly related to force at the p<.01 level (LSite3 and LSite4). Indianapolis officers who do not have a proclivity to overlook legal guidelines (LSite3) were more likely to apply force, while St. Petersburg officers with a similar proclivity (LSite4) were less likely to use higher forms of force. The former finding was especially unexpected since the opposite was predicted. As seen in Table 6-2, there is very little variation found in LSite1 (Indianapolis officers *with* a proclivity to overlook legal guidelines). In fact, looking at the variables where the strongest relationships were predicted (LSite1, LSuper1, and LWork1), we see that the percentages are almost identical. Further, looking at all of the hybrid factors, there are generally little differences found.

In sum, this analysis indicates that the use of force occurs more frequently in encounters involving males, nonwhites, younger citizens, lower class citizens, emotional citizens, and citizens displaying signs of drug or alcohol use. Force is also more likely in encounters where a citizen displays resistance, disrespect, or poses a threat to officer or citizen safety. In addition, Indianapolis officers, those with less education and experience, as well as those who feel legal guidelines serve as a constraint, were involved in more forceful encounters than their counterparts.

Those who perceived that their work partners felt constrained by legal guidelines were more likely to be involved in encounters where force was used. Surprisingly, officers with increased levels of verbal training were also more likely to be involved in encounters where force was used. Recall that it was expected that officers who had received increased levels of verbal meditation training would be more likely to use lower forms of force. The assumption was that they would rely on talking through various problems as opposed to relying on coercion to handle it. Force also occurred more frequently in encounters when an arrest occurred, where there was an increased number of officers on the scene, those involving fewer citizens, and those where an officer initiated the encounter or anticipated violence before the encounter began. Finally, Indianapolis officers who do not feel overlooking legal guidelines is necessary to do their job were more likely to use force while their St. Petersburg counterparts who do were not.

6.2 MULTIVARIATE ANALYSES

While the bivariate analysis provides an initial assessment of those factors related to force, it does not allow for an assessment of independent effects. This requires a multivariate analysis, which isolates the effects of each variable on force while statistically controlling other factors. For instance, while citizen race was related to force in a bivariate sense, once citizen resistance is controlled, this relationship may not hold.

Since force was conceived ordinally, this analysis was conducted using ordered probit. McKelvey and Zavonia (1975) have demonstrated the inherent weakness of using linear regression techniques with ordinally ranked dependent measures; namely that such models underestimate the effects of independent variables on the dependent measure. As a result, the preferred model for an ordinally ranked dependent measure is the ordered probit.[4] In addition to the estimates provided by the ordered probit, these estimates can be translated into predicted probabilities.[5] Predicted probabilities are used because of their intuitive appeal and for direct comparisons between categories among independent variables. (see Section C below).

Main Effects
Results from the ordered probit are presented in Table 6-3.[6] As a whole, the model was highly significant as evidenced by the chi-square statistic. As with the bivariate analysis, many of the citizen characteristic variables remain significant even when controlling for other factors. Several of these show a strong relationship to force. Citizen resistance is the strongest determinant of police force within this group.[7] This is not surprising given that resistance is one of the primary legal justifications for applying force; and the fact that resistance has been a consistent predictor of force in previous studies.

Besides resistance, several other variables were significantly related to force. These included citizen characteristics such as males, nonwhites, lower class citizens, young citizens, and those who appeared to have used some form of alcohol or drugs. As with citizen resistance, the use of force on those who appear to be under the influence of drugs or alcohol has been a consistent predictor of force in the past. Westley

Table 6-3: Ordered Probit Model Estimates - Main Effects

	Coefficient	S.E.	Significance
Citizen:			
Male	.295	.048	.000
NonWhite	.101	.043	.018
Age	- .097	.015	.000
Wealth	- .146	.035	.000
Anger/Fear	.090	.047	.054
Drug/Alcohol Use	.355	.048	.000
Mentally Impaired	- .042	.116	.716
Disrespect	- .056	.072	.430
Resistance	.360	.033	.000
Officer:			
Male	.081	.061	.182
White	.027	.053	.612
Experience	- .014	.003	.000
Education	- .040	.013	.002
Verbal Training	.028	.019	.148
Crimefighter	- .021	.029	.469
Citizens Trust	.015	.027	.569
Legal Guidelines	.024	.027	.373
Organization:			
Indianapolis	.192	.049	.000
911 Officer	- .091	.065	.158
Supervision	- .023	.030	.444
Workgroup	- .002	.027	.922

Table 6-3: Ordered Probit Model Estimates - Main Effects (cont.)

	Coefficient	S.E.	Significance
Control:			
# Officers	.057	.013	.000
# Bystanders	- .001	.003	.839
Ant. Violence	- .015	.071	.824
Proactive	.232	.041	.000
Type Problem	.034	.040	.394
Arrest	1.230	.058	.000
Officer Safety	.667	.161	.000
Citizen Conflict	.107	.042	.011

N = 3544
Intercept   - .093
Log Likelihood   - 3447.071
Chi-Square   1107.871 (p<.001)

(1953) and Reiss (1968) noted that "drunks" and other deviant types were particularly susceptible to police force. This was confirmed in subsequent studies (Friedrich, 1977, 1980; Worden, 1995; and Garner et al., 1996).

Nonetheless, in none of these earlier studies has there been such strong evidence about the use of force based on citizen traits. Friedrich (1977, 1980) concluded that much of police force depends on the *behavior* of citizens. Worden (1995), in his analysis of Police Services data, also uncovered this. However, he also found that force was more likely when citizens were male and nonwhite, something Friedrich (1977, 1980) did not find with the Black/Reiss data. Similarly, Garner and colleagues (1996) found that male citizens were subjected to force more often than females. Despite these findings, none of these inquiries produced such widespread evidence indicating that officers use force based on who the citizen is, rather than on his or her actions.

As the results from Table 6-3 show, even when controlling for citizen actions, officers were still more forceful toward youths, nonwhites, lower class citizens, and males. This finding provides support for Black's (1976) theory. Clearly, despite the circumstances such citizens present to officers, they are significantly more likely to be on the receiving end of some form of force. Much of police force does depend on the behavior of the citizen, but the findings uncovered here also show that certain individuals are more likely to be recipients of force despite the actions they present to officers.

In addition to these findings, perhaps the most surprising finding was that of citizen disrespect. *Citizens who displayed disrespectful behavior toward officers were no more likely to have force used on them than those who were respectful.* This runs counter to much of what has been found in previous force studies. Disrespect had been one of the most consistent predictors of police force, yet this was not the case here.

Possibly, the increased attention given toward measuring citizen disrespect and resistance may help to explain this finding. Perhaps adequate care had not been given to properly distinguishing the difference between citizen disrespect and resistance in previous work. It appears that these two similar, yet distinct, behaviors may have been improperly meshed together. For example, Reiss talked about "defying police authority" and the effect this had on police use of force. Yet, defying police authority can take the form of a legal justification for the use of police force or an illegal justification for force. Defying police authority can be perceived as either disrespect, citizen resistance, or both. A citizen who aggressively complains (e.g., what the hell is wrong with you MF cops?) to an officer about his or her treatment during an encounter may be defying police authority because of his or her displeasure with the officers' understanding of the situation. However, this may in no way mean that the citizen was resistant, just disrespectful. Conversely, a citizen who complains in the same manner while failing to respond to an officer's command may be considered both disrespectful and resistant. Each of these behaviors need to be properly distinguished, since one (disrespect) is an extra legal factor, while the other is a legal (resistance) justification for the application of force. Describing a citizen action as one that defies police authority or is antagonistic is not sufficiently clear.

Moving to officer explanations, it seems logical that officers with certain characteristics or background experiences would approach the use of force in different ways. It also makes intuitive sense that officers with particular views or beliefs would resort to force differently than those with dissimilar attitudes (Muir, 1977). However, there has been little support in the past for individual explanations of police force. Various individual factors have been found to be significantly related to force over the years, but there has been a tremendous inconsistency in these findings.

Until recently there has been little support concerning officer gender and the use of force. The Garner study (1996) in Phoenix was the first to show that male officers were more forceful in the course of their duties than female officers. One reason that officer gender has not been a primary predictor of force may be a result of few female officers being on the police force or working street assignments in the past. In some of the more dated studies (e.g., Reiss, 1966) there were not that many female officers with whom to make valid comparisons.

In the present study, female officers were involved in 537 or just over 15.1 percent of the observed encounters. While still not a very high percentage, there is certainly a sufficient number of encounters for comparative purposes. The results, as shown in Table 6-3, are that males were no more likely to be involved in forceful encounters than females. Thus, the Garner study is still the only inquiry to demonstrate a gender effect.

While officer race has been shown to be insignificant in a majority of previous studies (Friedrich, 1977, 1980; Croft, 1985; Worden, 1995; Garner et al., 1995), Cohen and Chaiken (1972) did uncover a race effect. And, although Friedrich (1980) stops short of claiming a race effect, he reported that black officers in the Black/Reiss study patrolled "more aggressively" (e.g., conducting more stops and questioning) than their white counterparts.

In the current analysis, officer race had no effect on forceful behavior. There was no difference in the number of forceful encounters involving white as compared to nonwhite officers. In addition to looking at race in this manner (e.g., officer and citizen race separately), this study also examined citizen and officer race together. Four combinations of officer/citizen race were tested: white officer/nonwhite citizen, white officer/white citizen, nonwhite officer/nonwhite citizen, nonwhite officer/white citizen.[8] This also failed to produce a significant difference. Hence, while nonwhite citizens were subjected to more force, this was not a function of officer race.

Examinations of officer education and police behavior have produced some puzzling findings in the past. Both Cohen and Chaiken (1972), as well as Cascio (1977), found that educated officers received *fewer* citizen complaints. Conversely, Worden (1995) found that educated officers (those with a Bachelor degree) were *more* likely to engage in force. The present research finds that encounters involving officers with higher levels of education were significantly less likely to involve force compared to those involving officers with lower levels of education.

Officer experience was another potential determinant of force tested. Friedrich (1977, 1989) and Worden (1995) discovered that less experienced officers were more likely to patrol aggressively, initiate contacts with citizens, and make arrests. The assumption here is that these officers may be at greater risk for using force. On the other hand, Niederhoffer (1967) hypothesized that experienced officers may be more prone to force because of the increased tendency for these officers to become more authoritarian.

As shown in Table 6-3, the finding from this study supports Friedrich and Worden's findings, in that force was used more often in encounters involving inexperienced officers. Curiously, none of the three "attitude" measures were significantly related to force. This supports previous findings that attitudes seem to be poor predictors of actual behavior. Officers' attitudes and how they may interact with organizational influences were also analyzed and the results presented below.

Of the organizational variables tested, only site emerged as a significant predictor. Indianapolis officers were more likely to resort to force than were St. Petersburg officers. This was predicted as a result of the differing organizational philosophies in each city. Indianapolis management stressed an aggressive get tough policy designed around crackdowns and aggressive stops. By contrast, St. Petersburg officials emphasized problem-solving and community organizing to a greater extent. Despite the hypothesized relationship between front-line supervision and workgroup influences on force, neither of these factors reached statistical significance

In regard to the control variables, all these factors were significantly related to force with the exception of the number of bystanders on the scene, the anticipation of violence, and type of problem. Arrest by far had the greatest impact on force. This is not surprising given the high number of arrests that involve physical restraint in the process of taking the suspect into custody. Similarly, it was expected that officer safety and citizen conflict would be determinants of force. Like citizen resistance, these two factors can be seen as legal justifications for force.

Finally, number of officers on the scene and proactivity were related to force. Worden (1995) and Garner and colleagues (1996) also found that an increased number of officers on the scene increased the likelihood of force. On the other hand, proactivity had not been closely examined in previous studies. However, it was posited that proactive stops had a greater likelihood of force since officers are placing the responsibility upon themselves to intervene in the lives of citizens. As hypothesized, encounters initiated by officers themselves did indeed involve a greater likelihood of force.

Interaction Effects - Perception of Legal Guidelines and Organizational Context

As seen in the main effects model, none of the officer attitude measures were significantly related to force and only one of the organizational measures was significant (e.g., site). However, there may be more at work here. As noted earlier, the impact of force decisions may be better explained by looking across levels of explanation. In other words, officers with certain proclivities may be more inclined to act on these when placed in a context that promotes such behavior.

To test the interaction hypotheses, three particular interactions were examined, each involving officer perceptions concerning the importance of legal guidelines. More specifically, the hypothesis that officers who feel legal guidelines presents an obstacle to carrying out their duties, when combined with an environment conducive to this line of reasoning, will be more inclined to apply force than those with dissimilar views and working environments.

Thus, officer views toward legal guidelines are combined with each of the first three organizational influences posited earlier. It was hypothesized that Indianapolis officers with a proclivity to overlook legal guidelines would be more coercive than their St. Petersburg counterparts. It was also hypothesized that officers with a proclivity to overlook legal guidelines and work for a supervisor that rarely intervenes or attempts to modify their behavior would be more coercive than those who work for a first-line supervisor that more closely monitors his or her behavior. Finally, it was posited that officers with a proclivity to overlook legal guidelines and work with a group of officers perceived to have the same beliefs would be more coercive. Each assumes that officers with an inclination toward viewing legal guidelines negatively may be further influenced by the organizational context in which they find themselves, which may more readily permit them to resort to forceful ways. Each assumes a different level of influence: site (department), supervisor (first-line), and workgroup (peer).

To test for these effects, three separate elaboration models were estimated - one for each hypothesized interactive relationship. In each case, three of the four interaction terms were introduced while one was excluded, which served as the reference category.[9] The reference categories were as follows: LSite1, LSuper1, and LWork1, as these were hypothesized to be the most coercive. Results are presented in Table 6-4.

As shown, *none of the interactions were significantly related to force.* As seen in the main effects model, officer proclivity to overlook legal guidelines was not significantly related to force. Nonetheless, it was hypothesized that different levels of perceived organizational influence combined with such a proclivity may help tip the scales toward more forceful behavior, but this clearly was not the case.

After viewing the similarity shown in the bivariate relationships, this was not overly surprising. Such a finding of "no effect" is encouraging, as it demonstrates that personal bias, in this case individual perceptions toward legal constraints, when combined with organizational perceptions, do not alter behavior. *Thus, negative officer belief systems are negated even when the organizational climate encourages such action.*

From an intuitive standpoint, this was somewhat surprising. The fact that neither upper-level management, mid-level management, nor the peer group (as perceived by the individual officer) influenced officer behavior, even when they were predisposed toward overlooking legal constraints, was unexpected and requires additional thought towards the interaction between the individual and varying potential external influences.

Table 6-4: Ordered Probit Model Estimates - Interaction Effects

	Site Model			Supervision Model			Workgroup Model		
	Coeff.	*SE*	*p*	*Coeff.*	*SE*	*p*	*Coeff.*	*SE*	*p*
Citizen:									
Male	.295	.048	.000	.295	.048	.000	.295	.048	.000
NonWhite	.099	.043	.021	.101	.043	.018	.098	.043	.022
Age	-.099	.015	.000	-.097	.016	.000	-.098	.016	.000
Wealth	-.145	.035	.000	-.147	.035	.000	-.143	.035	.000
Anger/Fear	.081	.047	.083	.089	.047	.057	.090	.047	.056
Drug/Alcohol	.354	.048	.000	.353	.048	.000	.357	.048	.000
Mental Impairment	-.047	.116	.683	-.041	.116	.719	-.034	.116	.767
Disrespect	-.052	.072	.469	-.055	.072	.439	-.059	.072	.409
Resistance	.360	.033	.000	.360	.033	.000	.360	.033	.000
Officer:									
Male	.081	.061	.189	.083	.061	.173	.096	.061	.116
White	.018	.053	.736	.025	.053	.634	.011	.054	.829
Experience	-.013	.004	.000	-.014	.003	.000	-.013	.003	.000
Education	-.040	.013	.002	-.040	.013	.002	-.035	.013	.007
Verbal Training	.027	.020	.174	.027	.020	.177	.026	.020	.187
Crimefighter	-.022	.029	.450	-.020	.029	.482	-.029	.029	.482

Table 6-4: Ordered Probit Model Estimates - Interaction Effects (cont.)

	Site Model			Supervision Model			Workgroup Model		
	Coeff	SE	p	Coeff	SE	p	Coeff	SE	p
Officer:									
Citizens Trust	.010	.027	.695	.015	.027	.581	.016	.027	.543
Legal Guidelines	--	--	--	--	--	--	--	--	--
Organization:									
Indianapolis	--	--	--	.191	.050	.000	.200	.049	.000
Supervision	-.023	.030	.448	--	--	--	-.019	.030	.526
Workgroup	-.008	.028	.763	.003	.027	.907	--	--	--
911 Officer	-.092	.064	.154	-.089	.065	.167	-.081	.065	.212
Control:									
# Officers	.059	.013	.000	.057	.013	.000	.058	.013	.000
# Bystanders	-.001	.003	.798	-.001	.003	.845	-.001	.003	.764
Anticipate Violence	-.022	.070	.755	-.014	.071	.833	-.011	.070	.873
Proactive	.233	.041	.000	.230	.041	.000	.229	.041	.000
Type Problem	.034	.040	.405	.035	.040	.386	.036	.040	.378
Arrest	1.237	.058	.000	1.238	.058	.000	1.237	.058	.000
Officer Safety	.668	.159	.000	.669	.161	.000	.670	.161	.000

Table 6-4: Ordered Probit Model Estimates - Interaction Effects (cont.)

	Site Model			Supervision Model			Workgroup Model		
	Coeff	*SE*	*p*	*Coeff*	*SE*	*p*	*Coeff*	*SE*	*p*
Control:									
Citizen Conflict	.108	.042	.011	.106	.042	.012	.106	.042	.013
Hybrid:									
Site2	- .016	.064	.876						
Site3	.115	.109	.110						
Site4	- .096	.072	.227						
Super2				.029	.171	.865			
Super3				.044	.061	.469			
Super4				.016	.099	.866			
Work2							.113	.101	.262
Work3							.153	.092	.099
Work4							.079	.062	.198
Intercept	.129			- .899			- .148		
Log Likelihood	- 3446.948			- 3447.952			- 3448.482		
Chi-Square	- 1108.116			- 1106.108			- 1105.048		
N	3544			3544			3544		

Predicted Probabilities

Another way to view the effects of the various determinants is to consider predicted probabilities on each level of force. This allows for a comparison of each independent variable category and the probability of following into each of the four levels of force. Table 6-5 presents the predicted probabilities of those factors found to be significantly related to force. Viewing citizen characteristics, we see that males have a greater chance of being on the receiving end of all forms of force. Here, the greatest difference lies in physical restraint. While males had a 19.3 percent chance of being recipients of physical restraint, the probability of officers using physical restraint on females was 12.4 percent. Officers were also more likely to use verbal force on males as opposed to females (45.0% versus 40.8%). The difference in the probability of force between white and nonwhite citizens was less than that of males and females. Although nonwhites had a higher chance of verbal and impact force, these differences were fairly small. The largest difference is found in physical restraint, and even here the difference in probability is 0.25.

Citizen wealth produced more pronounced differences in the probability that force would be used, especially with verbal force and physical restraint. Citizens in the chronic poverty category had a 36.7 percent and 9.0 percent chance of being recipients of verbal force and physical restraint force respectively, compared to 25.5 percent and 3.8 percent of those in the above middle category. However, the probability of impact force between categories of wealth was minimal. A similar pattern emerged with citizen age and drug/alcohol use, although the greatest difference in probability was found with physical restraint as opposed to verbal force. With age, young adults had approximately an 8 percent greater probability of physical restraint compared to middle-aged citizens; while those showing signs of drug/alcohol use were about 10 percent more likely to be a recipient of physical restraint compared to those who were not.

The probabilities uncovered within citizen resistance partially confirm what was found in the bivariate analysis - verbal resistance prompts verbal force, while physical resistance prompts physical force. For instance, as shown, those citizens who are verbally resistant have a 68.1 percent chance of being issued a command or threat by an officer.

Table 6-5: Predicted Probabilities
Level of Force

	No Force	Verbal	Restraint	Impact
Citizen:				
Gender				
Male	.352	.450	.193	.005
Female	.466	.408	.124	.002
Race				
NonWhite	.369	.446	.181	.004
White	.408	.433	.156	.003
Age				
Young Adult	.304	.459	.230	.007
Older Teen	.339	.453	.203	.005
Adult	.375	.444	.177	.004
Middle-Aged	.413	.430	.154	.003
Wealth				
Chronic Poverty	.542	.367	.090	.001
Low	.599	.331	.069	.001
Middle	.655	.293	.052	.000
Above Middle	.707	.255	.038	.000
Drug/Alcohol Use				
Yes	.282	.461	.249	.008
No	.412	.431	.154	.003
Resistance				
None	.412	.431	.154	.003
Passive	.281	.460	.250	.009
Verbal	.174	.681	.124	.021
Defensive	.096	.375	.481	.048
Active	.048	.285	.571	.096
Officer:				
Experience				
One year	.349	.451	.195	.005
Five Year	.370	.445	.181	.004
Ten Year	.398	.436	.163	.003

Table 6-5: Predicted Probabilities
Level of Force (cont.)

	No Force	Verbal	Restraint	Impact
Officer:				
Education				
High School	.348	.451	.196	.005
Associate Degree	.379	.442	.175	.004
Bachelor Degree	.409	.417	.171	.003
Organization:				
Site				
Indianapolis	.351	.450	.194	.005
St. Petersburg.	.425	.426	.146	.003
Control:				
Officers on Scene				
One	.410	.432	.155	.003
Two	.388	.439	.169	.004
Three	.366	.446	.184	.004
Proactive Stop				
Yes	.335	.454	.205	.006
No	.424	.426	.147	.003
Arrest				
Yes	.081	.351	.509	.059
No	.436	.421	.140	.003
Officer Safety				
Yes	.170	.438	.370	.022
No	.387	.440	.169	.004
Citizen Conflict				
None	.388	.439	.169	.004
Calm Verbal	.348	.451	.196	.005
Agitated Verbal	.309	.458	.226	.007
Threatened	.272	.461	.258	.009
Assaulted	.239	.459	.290	.012

However, there is only a 14.5 percent chance that the officer will use physical force on a verbally resistant citizen. Conversely, those citizens who display defensive resistance have a 52.9 percent chance of physical force and those who actively resist have 66.7 percent chance of being a recipient of physical force. Somewhat surprisingly, citizens who are passively resistant face a 25 percent chance of physical restraint, double the chance of a verbally resistant citizen. Hence, there is a much greater chance of physical restraint being applied when citizens passively resist as opposed to verbally resist.

Two other points are worth noting. First, there is nearly a 16 percent chance that officers will use some form of physical force on completely nonresistant citizens - citizens who are never resistant in any form nor at any point during the encounter. Second, even when citizens resist in the most aggressive manner, there is still a 33.3 percent chance that officers do not match such resistance with the highest form of force (impact methods). These two extremes point to fairly widespread variation in officer behavior. A substantial number of cases seem to fall outside the norm of what may be the expected response. In one set of cases it appears officers are responding somewhat harshly while in the other they seem to be responding somewhat lightly. Such a finding serves to highlight the importance of the analyses performed in the following chapter - more closely linking citizen behavior with police behavior.

The two officer characteristics related to force were education and experience. Looking at Table 6-5 we see that those encounters involving less educated and less experienced officers were more likely to involve each form of force. For instance, in encounters involving officers with high school educations there was a 45.1 percent and 19.6 percent chance of verbal and physical force being applied compared to 41.7 percent and 17.1 percent respectively for those involving officers with a Bachelor's degree. This same pattern exists for officer experience as well, producing almost the same exact probabilities.

It was also discovered that Indianapolis officers were more coercive than St. Petersburg officers. This finding held for all types of force. Indianapolis officers had a 45 percent chance of using verbal force, nearly 20 percent chance of restraint, and 0.5 percent chance of applying impact methods in their encounters with suspects. In contrast, the probability of verbal force was 42.6 percent, physical restraint 14.6

percent, and impact force 0.3 percent for those encounters involving St. Petersburg officers. As with many of the significant factors, we see that the greatest difference is found in the use of physical restraint.

Of the control variables, the number of officers on the scene and whether an encounter was initiated by the officer produced consistent, but moderate differences in probabilities. More pronounced differences emerged in the remaining three significant determinants. As shown in Table 6-5, the probability of physical restraint was .50 for those arrested and only .14 for those not arrested. On the other hand, the probability of verbal force was greater for those suspects not arrested (.42 versus .35). Also, the chance of an arrested citizen being subjected to impact force was much greater than those who were not arrested (.059 versus .003). An officer safety issue also produced a much greater chance of physical force. Citizens possessing some sort of weapon were twice as likely to be physically restrained compared to those who did not (37.0% versus 16.9% respectively). Finally, the probability of physical force was also substantially higher when citizens on the scene were in conflict with one another.

6.3 SUMMARY

Several interesting findings emerged from this analysis. It was no surprise that much of police force behavior is driven by the citizen behavior that preceded it. This comes mainly in the form of citizen resistance, in the process of arrest, as well as when a threat to citizen or officer safety is presented. However, the fact that officers do not, on average, respond with force to disrespectful citizens is a surprise - and a rather substantial one. This is certainly encouraging from a police professionalism standpoint. Responding to a legal factor (resistance) as opposed to an extra legal factor (disrespect) is a finding any police chief would applaud. Despite this, not all of the findings are so encouraging. Particularly troubling is that officers applied more force to certain individuals despite his or her behavior. Specifically, officers were more coercive toward males, nonwhites, citizens of lower wealth, and younger citizens.

From an individual officer perspective, several factors play a role in forceful behavior. Both officer education and experience had an effect on force in the predicted direction. Encounters involving officers with increased levels of education, as well as those with more years on the job resulted in less force. Of the organizational factors, encounters involving Indianapolis officers resulted in more force. As seen in the predicted probabilities table, Indianapolis officers were more likely to apply verbal and physical restraint. This was actually the case for most of the significant factors. When significant differences were present, it was primarily found in verbal force and physical restraint.

Finally, no differences were found when testing the various interactive relationships. In fact, very little variation was uncovered. It was originally believed that officers with a proclivity to see legal guidelines as a constraint may be more inclined toward forceful behavior given their organizational environment. However, regardless of the officer's view, organizational influences did not promote differences in forceful behavior.

## CHAPTER 7

Application of the Force Continuum

The concept of a force continuum has been fully explained in previous chapters. The continuum provides a means or analytic tool for measuring and examining police use of force relative to citizen resistance. The benefit of examining police force through use of a force continuum is that it identifies instances when officers fail to escalate and de-escalate force in small increments in relation to citizen resistance. Concern over the proper use of force is most pronounced when it appears that the level of police force is not congruent with the level of resistance that preceded it: instances when a citizen is compliant, but the officer chooses to use physical restraint; instances when a citizen passively resists, but is thrown to the ground; instances when a citizen verbally resists and the officer delivers a blow to the head; and, even instances when a citizen refuses to adhere to a command, but the officer chooses to ignore such resistance. In general, it is one thing for an officer to tackle a fleeing suspect. It is quite another for an officer to tackle a fleeing suspect, place him in handcuffs, and then proceed to mace him. Using the force continuum as a measuring device is nothing more than a way to more adequately identify those instances when resistance and force appear to diverge.

This chapter covers the extent to which police behavior adheres to a force continuum. Encounters are "sequenced out" to account for successive citizen and police behaviors. This allows for the examination of what factors are related to those instances when officers refrain from moving up the continuum despite resistance, move up and down the continuum incrementally based on resistance, or apply higher forms of force given the level of resistance. Throughout the chapter these responses are referred to as: *refraining* from following the continuum, *following* the continuum, and *jumping* the continuum respectively. In short, an officer has one of three options when faced with a resistant citizen:

- apply less force (refrain) than the continuum criteria provides,
- apply force (follow) in accordance with the continuum criteria,
- apply more force (jump) than the continuum criteria provides.[1]

Descriptive statistics are presented in Table 7-1 for each of the variables under study, including the range, mean, and standard deviations. The hypothesized relationships are the same as in the previous chapter. For example, it is hypothesized that officers will be more likely to jump the continuum when dealing with nonwhite citizens as opposed to white citizens. However, in the current analysis it is also posited that officers will be more likely to refrain from following the continuum when dealing with white citizens. One of the models tested here provides for not only whether nonwhite citizens are more likely to be subjected to force in the sense of an officer jumping the continuum, but also whether white citizens are on the opposite end of the spectrum when officers hold back from using force in accordance with the continuum criteria. This is a novel of way of examining how force is applied. Certain citizens (e.g., whites) may not only be less likely to be on the receiving end of more extreme force, but they may actually be more likely to be recipients of little to no force despite presenting the same levels of resistance to officers.

As seen in Table 7-1, statistics are listed for two separate models. Given the design of the question posed in this chapter it is necessary to estimate two models. Force1 is used in the model involving those cases where the citizen never displayed resistance at any point during the encounter. The research question seeks to answer whether an officer refrains, follows, or jumps the continuum. However, the first of these options is unavailable to an officer who never encounters resistance. An officer cannot refrain from following the continuum when the citizen never presents the opportunity to do so. As a result, an officer is left with one of two options: follow the continuum or jump the continuum.

Table 7-1: Continuum Descriptive Statistics

		Non-Resistant Citizen Logistic Model		Resistant Citizen Multinomial Logit	
Outcome Variables:	Range	Mean	S.D.	Mean	S.D.
Force1 (Logistic) (Follow=0; n=2519) (More=1; n=595)	0-1	.191	.393	-----	-----
Force2 (Multinomial) (Follow=0; n=68) (Less=1; n=250) (More=2; n=25)	0-2	-----	-----	.874	.506
Citizen:					
Gender	0-1	.714	.415	.731	.443
Race	0-1	.613	.487	.702	.457
Age	1-8	5.207	1.356	5.274	1.412
Wealth	1-4	2.383	.561	2.227	.546
Emotional State	0-1	.281	.449	.588	.492
Drug/Alcohol Impaired	0-1	.177	.381	.448	.498
Mentally Impaired	0-1	.025	.158	.081	.274
Disrespect	0-1	.066	.249	.428	.495
Officer:					
Gender	0-1	.850	.356	.833	.372
Race	0-1	.195	.396	.215	.411
Experience	1-32	7.406	6.081	6.233	5.818
Education	1-8	4.321	1.890	3.912	2.161
Verbal Training	1-4	1.687	1.174	1.577	1.171
Crimefighter	1-4	1.755	.829	1.615	.900
Distrust	1-4	2.693	1.144	2.626	1.216
Individual Legal Guidelines	1-4	3.184	1.204	2.900	1.394

Table 7-1: Continuum Descriptive Statistics (cont.)

	Range	Non-Resistant Citizen Logistic Model		Resistant Citizen Multinomial Logit	
		Mean	S.D.	Mean	S.D.
Organization:					
Site	0-1	.555	.496	.603	.489
Assignment	0-1	.867	.339	.895	.306
Supervisor Criticism	1-4	1.282	.739	1.309	.832
Workgroup Legal Guidelines	1-4	2.766	1.137	2.481	1.272
Control:					
Number of Officers	1-26	2.122	1.438	2.813	2.571
Number of Bystanders	1-99	3.930	4.713	6.037	10.088
Anticipate Violence	0-1	.077	.266	.157	.364
Proactive Encounter	0-1	.471	.499	.306	.461
Type Problem	0-1	.473	.499	.448	.498
Pattern1	0-1	.181	.385	--	--
Pattern2	0-1	.060	.237	--	--
Pattern3	0-1	.758	.427	--	--
Pattern1	0-1	--	--	.530	.499
Pattern2	0-1	--	--	.090	.287
Pattern3	0-1	--	--	.102	.303
Pattern4	0-1	--	--	.276	.448
Missing	0-1	.125	.331	.119	.324
Hybrid:					
LSite1	0-1	.123	.328	.180	.385
LSite2	0-1	.005	.218	.055	.229
LSite3	0-1	.390	.487	.370	.483
LSite4	0-1	.366	.481	.314	.465
LSuper1	0-1	.162	.369	.201	.401
LSuper2	0-1	.001	.009	.029	.168
LSuper3	0-1	.685	.464	.603	.489

Table 7-1: Continuum Descriptive Statistics (cont.)

		Non-Resistant Citizen Logistic Model		Resistant Citizen Multinomial Logit	
Hybrid:	Range	Mean	S.D.	Mean	S.D.
LSuper4	0-1	.006	.249	.072	.260
LWork1	0-1	.114	.318	.183	.387
LWork2	0-1	.005	.235	.052	.223
LWork3	0-1	.007	.269	.064	.245
LWork4	0-1	.676	.468	.620	.485

Therefore, these cases are analyzed using a logistic regression model. Force2 is used in the model involving cases where a citizen displayed some form of resistance. In these cases the officer is presented with each of the three options from which to choose and a multinomial logit model is employed.[2]

Before presenting the relationship between each of the independent factors and the continuum, it is important to note that, on the whole, *officers rarely strayed far from the continuum even in those cases where they did not follow it.* A vast majority of the cases where officers refrained from moving up or jumped the continuum involved minimal deviation. For example, in 103 of the 250 (41.2%) cases where officers refrained from moving up the continuum, the nature of refraining was in the form of a citizen mildly resisting (passive or verbal) and the officer countering with no force.[3] In another 68 cases (27.2%), the form taken was that of a verbally resistant citizen and the officer following with a command. Therefore, in over two-thirds of the refraining cases (68.4%) the manner in which the officer held back was minimal. In fact, officers refrained from increasing their use of force on the continuum, in a more pronounced manner, in only 4 of the 250 cases (1.6%). In one case a citizen struck an officer who responded with no force; in another a citizen defensively resisted and the officer applied no force; and in the remaining two, a citizen struck an officer and the officer issued a command. Thus, the "typical" refraining case could be categorized as that of involving "minimal" refraining. The following examples illustrate such cases:

Encounter 1 (officer sees people drinking outside a government housing complex and after questioning five individuals turns her attention to C6)

O1 then turned to C6, a black male approximately 25 years old, who had come over to the group and sat on the trunk of the unoccupied car about the time that O1 was questioning C2. *O1 proceeded to ask C6 if he lived at the complex and his response to her was that she did not need to know.* O1, who's demeanor up to this point had been-like I said-curt yet still quite pleasant, changed a degree to a more authoritative tone. C6 got up off the hood of the car and began to walk away and O1 began to follow. O1 asked C6 for his name to which he exclaimed in a rather nasty and defensive tone with a scowl on his face, *"I don't gotta talk to you!"* O1 then got on the radio and requested for a backup unit to watch the group of people while she went to talk to management. O1 just looked to C6 and seemed to threaten him by saying "Ok, if you don't want to cooperate." At this point C4 told O1 that the management had walked by minutes before she arrived and had seen the group in the parking lot and had said nothing so they apparently had no problem with their actions.

Encounter 2 (while investigating a dispute)

O1 asked C2 for her name, date of birth, and SSN. O1 wrote the information down and asked C2 for her ID. O1 took the ID and went over to C1 and asked him his name. *C1 ignored O1's questions so O1 went back over to C2 and asked her for C1's information.* O1 wrote the information down and started writing the report.

Encounter 3 (dispute)

O1 and O2 met C1(BM 30's) outside the inner-city lower-class apartment building that he resided in. The three of them walked into the building lobby together. C1 told O1 that he was the person that called. O1 asked what the problem was. C1 began to tell how another resident in the building told him that he could not walk through the lobby without a shirt on and that an argument ensued at which time the man poked him in the chest and in return C1 asked the man not to touch him and that if he wanted they could go outside and he would 'kick his ass'. O1 asked C1 for his identification information. C1 complied until O1 asked for his social security number. *C1 said that he was not going to give him his social security number. O1 said that he would be able to find it out on his own. C1 said that he knew he could but that he knew his rights and that he did not have to disclose it. C1 appeared emotionally distraught and with exaggerated body movements said that he was tired of speaking his social security number so that anyone could hear it then punch into a computer. O1 shrugged off C1's tirade.*

Encounter 4 (police custody)

O1 and O2 then led C1 to the rear of the ambulance where they helped him climb up. O1 looked at C1 and told him to calm down and that they were not going to hurt him. *C1 agreed to calm down at O1's request but must have forgotten once he got into the ambulance because he started being belligerent again.* It appeared as though C1 was going to cooperate as O2 and the EMS workers began restraining him. *C1 then started screaming and flailing about in the back of the ambulance. C1's arms were handcuffed to the gurney but his legs were not yet restrained and he had some sort of breathing apparatus placed on his face [which seemed to be placed there only in an effort to muffle C1's objections and screams.] O1, who was outside of the ambulance rinsing his hands with disinfectant, now climbed back into the side of the ambulance and told C1 to calm down again and that he was not going to allow C1 to hurt anyone.* C1 was screaming and straining to the point of making his face red. C1 was also foaming at the mouth as he screamed "HELP ME, HELP ME!." In the struggle O2 attempted to restrain C1's artificial leg and it came off. O2 handed the leg to O1 who pretended it was kicking him in the butt while C1 screamed as if he was in terrible pain.

O2 agreed to ride in the ambulance with C1 and O1 decided to
follow in his patrol car.

    In the first three examples the officer just ignores the resistant
behavior or seeks an alternative way to deal with the situation. In the last
example, the citizen continues his attempt to resist (although limited since
he is already partially restrained) and the observed officer still initially
attempts to verbally seek compliance upon entering the ambulance. The
backup officer goes on to use further physical restraint.

    A similar pattern emerged in reference to jumps in the
continuum. Of the 595 cases where an officer jumped the continuum when
dealing with a "nonresistant" citizen, only 10 (1.6%) would be classified
as extreme jumps (e.g., officer striking a nonresistant citizen with a
flashlight to the head). In eight of these cases the observed officer used
level five force (pain compliance/takedown) on a nonresistant citizen. In
the other two cases the officer used impact methods on a nonresistant
citizen. In the remaining 585 (98.4%) cases, officers either issued a threat
or applied physical restraint to a nonresistant citizen. Thus, in a great
majority of cases the form of the jump was minimal.[4] Further, of the 343
cases involving a "resistant" citizen, officers jumped the continuum in 25
(7.2%). Of these 25, eight may be categorized as extreme jumps. In four,
officers used level five force (pain compliance/takedown) on a citizen
displaying level two resistance (passive); three involved impact force on
a passively resistant citizen; and one involved impact force on a citizen
who was verbally resistant. The following examples illustrate the typical
jump:

Encounter 1 (officer suspects involvement with drugs)
O1 left his cruiser, and began walking towards the group of kids,
who did not run, but groaned at the police presence and stayed
where they were at. *O1 began frisking the kids* to see if they had
drugs or weapons on their person. He began with C1, a black
male in his mid twenties and in the lower class strata based on
his appearance. He then went on the C2, C3, and C4, who were
all black male in their mid teens and in the lower class strata

judging by their clothing. O1 spent very little time on each citizen, and when he was finished, he collected them all so that he could see them. He then began talking very calmly to them, assuring them that they weren't going to be arrested. The teens were very riled up, and O1 was talking to them in a cool dialect, using phrases and terminology that younger people use.

Encounter 2 (officer suspects citizen is involved with drugs)
O1 pulled up to C1 (WM37, low SES based on dirty dress; nervous demeanor based on talking fast) (reference activity 19), stopped him and asked him where he was going. C1 said he was just trying to get paid for some jobs that he had done and was on his way home. O1 said that C1 had ridden his bike through several stop signs without stopping, and that was why O1 had stopped C1. O1 asked if he could search C1 and C1 agreed. *O1 patted C1 down*, searched his hat, and then let him go. C1 left without indicating any emotion or saying anything.

Encounter 3 (Officer dealing with a juvenile involved in an suspected altercation)
C2 began to say at this point that they would not "whip" her because the police were there and she would have them arrested for abusing her. O1 immediately jumped in the conversation and said "young lady, there is nothing wrong with being disciplined and if your grandma wants me to *I will hold you down while she whips your little ass.*"

As seen in these examples none of the actions are drastic in the sense of extreme force on a minimally resistant citizen. The first two involve simple pat downs, while the latter involves a threat. In sum, although refraining or "holding back" cases, as well as those involving a jump of the continuum are presented here, it must be remembered that while falling outside the continuum criteria, most deviations are minimal.

7.1 FORCE AND THE NONRESISTANT CITIZEN

Bivariate Relationships

As a whole, officers chose to jump the continuum in nearly 20 percent of the nonresistant cases (595 of 3114 cases). Table 7-2 presents the bivariate relationships, for those encounters where the citizen was nonresistant, between each of the independent variables and whether the officer followed or jumped the continuum. Many of the findings found here are similar to those found in the previous chapter when examining the highest level of force.

Citizen gender, race, age, wealth, and indication of alcohol/drug use were all significantly related to force in the predicted direction (at the $p<.01$ level). For instance, while officers jumped the continuum in 11.5 percent of the encounters involving female citizens, they did so in 22.2 percent of those involving male citizens. Officers were also more likely to jump the continuum in encounters involving nonwhites compared to whites (20.6% versus 16.8%). Further, while 30.5 percent of the citizens classified as yong adults (13-17 years old) were subjected to more force, only 15.2 percent of adults (30-44 years old) were. A similar pattern emerges for both citizen wealth and alcohol/drug use. For instance, while officers jumped the continuum on 25% of those classified as having chronic low wealth, officers jumped the continuum on 16% of those classified as middle class, and on none of the suspects deemed above middle class wealth.

Several of the officer characteristic variables were significant. Three were related to force at the $p<.05$ level (gender, race, and verbal training), while four were related at the $p<.01$ level (experience, education, crimefighter, and views toward legal guidelines). For example, while nearly 20 percent of the encounters involving male officers resulted in a jump of the continuum, the same outcome occurred in only 15 percent of those involving female officers. Also, encounters involving officers who perceive their role as one of a crimefighter (agree strongly) were more likely to result in a jump of the continuum, compared to those who did not (disagree strongly). The greatest difference can be found in the legal guidelines variable.

Table 7-2: Bivariate Relationships by the Continuum
Encounters Involving No Resistance (N=3114)

	Follow	Jump
Citizen:		
Gender		
Male (2224)	1731 (77.8)	493 (22.5)
Female (890)	788 (88.5)	102 (11.5)
Chi Sq.=47.14, d.f.=1, p=.000		
Race		
White (1205)	1003 (83.2)	202 (16.8)
NonWhite (1909)	1516 (79.4)	393 (20.6)
Chi Sq.=6.98, d.f.=1, p=.008		
Age		
Pre-School, 0-5 years (6)	6 (100)	--
Child, 6-12 years (74)	57 (77.0)	17 (23.0)
Young Adult, 13-17 years (400)	278 (69.5)	122 (30.5)
Older Teen, 18-20 years (329)	243 (73.9)	86 (26.1)
Young Adult, 21-29 years (768)	614 (79.9)	154 (20.1)
Adult, 30-44 years (1143)	969 (84.8)	174 (15.2)
Middle-Aged, 45-59 years (303)	265 (87.5)	38 (12.5)
Senior, 60+ years (91)	87 (95.6)	4 (4.4)
Chi Sq.=79.04, d.f.=7, p=.000		
Wealth		
Chronic (104)	78 (75.0)	26 (25.0)
Low (1732)	1365 (78.8)	367 (21.2)
Middle (1259)	1057 (84.0)	202 (16.0)
Above Middle (19)	19 (100)	--
Chi Sq.=19.32, d.f.=3, p=.000		

Table 7-2: Bivariate Relationships by the Continuum Encounters Involving No Resistance (N=3114) (cont.)

	Follow	Jump
Emotional State		
Fear/Anger (877)	722 (82.3)	155 (17.7)
No (2237)	1797 (80.3)	440 (19.7)
Chi Sq.=1.62, d.f.=1, p=.203		
Drug/Alcohol Use		
Yes (552)	401 (72.6)	151 (27.4)
No (2562)	2118 (82.7)	444 (17.3)
Chi Sq.=29.52, d.f.=1, p=.000		
Mentally Impaired		
Yes (80)	70 (87.5)	10 (12.5)
No (3034)	2449 (80.7)	585 (19.3)
Chi Sq.=2.31, d.f.=1, p=.128		
Disrespectful		
Yes (207)	172 (83.1)	35 (16.9)
No (2907)	2347 (80.7)	560 (19.3)
Chi Sq.=.69, d.f.=1, p=.405		
Officer:		
Gender		
Male (2648)	2123 (80.2)	496 (19.8)
Female (466)	396 (85.0)	70 (15.0)
Chi Sq.=5.91, d.f.=1, p=.015		
Race		
White (2506)	2010 (80.2)	496 (19.8)
NonWhite (608)	509 (83.7)	99 (16.3)
Chi Sq.=3.89, d.f.=1, p=.048		

Table 7-2: Bivariate Relationships by the Continuum Encounters Involving No Resistance (N=3114) (cont.)

	Follow	Jump
Experience (Years on Job)		
One (166)	143 (86.1)	23 (13.9)
Five (426)	345 (81.0)	81 (19.0)
Ten (102)	84 (82.4)	18 (17.6)
Chi Sq.=55.90, d.f.=31, p=.004		
Education		
< than High School (49)	39 (79.6)	10 (20.4)
High School Grad/GED (372)	298 (80.1)	74 (19.9)
Some College, no degree (648)	544 (84.0)	104 (16.0)
Assoc. Degree (137)	104 (75.9)	33 (24.1)
>2 years college, no B.S. (507)	408 (80.5)	99 (19.5)
B.S./B.A. (1078)	899 (83.4)	179 (16.6)
Some Graduate, no degree (160)	109 (68.1)	51 (31.9)
Graduate Degree (6)	5 (83.3)	1 (16.7)
Chi Sq.=35.72, d.f.=8, p=.000		
Verbal Training		
None (1711)	1410 (82.4)	301 (19.6)
<1 day (516)	400 (77.5)	116 (22.5)
1-2 days (405)	336 (83.0)	69 (17.0)
3-5 days (187)	151 (80.7)	36 (19.3)
>5 days (110)	85 (77.3)	25 (22.7)
Chi Sq.=13.99, d.f.=5, p=.016		
Crimefighter		
Agree Strongly (967)	802 (82.9)	165 (17.1)
Agree Somewhat (1543)	1223 (79.3)	320 (20.7)
Disagree Somewhat (351)	294 (83.8)	57 (16.2)
Disagree Strongly (90)	81 (90.0)	9 (10.0)
Chi Sq.=18.52, d.f.=4, p=.001		

Table 7-2: Bivariate Relationships by the Continuum Encounters Involving No Resistance (N=3114) (cont.)

	Follow	**Jump**
Distrust		
Agree Strongly (64)	50 (78.1)	14 (21.9)
Agree Somewhat (736)	588 (79.9)	148 (20.1)
Disagree Somewhat (1248)	1028 (82.4)	220 (17.6)
Disagree Strongly (777)	620 (79.8)	157 (20.2)
Chi Sq.=3.18, d.f.=4, p=.528		
Individual Legal Guidelines		
Agree Strongly (88)	63 (71.6)	25 (28.4)
Agree Somewhat (452)	370 (81.9)	82 (18.1)
Disagree Somewhat (500)	418 (83.6)	82 (16.4)
Disagree Strongly (1856)	1517 (81.7)	339 (18.3)
Chi Sq.=27.48, d.f.=4, p=.000		
Organization:		
Site		
Indianapolis (1730)	1350 (78.0)	380 (22.0)
St. Petersburg (1384)	1169 (84.5)	215 (15.5)
Chi Sq.=20.57, d.f.=1, p=.000		
Assignment		
911 (2700)	2181 (80.8)	519 (19.2)
CPO (414)	338 (81.6)	76 (18.4)
Chi Sq.=.17, d.f.=1, p=.677		
Supervisor Criticism		
Agree Strongly (2171)	1761 (81.1)	410 (18.9)
Agree Somewhat (514)	427 (83.1)	87 (16.9)
Disagree Somewhat (194)	151 (77.8)	43 (22.2)
Disagree Strongly (53)	47 (88.7)	6 (11.3)
Chi Sq.=12.09, d.f.=4, p=.017		

Table 7-2: Bivariate Relationships by the Continuum Encounters Involving No Resistance (N=3114) (cont.)

	Follow	Jump
Workgroup Legal Guidelines		
All of most (298)	225 (75.5)	73 (24.5)
About half (319)	270 (84.6)	49 (15.4)
A few (1477)	1216 (82.3)	261 (17.7)
None (812)	668 (82.3)	144 (17.7)
Chi Sq.=36.29, d.f.=4, p=.000		
Control:		
Number of Officers		
One (1131)	943 (83.4)	118 (16.6)
Two (1250)	1014 (81.1)	236 (18.9)
Three (401)	315 (78.6)	86 (21.4)
Chi Sq.=31.03, d.f.=13, p=.003		
Number of Bystanders		
One (688)	580 (84.3)	108 (15.7)
Two (832)	693 (83.3)	139 (16.7)
Three (505)	390 (77.2)	115 (22.8)
Chi Sq.=47.45, d.f.=29, p=.017		
Anticipate Violence		
Yes (240)	200 (83.3)	40 (16.7)
No (2874)	2319 (80.7)	555 (19.3)
Chi Sq.=1.00, d.f.=1, p=.317		
Proactive Encounter		
Yes(1469)	1141 (77.7)	328 (22.3)
No (1645)	1378 (83.8)	267 (16.2)
Chi Sq.=18.66, d.f.=1, p=.000		

Table 7-2: Bivariate Relationships by the Continuum Encounters Involving No Resistance (N=3114) (cont.)

	Follow	Jump
Potentially Violent Problem		
Yes (1474)	1201 (81.5)	273 (18.5)
No (1640)	1318 (80.4)	322 (19.6)
Chi Sq.=.62, d.f.=1, p=.430		
Pattern1		
Yes (564)	325 (57.6)	239 (42.4)
No (2250)	2194 (86.0)	356 (14.0)
Chi Sq.=241.26, d.f.=1, p=.000		
Pattern2		
Yes (187)	171 (91.4)	16 (8.6)
No (2927)	2348 (80.2)	579 (19.8)
Chi Sq.=14.32, d.f.=1, p=.000		
Pattern3		
Yes (2363)	2023 (85.6)	340 (14.4)
No (751)	496 (66.0)	255 (34.0)
Chi Sq.=141.15, d.f.=1, p=.000		
Missing		
Yes (390)	301 (77.2)	89 (22.8)
No (2731)	2218 (81.3)	506 (18.6)
Chi Square=3.70, d.f.=1, p=.054		
Hybrid:		
LSite1		
Yes (383)	299 (78.1)	84 (21.9)
No (2731)	2220 (81.3)	511 (18.7)
Chi Sq.=2.25, d.f.=1, p=.133		

Table 7-2: Bivariate Relationships by the Continuum Encounters Involving No Resistance (N=3114) (cont.)

	Follow	Jump
LSite2		
Yes (157)	134 (85.4)	23 (14.6)
No (2957)	2385 (80.7)	572 (19.3)
Chi Sq.=2.12, d.f.=1, p=.145		
LSite3		
Yes (1216)	976 (80.3)	240 (19.7)
No (1898)	1543 (81.3)	355 (18.7)
Chi Sq.=.51, d.f.=1, p=.474		
LSite4		
Yes (1140)	959 (84.1)	181 (15.9)
No (1974)	1560 (79.0)	414 (21.0)
Chi Sq.=12.13, d.f.=1, p=.000		
LSuper1		
Yes (506)	411 (81.2)	95 (18.8)
No (2608)	2108 (80.8)	500 (19.2)
Chi Sq.=.04, d.f.=1, p=.835		
LSuper2		
Yes (31)	19 (61.3)	12 (38.7)
No (3083)	2500 (81.1)	583 (18.9)
Chi Sq.=7.78, d.f.=1, p=.005		
LSuper3		
Yes (2133)	1749 (82.0)	384 (18.0)
No (981)	770 (78.5)	211 (21.5)
Chi Sq.=5.34, d.f.=1, p=.021		

Table 7-2: Bivariate Relationships by the Continuum
Encounters Involving No Resistance (N=3114) (cont.)

	Follow	**Jump**
LSuper4		
Yes (207)	175 (84.5)	32 (15.5)
No (2907)	2344 (80.6)	563 (19.4)
Chi Sq.=1.91, d.f.=1, p=.167		
LWork1		
Yes (357)	287 (80.4)	70 (19.6)
No (2757)	2232 (81.0)	558 (19.0)
Chi Sq.=.06, d.f.=1, p=.798		
LWork2		
Yes (183)	146 (79.8)	37 (20.2)
No (2931)	2373 (81.0)	558 (19.0)
Chi Sq.=.15, d.f.=1, p=.693		
LWork3		
Yes (246)	194 (78.9)	52 (21.1)
No (2868)	2325 (81.1)	543 (18.9)
Chi Sq.=.71, d.f.=1, p=.399		
LWork4		
Yes (2106)	1738 (82.5)	368 (17.5)
No (1008)	781 (77.5)	227 (22.5)
Chi Sq.=11.23, d.f.=1, p=.001		

Three of the four organizational factors were significant, two at the p<.01 level (site and workgroup) and one at the p<.05 level (supervisor). Twenty-two percent of the encounters involving Indianapolis officers resulted in the officer using more force, while 15.5 percent of the encounters involving St. Petersburg officers resulted in the officer jumping the continuum. Moreover, encounters involving officers who felt that all or most of the officers within their workgroup felt constrained by legal guidelines were also more likely to result in the use of more force (24.5%) compared to those who felt that none of the officers in their workgroup perceived such a constraint (17.7%).

All of the control factors were significant at the p<.01 level with the exception of those where the officer anticipated violence, it was a potentially violent problem, and the missing case variable. Of particular interest is the significance of the pattern variables. Encounters where officers initially used some form of verbal force (Pattern1) were significantly (and substantially) more likely to result in the officer eventually resorting to a jump of the continuum (42.4% versus 14.0%). Conversely, those where officers used physical force initially were significantly less likely to end up using more force (19.8% versus 8.6%), as were those where no force (Pattern3) was initially used (34.0 versus 14.4%).[5]

Four of the twelve hybrid variables were significantly related to a jump with three at the p<.01 level (LSite4, LSuper2, and LWork4) and one at the p<.05 level (LSuper3). As expected, St. Petersburg officers who do not believe overlooking legal guidelines is necessary to do their jobs (LSite4) were significantly less likely to jump the continuum (15.9% versus 21.0%). Also, officers who do not believe overlooking legal guidelines is necessary who work with a group of officers who they perceive to have the same views (LWork4) were less likely to jump the continuum (17.5% versus 22.5%).

The remaining two relationships are somewhat contradictory. Officers with a proclivity to overlook legal guidelines and who work for a supervisor they feel closely monitors their decision making (LSuper2) were more likely to jump the continuum. Conversely, officers without such a proclivity who work for a supervisor they feel rarely modifies their decisions were less likely to jump the continuum. The influence of perceived supervision appears irrelevant in the context of how officers feel toward legal constraints.

Multivariate Analyses

The dependent measure for this model is dichotomous - followed continuum, jumped continuum. As a result, a logistic regression is used (Liao, 1994). Since the regression coefficients of a logistic model are not particularly interpretable with respect to changes in the probability of jumping the continuum, a multiplier of the odds (better known as the "odds ratio") are presented.[6] This provides the odds that the officer will jump the continuum given a unit change in an independent variable while other factors are controlled (e.g., held at their mean). When odds ratios are greater than one, it signifies that the odds of an officer jumping the continuum increases as the independent variable increases. Conversely, odds ratios less than one signify that the odds of an officer jumping the continuum decrease as the independent variable increases.

Main Effects

Table 7-3 presents the estimates from the logistic regression. While the model was significant as a whole, it offers a somewhat weak fit to the data. Only slightly more than 13 percent of the variance is explained as illustrated by the pseudo-R square. Several individual predictors achieved statistical significance, many of which have been consistent predictors regardless of how force has been conceptualized at various points throughout this research.

Four of the citizen variables were significantly related to jumps in the continuum. The odds of officers jumping the continuum are increased when encounters involved citizens who were young, poor, and male, as well as those who displayed signs of alcohol/drug use. While each of these variables was statistically significant at the $p<.001$ level, we see from the odds ratios that none were dramatically more likely to involve a jump in the continuum. The odds of an officer jumping the continuum when dealing with male citizens as compared with female citizens were two to one. The same is true of those involving citizens who displayed signs of alcohol/drug use. Further, younger citizens and those perceived to be of lower wealth were also more likely to be recipients of a continuum jump.

With respect to officer behavior toward younger, lower wealth, and male suspects, it is difficult to ascertain a direct link to an officer's motivation based solely on these characteristics. In terms of alcohol use, it may be that officers become more frustrated when dealing with these individuals. In the case highlighted below it appears that the citizen had difficulty communicating with the officer:

Table 7-3: Estimates from Logistic Model - Main Effects
Nonresistant Citizens, Jump of the Continuum

	Coeff	SE	*p*-value	Odds Ratio
Citizen:				
Male	.640	.125	.000	1.897
NonWhite	.093	.109	.394	1.097
Age	- .297	.038	.000	.742
Wealth	- .396	.092	.000	.672
Anger/Fear	.116	.120	.335	1.123
Drug/Alcohol Use	.679	.126	.000	1.973
Mentally Impaired	- .338	.366	.354	.712
Disrespect	- .149	.215	.486	.860
Officer:				
Male	.196	.159	.216	1.217
White	- .263	.136	.053	.768
Experience	- .003	.009	.683	.996
Education	.021	.028	.459	1.021
Verbal Training	- .037	.047	.434	.963
Crimefighter	- .079	.072	.270	.923
Citizens Trustworthy	.107	.064	.096	1.113
Legal Guidelines	.032	.066	.632	1.032
Organization:				
Indianapolis	.244	.127	.055	1.276
911 Officer	- .017	.169	.522	.897
Supervision	- .092	.074	.214	.911
Workgroup	- .106	.069	.125	.899
Control:				
# Officers	.065	.035	.067	1.067
# Bystanders	- .017	.012	.166	.982
Anticipate Violence	.151	.200	.451	1.163
Proactive	.388	.105	.000	1.474

**Table 7-3: Estimates from Logistic Model - Main Effects
Nonresistant Citizens, Jump of the Continuum (cont.)**

Control:	Coeff	SE	p-value	Odds Ratio
Type Problem	- .106	.101	.295	.898
Pattern1	1.284	.111	.000	3.611
Pattern2	- .983	.281	.000	.374
Missing	.248	.227	.275	1.276
Constant	- .265	.456		

N = 3114
Pseudo R Square   .133
Model Chi-Square 404.410 (p<.000)

Encounter (information gathering)
O2 had C1 (Hispanic Male, 29 yrs old, lower class based on his worn clothes and body odor) handcuffed and sitting on someone's front lawn. There were 15 bystanders and 2 EMS techs with an ambulance. C1 was extremely intoxicated. O2 was trying to get C1's information, but C1 was almost unconscious. *O1 approached C1, smacked him on his chest to get his attention, and asked what his name was.* C1 slurred back something in Spanish. O2 said he didn't understand Spanish and couldn't get his information. (The EMS guys were laughing at how drunk C1 was.) O1 tried to get C1's name and address, but either C1 couldn't understand English or he was too drunk to understand English.

In this particular case the officer chose to strike the citizen probably in order to get his attention. The officer may have chosen to nudge or shake him instead. Another alternative may have been to issue a threat before initiating any type of physical force. Perhaps the officer felt that neither alternative would have been effective due to his state of intoxication.

None of the officer or organizational variables tested were significantly related to a jump in the continuum. However, three control variables were significantly related to officers jumping the continuum.

Encounters where the officer initiated citizen contact were about one and a half times more likely to result in the officer jumping the continuum compared to those that were citizen or dispatch initiated. Further, both of the pattern variables were significant. Compared to the reference category (pattern3 - no force used prior), encounters in which an officer on the scene initially used verbal force (pattern1) were over three and a half times more likely to result in a jump of the continuum. Since all these cases involve no citizen resistance, we know that the use of verbal force early in the encounter could not have prompted resistance from the citizen thereby leading to the increased chance of the officer using more force. Rather, it appears that commands are often used to maintain initial control of a suspected offender, which then leads to an eventual threat. In many cases it appears the threat is used as an "added effect." For example:

Encounter (problem individual dispatch)
O1 pulled up behind a parked city bus. The bus was parked in the right lane on a fairly busy road. The bus was fully painted and you couldn't see inside the bus (all the way around the entire bus) because of the painting. O1 walked up one of the bus steps and asked the bus driver what the problem was. C1, a 53 year-old middle income white male was sitting in the driver's seat. He stated that the guy sitting behind him was bleeding and that he couldn't be on the bus. C2, a 41 year-old low income black male was sitting in the seat behind the bus driver. C2 had on a raggedy old wig with a white cap. He wore dirty white clothes and hiking boots. He carried two beat up old bags which were filled with junk. He had drawn on a mustache, and eyebrows.

C1 stated the guy couldn't be on the bus because he was bleeding and that was against the rules of the bus company. He informed O1 that they were waiting for another bus, and the guy wouldn't get off. *O1 looked at C2 and very sternly told him to get off the bus.* C2 held up his hands, and said, what, what, all I want to do is go home. There was a newspaper on his arm where he had been bleeding, and there was a little blood on one of his white shirts. C2 stood up and began stumbling off the bus. O1 asked if he was bleeding. C2 held up his left arm and showed O1, it's just bleeding a little, he slurred, I just fell down and scraped it.

By this time a fire engine and an ambulance came to the scene. Four white firefighters hopped off the truck and walked over to the scene. Two paramedics, one white female, age 32, walked over to C2. O1 stated to the paramedic that she probably wouldn't need to take him because the cut wasn't that bad. O1 asked the paramedic if she could take the guy. She replied if he wanted to go they could take him. O1 asked C2 if he had any ID, C2 pulled out a gray electrical cord that was tied around a picture ID, he took it off and handed it to O1. He kept repeating how he just wanted to go home. The bus driver got off the bus and told O1 he was waiting for another bus because that's what his supervisor said. O1 told C1 she didn't like the covered up windows because she felt unsafe. C1 claimed you can see out the windows just not in. O1 told C1 she'd seen the movie "Speed" six times.

O1 walked over to her car and got out some hand cleaner, she cleaned her hands and put on some gloves. She began filling out an arrest slip for public intoxication. Another officer pulled up by this time. He walked over to the guy. He told C2 if he could stand like a crane, and stood like one then he could go home. O1 walked back over to the guy sitting on the ground. (The fire engine and paramedics had left by now, they put a gauze bandage on his arm.) She asked C2 what his phone number was, he replied he didn't know, but wanted to just go home, and that his mother knew the phone number. O2 carried his things over because C2 could hardly walk. O1 escorted C2 over to a spot near her car. *Sit on the ground, she commanded, and if you move from this spot, I'll spray you with mace, she told C2 sternly.*

In other cases, commands are used prior to the eventual use of physical restraint. It appears verbal force is used as the initial means of control until physical force can be applied.

> *Encounter (Officer observes car with two citizens in park)*
> O1 got out of his car and approached the suspects car. *O1 approached the passenger side door and as he got within a few feet of the car he pulled his gun and yelled at the driver and passenger to put their hands where he could see them.* O1 radioed for another car to assist him and told the passenger, C1, a 50 year old black male, to get out of the car while keeping his hands where he could see them. C1 got out of the car and *O1 ordered C1 to walk to the front of the car and put his hands on the hood.* As this was happening O2 arrived and walked to the driver's side of the car. *O2 told C2, a 40 year old black female, to get out of the car and ordered her to walk to the front of the car. At this point O1 patted down C1 and O2 patted down* C2.

Debriefing O1. I asked O1 what prompted him to draw his weapon and he explained that when he walked up on the car he noticed that the car was running without the keys in it and there was a screwdriver on the dashboard. O1 stated that the ignition had been punched which made him think that it had probably been stolen. O1 mentioned that many people who steal cars carry weapons and he just wanted to be safe. O1 stated that he would rather draw his weapon and not have to use it than not draw it when he needed to use it.

I then asked O1 what drew his attention to the car in the first place and he explained that he usually checks on cars sitting in parks late at night. O1 also mentioned that when he had pulled up on the car he saw a bright light inside that looked like they were smoking something other than a cigarette. O1 stated that marijuana joints and crack pipes have a more intense light to them than a cigarette.

Neither of these examples demonstrate an overly drastic use of force in the sense of takedowns, pain compliance, or striking (as mentioned previously, most deviations from the continuum do not). However, in both cases an added element of force is used on a nonresistant citizen. Did the officer in the first example have to add in a threat to mace? Did the officer in the second example have to pull his gun and then move on to a search of the suspect because people who steal cars supposedly also steal guns? Perhaps, perhaps not. This may very well be considered good police work.

On the other hand, the law concerning the pat down of a citizen stipulates that officers can frisk someone if he or she believes the person is armed and a threat. Was that the case here? The officer refers to such a threat in this example, but certainly not everyone may agree. The purpose here is not one of judging, but rather the actions prior to the point that the "added" element of force is used. As noted before, many police officials may consider such uses of force as perfectly proper, while others may be troubled by such actions.

Those cases involving the initial use of physical force (pattern2) were less likely to involve a jump in the continuum compared to no force. This may be a result of the observed officer recognizing that the force already used was sufficient to maintain control of the citizen; and, since the citizen never becomes resistant, no need for more force. For example:

Encounter (dispatch domestic argument)
O1 arrived at the location of a domestic argument and stopped the car in front of the house, an older model duplex. There was already one officer on scene, who was talking to the disputants, in the walkway along the side of the house. Just as O1 arrived O2 placed C2, a white male lower class in his 30's, claimed to be a roofer, but fiancee claimed that he did not work, against the outside wall of the house and *placed him in handcuffs.*

C1, a white female lower class in her 30's, works as an attendant in a hospital, was sitting on the back steps. O2 took O1 about 20-25 ft away, but still in the yard, to keep C1 and C2 from arguing. O1 talked to C1 while O2 talked to C2. O1 asked C1 what had happened. C1 said that C2 had been hitting her about the face and on her arm. O1 asked C1 if she was injured and would be requiring and ambulance. C1 said that she did not, and said that she was mostly just hurt on her arm. C1 raised the sleeve of her shirt to reveal finger marks and bruises. O1 asked how C2 had hit C1 in the face. C1 said that C2 had hit her with a fist, but she was O.K. C1's face was very red and looked like it might bruise up, later. O1 then asked what C1 and C2 had been fighting about. C1 said that they had gotten into an argument about going fishing. C1 had wanted to go and C1 had not, so C1 had gotten abusive. O1 then began to take down C1's personal information for a report. *O1 told C1 to stay where she was at and walked over to O2 and C2.*

The observed officer goes on to deal with citizen one while the other officer deals with citizen two. However, it appears that citizen two has already been restrained and never resists, so there is no need to use any further force - especially a higher level.

Interaction Effects

As seen in Table 7-2, several of the hybrid variables were significantly related to a jump in the continuum in the bivariate sense. Multivariate analyses of these effects are presented in Table 7-4. As was done in the previous chapter, to test for interaction effects, three separate elaboration models are estimated - one for each hypothesized interactive relationship.

In each of the models, three of the four interaction terms were introduced while one was excluded. LSite1, LSuper1, and LWork1 were the reference categories in each of the respective models. As shown, none of the interactions were significant controlling for independent effects. Upon closer examination, we see that none of these variables even come close to significance. How officers perceive legal constraints simply does not interact with either of the organizational influences tested.

Table 7-4: Estimates from Logistic Model - Interaction Effects Nonresistant Citizens, Jump of the Continuum

	Site Model			Supervision Model			Workgroup Model		
	Coeff.	*SE*	*p*	*Coeff.*	*SE*	*p*	*Coeff.*	*SE*	*p*
Citizen:									
Male	.644	.125	.000	.640	.125	.000	.647	.125	.000
NonWhite	.094	.109	.388	.096	.109	.337	.099	.109	.362
Age	-.298	.038	.000	-.295	.038	.000	-.299	.038	.000
Wealth	-.395	.091	.000	-.390	.092	.000	-.381	.092	.000
Anger/Fear	.096	.120	.425	.115	.120	.341	.100	.121	.407
Drug/Alcohol	.676	.126	.000	.675	.125	.000	.686	.126	.000
Mental Impairment	-.354	.366	.333	-.329	.365	.368	-.313	.366	.391
Disrespect	-.152	.215	.499	-.150	.215	.483	-.146	.215	.497
Officer:									
Male	.195	.161	.226	.185	.160	.247	.174	.160	.278
White	-.249	.137	.068	-.253	.136	.063	-.287	.137	.036
Experience	-.002	.009	.765	-.003	.009	.686	-.006	.009	.522
Education	.025	.028	.383	.015	.028	.596	.018	.028	.511
Verbal Training	-.020	.047	.662	-.053	.048	.267	-.049	.048	.309
Crimefighter	-.061	.072	.127	-.092	.073	.209	-.087	.072	.224

Table 7-4: Estimates from Logistic Model - Interaction Effects
Nonresistant Citizens, Jump of the Continuum (cont.)

	Site Model			Supervision Model			Workgroup Model		
	Coeff.	*SE*	*p*	*Coeff.*	*SE*	*p*	*Coeff.*	*SE*	*p*
Officer:									
Citizens Trust	.098	.064	.127	.106	.064	.097	.110	.064	.088
Legal Guidelines	--	--	--	--	--	--	--	--	--
Organization:									
Indianapolis	--	--	--	.259	.128	.043	.280	.125	.025
Supervision	-.089	.074	.229	--	--	--	-.087	.074	.243
Workgroup	-.099	.067	.139	-.075	.065	.246	--	--	--
911 Officer	-.060	.169	.721	-.128	.170	.449	-.105	.170	.534
Control:									
# Officers	.068	.035	.054	.066	.035	.063	.065	.035	.066
# Bystanders	-.017	.012	.167	-.017	.012	.168	-.018	.012	.157
Anticipate Violence	.152	.200	.447	.146	.200	.464	.150	.200	.453
Proactive	.388	.105	.000	.390	.105	.000	.383	.105	.000
Type Problem	-.103	.102	.310	-.110	.102	.277	-.105	.101	.298

Table 7-4: Estimates from Logistic Model - Interaction Effects Nonresistant Citizens, Jump of the Continuum (cont.)

	Site Model			Supervision Model			Workgroup Model		
	Coeff	*SE*	*p*	*Coeff*	*SE*	*p*	*Coeff*	*SE*	*p*
Control:									
Pattern1	1.300	.111	.000	1.280	.111	.000	1.288	.111	.000
Pattern2	-.967	.281	.000	-.975	.281	.000	-.973	.281	.000
Missing	.173	.218	.427	.261	.216	.228	.338	.222	.127
Hybrid:									
Site2	-.289	.287	.313						
Site3	-.011	.182	.948						
Site4	-.117	.204	.565						
Super2				.215	.428	.614			
Super3				.014	.156	.927			
Super4				-.217	.255	.287			

Table 7-4: Estimates from Logistic Model - Interaction Effects Nonresistant Citizens, Jump of the Continuum (cont.)

	Site Model			Supervision Model			Workgroup Model		
	Coeff	*SE*	*p*	*Coeff*	*SE*	*p*	*Coeff*	*SE*	*p*
Hybrid:									
Work2							.148	.244	.544
Work3							.142	.222	.521
Work4							-.079	.148	.592
Constant	-.080			-.294			-.418		
Model Chi-Square	404.662			404.151			403.965		
Pseudo R Square	13.3			13.2			13.2		
N	3114			3114			3114		

7.2 FORCE AND THE RESISTANT CITIZEN

There were 343 cases involving a resistant citizen.[7] When dealing with such citizens, what stands out most is the fact that an overwhelming number of cases fall into the category of holding back from applying force in accordance with the continuum criteria. Of the 343 cases involving a resistant citizen, 72.8 percent (n=250) result in the officer restraining or holding back from following the continuum. *In nearly three of every four encounters, the officer attempted to de-escalate a situation where a citizen was attempting to escalate it.* This is rather remarkable, as it says that not only are officers choosing not to use more extreme levels of force on resistant citizens, they do not even apply as much force as the continuum allows. Furthermore, in only 25 of the 343 cases (7.2%) did the officer go to the other extreme of jumping the continuum. Thus, officers chose to jump the continuum in nearly 20 percent of the cases where citizens were nonresistant, at any point during the encounter, yet when citizens display resistance the percentage drops to just over seven percent. However, recall that 87 cases are excluded here. In each of these cases there was at least one instance of resistance.[8] If percentages are calculated adding in these cases, 112 of the 430 (26.0%) encounters involving a resistant citizen involved a jump. Similarly, 337 of 430 involved refraining behavior (76.5%).[9] Hence, regardless of how the figures are calculated, officers refrained much more often than that of jumping the continuum.

Bivariate Relationships

Results of the bivariate relationships for encounters involving resistant citizens are presented in Table 7-5. Few of the variables were significantly related to force according to the continuum format laid out.[10] Number of officers and pattern3 were related to force at the p<.01 level, while site and pattern4 were significantly related at the p<.05 level. In terms of site, 81.6 percent of the encounters occurring in St. Petersburg resulted in the use of less force compared to 67.1 percent in Indianapolis. Indianapolis officers were more likely to follow or jump the continuum. Further, early actions during an encounter help predict a later response from an officer.

Table 7-5: Bivariate Relationships by the Continuum Encounters Involving Citizen Resistance (N=343)

	Less	**Follow**	**More**
Citizen:			
Gender			
Male (92)	176 (70.1)	53 (21.1)	22 (8.8)
Female (251)	74 (80.4)	15 (16.3)	3 (3.3)
Chi Sq.=4.56, d.f.=2, p=.102			
Race			
White (102)	76 (74.5)	17 (16.7)	9 (8.8)
NonWhite (241)	174 (72.2)	51 (21.2)	16 (6.6)
Chi Sq.=1.25, d.f.=2, p=.535			
Age			
Pre-School, 0-5 years (12)	--	--	--
Child, 6-12 years (12)	9 (75.0)	--	3 (25.0)
Young Adult, 13-17 years (41)	29 (70.7)	10 (24.4)	2 (4.9)
Older Teen, 18-20 years (35)	25 (71.4)	7 (20.0)	3 (8.6)
Young Adult, 21-29 years (69)	50 (72.5)	15 (21.7)	4 (5.8)
Adult, 30-44 years (141)	100 (70.9)	30 (21.3)	11 (7.8)
Middle-Aged, 45-59 (29)	24 (82.8)	4 (13.8)	1 (3.4)
Senior, 60+ years (16)	13 (81.3)	2 (12.5)	1 (6.3)
Chi Sq.=11.15, d.f.=12, p=.516			

Table 7-5: Bivariate Relationships by the Continuum Encounters Involving Citizen Resistance (N=343) (cont.)

	Less	Follow	More
Wealth			
Chronic Poverty (21)	15 (71.4)	5 (23.8)	1 (4.8)
Low (223)	159 (71.3)	45 (20.2)	19 (8.5)
Middle (99)	76 (76.8)	18 (18.2)	5 (5.1)
Above Middle (0)	--	--	--

Chi Sq.=1.93, d.f.=4, p=.748

	Less	Follow	More
Emotional State			
Fear/Anger (202)	146 (72.3)	39 (19.3)	17 (8.4)
No (141)	104 (73.8)	29 (20.6)	8 (5.7)

Chi Sq.=.94, d.f.=2, p=.622

	Less	Follow	More
Drug/Alcohol Use			
Yes (154)	107 (69.5)	35 (22.7)	12 (7.8)
No (189)	143 (75.7)	33 (17.5)	13 (6.9)

Chi Sq.=1.72, d.f.=2, p=.421

	Less	Follow	More
Mentally Impaired			
Yes (28)	22 (78.6)	3 (10.7)	3 (10.7)
No (315)	228 (72.4)	65 (20.6)	22 (7.0)

Chi Sq.=1.90, d.f.=2, p=.386

	Less	Follow	More
Disrespectful			
Yes (147)	110 (74.8)	29 (19.7)	8 (5.4)
No (196)	140 (71.4)	39 (19.9)	17 (8.7)

Chi Sq.=1.33, d.f.=2, p=.512

	Less	Follow	More
Officer:			
Gender			
Male (286)	206 (72.0)	55 (19.2)	25 (8.7)
Female (57)	44 (77.2)	13 (22.8)	--

Chi Sq.=5.46, d.f.=2, p=.065

Table 7-5: Bivariate Relationships by the Continuum Encounters Involving Citizen Resistance (N=343) (cont.)

	Less	Follow	More
Race			
White (269)	191 (71.0)	59 (21.9)	19 (7.1)
NonWhite (74)	59 (79.7)	9 (12.2)	6 (8.1)
Chi Sq.=3.48, d.f.=2, p=.175			
Experience (Years on Job)			
One (15)	12 (80.0)	2 (13.3)	1 (6.7)
Five (25)	17 (68.0)	7 (28.0)	1 (4.0)
Ten (15)	12 (80.0)	2 (13.3)	1 (6.7)
Chi Sq.=52.44, d.f.=48, p=.306			
Education			
< than High School (8)	6 (75.0)	2 (25.0)	--
High School Grad/GED (41)	28 (68.3)	10 (24.4)	3 (7.3)
Some College, no degree (72)	54 (75.0)	12 (16.7)	6 (8.3)
Associate Degree (13)	10 (76.9)	3 (23.1)	--
>2 years college, no B.S. (40)	29 (72.5)	7 (17.5)	4 (10.0)
Bachelors Degree (114)	84 (73.7)	23 (20.2)	7 (6.1)
Some Graduate, no degree (12)	5 (41.7)	5 (41.7)	2 (16.7)
Graduate Degree (2)	2 (100)	--	--
Chi Sq.=10.93, d.f.=16, p=.814			

Table 7-5: Bivariate Relationships by the Continuum Encounters Involving Citizen Resistance (N=343) (cont.)

	Less	**Follow**	**More**
Verbal Training			
None (168)	132 (78.6)	27 (16.1)	9 (5.4)
<1 day (64)	38 (59.4)	18 (28.1)	8 (12.5)
1-2 days (47)	33 (70.2)	10 (21.3)	4 (8.5)
3-5 days (11)	7 (63.6)	4 (36.4)	--
>5 days (12)	8 (66.7)	3 (25.0)	1 (8.3)

Chi Sq.=12.60, d.f.=10, p=.247

	Less	Follow	More
Crimefighter			
Agree Strongly (102)	78 (76.5)	18 (17.6)	6 (5.9)
Agree Somewhat (153)	104 (68.0)	37 (24.2)	12 (7.8)
Disagree			
Somewhat(42)	33 (78.6)	5 (11.9)	4 (9.5)
Disagree Strongly (5)	3 (60.0)	2 (40.0)	--

Chi Sq.=6.75, d.f.=8, p=.564

	Less	Follow	More
Distrust			
Agree Strongly (8)	7 (87.5)	--	1 (12.5)
Agree Somewhat (71)	49 (69.0)	15 (21.1)	7 (9.9)
Disagree			
Somewhat(141)	103 (73.0)	29 (20.6)	9 (6.4)
Disagree Strongly (82)	59 (72.0)	18 (22.0)	5 (6.1)

Chi Sq.=4.23, d.f.=8, p=.836

	Less	Follow	More
Individual Legal Guidelines			
Agree Strongly (14)	10 (71.4)	4 (28.6)	--
Agree Somewhat (63)	48 (76.2)	12 (19.0)	3 (4.8)
Disagree			
Somewhat(45)	26 (57.8)	12 (26.7)	7 (15.6)
Disagree			
Strongly (180)	134 (74.4)	34 (18.9)	12 (6.7)

Chi Sq.=9.86, d.f.=8, p=.275

Table 7-5: Bivariate Relationships by the Continuum Encounters Involving Citizen Resistance (N=343) (cont.)

	Less	Follow	More
Organization:			
Site			
Indianapolis (207)	139 (67.1)	51 (24.6)	17 (8.2)
St. Petersburg (136)	111 (81.6)	17 (12.5)	8 (5.9)
Chi Sq.=9.06, d.f.=2, p=.011			
Assignment			
911 (307)	219 (71.3)	64 (20.8)	24 (7.8)
CPO (36)	31 (86.1)	4 (11.1)	1 (2.8)
Chi Sq.=3.62, d.f.=2, p=.163			
Supervisor Criticism			
Agree Strongly (192)	138 (71.9)	41 (21.4)	13 (6.8)
Agree Somewhat (77)	59 (76.6)	12 (15.6)	6 (7.8)
Disagree			
Somewhat (29)	18 (62.1)	9 (31.0)	2 (6.9)
Disagree Strongly (4)	3 (75.0)	--	1 (25.0)
Chi Sq.=6.73, d.f.=8, p=.566			
Workgroup Legal Guidelines			
All of most (42)	28 (66.7)	11 (26.2)	3 (7.1)
About half (40)	34 (85.0)	3 (7.5)	3 (7.5)
A few (151)	106 (70.2)	33 (21.9)	12 (7.9)
None (69)	50 (72.5)	15 (21.7)	4 (5.8)
Chi Sq.=6.55, d.f.=8, p=.585			
Control:			
Number of Officers			
One (64)	55 (85.9)	6 (9.4)	3 (4.7)
Two (150)	107 (71.3)	31 (20.7)	12 (8.0)
Three (65)	48 (73.8)	13 (20.0)	4 (6.2)
Chi Sq.=50.60, d.f.=26, p=.003			

Table 7-5: Bivariate Relationships by the Continuum
Encounters Involving Citizen Resistance (N=343) (cont.)

	Less	Follow	More
Number of Bystanders			
One (46)	29 (63.0)	13 (28.3)	4 (8.7)
Two (81)	61 (75.3)	14 (17.3)	6 (7.4)
Three (57)	42 (73.7)	9 (15.8)	6 (10.5)
Chi Sq.=44.74, d.f.=54, p=.811			
Anticipate Violence			
Yes (54)	39 (72.2)	9 (16.7)	6 (11.1)
No (289)	211 (73.0)	59 (20.4)	19 (6.6)
Chi Sq.=1.61, d.f.=2, p=.447			
Proactive Encounter			
Yes(105)	73 (69.5)	22 (21.0)	10 (9.5)
No (238)	177 (74.4)	46 (19.3)	15 (6.3)
Chi Sq.=1.36, d.f.=2, p=.504			
Potentially Violent Problem			
Yes (154)	115 (74.7)	30 (19.5)	9 (5.8)
No (189)	135 (71.4)	38 (20.1)	16 (8.5)
Chi Sq.=.94, d.f.=2, p=.625			
Pattern1			
Yes (182)	141 (77.5)	32 (17.6)	9 (4.9)
No (161)	109 (67.7)	36 (22.4)	16 (9.9)
Chi Sq.=5.02, d.f.=2, p=.081			
Pattern2			
Yes (31)	21 (67.7)	9 (29.0)	1 (3.2)
No (312)	229 (73.4)	59 (18.9)	24 (7.7)
Chi Sq.=2.35, d.f.=2, p=.308			

Table 7-5: Bivariate Relationships by the Continuum Encounters Involving Citizen Resistance (N=343) (cont.)

	Less	Follow	More
Pattern3			
Yes (35)	18 (51.4)	14 (40.0)	3 (8.6)
No (308)	232 (75.3)	54 (17.5)	22 (7.1)
Chi Sq.=10.55, d.f.=2, p=.005			
Pattern4			
Yes (95)	70 (73.7)	13 (13.7)	12 (12.6)
No (248)	180 (72.6)	55 (22.2)	13 (5.2)
Chi Sq.=7.65, d.f.=2, p=.022			
Missing			
Yes (41)	32 (78.0)	6 (14.6)	3 (7.3)
No (302)	218 (72.2)	62 (20.5)	22 (7.3)
Chi Sq.=.80, d.f.=2, p=.669			
Hybrid:			
LSite1			
Yes (62)	44 (71.0)	15 (24.2)	3 (4.8)
No (281)	206 (73.3)	53 (18.9)	22 (7.8)
Chi Sq.=1.39, d.f.=2, p=.499			
LSite2			
Yes (19)	18 (94.7)	1 (5.3)	--
No (324)	232 (71.6)	67 (20.7)	25 (7.7)
Chi Sq.=4.93, d.f.=2, p=.085			
LSite3			
Yes (127)	83 (65.4)	32 (25.2)	12 (9.4)
No (216)	167 (77.3)	36 (16.7)	13 (6.0)
Chi Sq.=5.79, d.f.=2, p=.055			

Table 7-5: Bivariate Relationships by the Continuum Encounters Involving Citizen Resistance (N=343) (cont.)

	Less	Follow	More
LSite4			
Yes (108)	84 (77.8)	16 (14.8)	8 (7.4)
No (235)	166 (70.6)	52 (22.1)	17 (7.2)
Chi Sq.=2.51, d.f.=2, p=.284			
LSuper1			
Yes (69)	53 (76.8)	13 (18.8)	3 (4.3)
No (274)	197 (71.9)	55 (20.1)	22 (8.0)
Chi Sq.=1.25, d.f.=2, p=.535			
LSuper2			
Yes (10)	7 (70.0)	3 (30.0)	--
No (333)	243 (73.0)	65 (19.5)	25 (7.5)
Chi Sq.=1.30, d.f.=2, p=.522			
LSuper3			
Yes (207)	148 (71.5)	42 (20.3)	17 (8.2)
No (136)	102 (75.0)	26 (19.1)	8 (5.9)
Chi Sq.=8.06, d.f.=2, p=.668			
LSuper4			
Yes (25)	16 (64.0)	6 (24.0)	3 (12.0)
No (318)	234 (73.6)	62 (19.5)	22 (6.9)
Chi Sq.=1.35, d.f.=2, p=.509			
LWork1			
Yes (63)	49 (77.8)	12 (19.0)	2 (3.2)
No (280)	201 (71.8)	56 (20.0)	23 (8.2)
Chi Sq.=2.06, d.f.=2, p=.355			

Table 7-5: Bivariate Relationships by the Continuum
Encounters Involving Citizen Resistance (N=343) (cont.)

	Less	Follow	More
Work2			
Yes (18)	13 (72.2)	4 (22.2)	1 (5.6)
No (325)	237 (72.9)	64 (19.7)	24 (7.4)
Chi Sq.=134, d.f.=2, p=.935			
LWork3			
Yes (22)	16 (72.7)	2 (9.1)	4 (18.2)
No (321)	234 (72.9)	66 (20.6)	21 (6.5)
Chi Sq.=5.19, d.f.=2, p=.075			
LWork4			
Yes (213)	151 (70.9)	46 (21.6)	16 (7.5)
No (130)	99 (76.2)	22 (16.9)	9 (6.9)
Chi Sq.=1.23, d.f.=2, p=.539			

For instance, officers held back from following the continuum in 51.4 percent of the encounters when the citizen initially displayed some form of physical resistance (pattern3) compared to 75.3 percent of those where the citizen did not.

Multivariate Analyses

The dependent measure for this model takes on more than two discrete values that cannot be naturally ordered - refrained from following the continuum, followed the continuum, jumped the continuum. As a result, a multinomial logit model is employed (Aldrich and Nelson, 1984; Long, 1997). The model is also known as MNL.

While an argument may be made that the dependent measure applied here can be ordered, this is not necessarily straightforward so a potential loss of efficiency was chosen instead of introducing possible bias (see Long, 1997, 149). First, as discussed previously, refraining or holding back from following the continuum does not necessarily equate to lower levels of force being applied. Similarly, jumping the continuum does not always mean applying higher forms of force.

Second, the intent is to distinguish differences in the probability in comparison to that of "following the continuum." The multinomial logit is an extension of the binary logit. The model determines the odds of an observation falling into one category compared to the omitted category.[11]

Use of the multinomial logit allows for "following" the continuum to be the omitted category, against which to compare both refraining from and jumping the continuum. The possibility exists that officers may be both significantly more likely to refrain from following the continuum *and* significantly more likely to jump the continuum when compared to following. Interest lies in explaining deviations from the continuum, which can be found at either end: refraining or jumping.

Table 7-6 presents results from the Multinomial logit model. Consider two specific points about the model. First, it must be remembered that a great majority of cases fall into the category of the officer holding back or refraining from using force (72.8%). Nonetheless, there was a fair amount of variation especially in terms of following the continuum (19.8%). Second, while 7.4 percent of the cases fall into the category of the officer jumping the continuum, it must be remembered that this is based on a relatively small number of cases (n=25).[12]

Main Effects
As seen in Table 7-6, the model was significant as a whole at p<.01 as shown by the chi-square statistic. Looking initially at those factors related to instances when officers choose to use less force as per the continuum criteria, we see that only two variables are significant, both control variables. Officers were not more likely to refrain from following the continuum when dealing with any number of citizen characteristics (e.g., whites, older citizens, higher income citizens, etc.). Similarly, none of the officer or organizational variables were significantly related to refraining from the continuum.

Nonetheless, as shown in Table 7-6, officers are significantly more likely to refrain from following the continuum when involved in encounters with few backup officers on the scene. Perhaps officers are more cautious in their approach to using force when they feel they do not have enough backup officers should the citizen become overly resistant.[13]

Table 7-6: Estimates from Multinomial Logit Model - Main Effects

	Prob of Less Force			Prob of More Force		
	Coeff.	*S.E.*	*p*	*Coeff.*	*S.E.*	*p*
Citizen:						
Male	-.067	.374	.856	1.629	.827	.048
NonWhite	-.377	.361	.296	-.546	.624	.381
Age	-.035	.131	.784	-.282	.231	.222
Wealth	.140	.294	.632	-.218	.529	.680
Anger/Fear	.101	.360	.778	1.606	.697	.021
Drug/Alcohol	-.281	.342	.410	.479	.645	.458
Mental Impairment	.378	.697	.587	1.425	1.08	.190
Disrespect	.007	.348	.982	-1.179	.653	.070
Officer:						
Male	.562	.425	.186	--	--	.076
White	.833	.431	.053	1.310	.738	.076
Experience	.011	.031	.717	.036	.051	.481
Education	.106	.100	.288	.073	.188	.697
Verbal Training	-.143	.160	.372	.097	.292	.739

Table 7-6: Estimates from Multinomial Logit Model - Main Effects (cont.)

	Prob of Less Force			Prob of More Force		
	Coeff	*S.E.*	*p*	*Coeff*	*S.E.*	*p*
Officer:						
Crimefighter	- .115	.246	.639	.020	.470	.965
Citizens Trust	- .173	.213	.416	- .407	.405	.314
Legal Guidelines	.240	.240	.316	.869	.441	.048
Organization:						
Indianapolis	- .614	.406	.130	.168	.734	.818
911 Officer	- .719	.657	.273	.300	1.47	.838
Supervision	.055	.231	.809	.468	.388	.228
Workgroup	- .308	.242	.203	- .301	.416	.469
Control:						
# Officers	- .172	.072	.016	.090	.134	.500
# Bystanders	.011	.019	.535	- .044	.043	.301
Anticipate Violence	.265	.498	.594	.799	.812	.325
Proactive	- .152	.353	.667	.375	.660	.569

Table 7-6: Estimates from Multinomial Logit Model - Main Effects (cont.)

Control:	Prob of Less Force			Prob of More Force		
	Coeff	_S.E._	_p_	_Coeff_	_S.E._	_p_
Type Problem	- .064	.331	.847	-1.036	.653	.112
Pattern1	- .129	.386	.737	-1.731	.659	.008
Pattern2	- .531	.581	.360	-2.906	1.36	.032
Pattern3	-1.303	.547	.017	-3.318	1.06	.001
Missing	- .035	1.27	.978	2.325	2.42	.338
Constant	- .093			-33.689		

N	343	
Log Likelihood	-211.366	
Chi-Square	86	.423 (p=.009)

Conversely, officers are less likely to refrain from following the continuum when citizens initially become physically resistant (pattern3) compared to when they initially display either passive or verbal resistance. That is, an aggressive physical form of resistance is likely to prompt a similar form of force. For example:

> *Encounter (domestic dispute suspect flees from officers)*
> O1 and O2 jumped into their cars, turned on their lights and sirens, and took off in pursuit of the suspect. O1 went one way and O2 went the other, but they communicated via radio. About three blocks away, O2 said he caught C2 (white male age 23 who was lower class based on his dress, speech, and quality of his apartment). O1 pulled up behind O2's car, handcuffed C2 (who was standing beside O2's car), put C2 in his car, and returned to the original scene of the encounter where C1 was.

As a whole, the overall lack of variables related to cases where officers chose to refrain from moving up the continuum signifies that many of the extra legal factors tested simply do not account for why officers chose to take such action. Rather, the general pattern is for officers to hold back most of the time regardless of citizen, officer, and organizational factors.

Viewing results from those cases where officers jumped the continuum, six of the predictors were significant. As found in cases where officers jumped the continuum when faced with nonresistant citizens, encounters involving male citizens were also significantly more likely to lead to a jump in the continuum by the officer. However, the other citizen variables drop out in this model.

Neither citizen age, wealth, or alcohol/drug use were found to be significantly related to officers jumping the continuum. On the other hand, citizens who were fearful or angry were significantly more likely to be on the receiving end of an officer jumping the continuum. Perhaps officers felt that emotional citizens who have shown signs of resistance warrant an extra degree of force.

Encounter (dispute)

O1 then spoke to C1 and asked him if he had any identification and C1 said that he did not. O1 asked C1 what happened and C1 said that he had got into a fight with his girlfriend. C1 claimed that his girlfriend had started the fight by slapping him. O1 then turned to C2 and asked her what her name and date of birth was. C1 interrupted and attempted to give O1 the information. *While looking at O1, he moved closer, with an ugly sneer on his face.*

O1 told C1 to back off and let C2 answer the questions. C1 said that "[he] would do the talking for his woman." *O1 then grabbed C1's arm and slammed him up against the patrol car. C1 struggled to escape and O1 twisted his wrist, using pain compliance to subdue him.*

Of the officer and organizational factors, individual legal guidelines was significantly related to a jump in the continuum. Encounters involving officers who strongly felt that legal guidelines served as a constraint to doing their jobs resulted in the officer using more force in comparison to those where the officer strongly disagreed with this assessment. The other factors within these sections were not significantly related.

The most powerful factor, it seems, was that of initial force or resistance. All three of the pattern variables were significant. Officers were less likely to jump the continuum in those cases where the officer initially used force (both verbal and physical, pattern1 and pattern2) as well as those where the citizen was initially physically resistant (pattern3) when compared to those cases where the citizen was initially passively or verbally resistant (pattern4, reference category). That officers were *less* likely to jump the continuum in encounters where the officer began by using verbal force is somewhat surprising. Recall that in the analysis of nonresistant citizens, officers were *more* likely to jump continuum when beginning with verbal force. It must be remembered that the point of reference in the former cases was no force while in the latter the comparison is with citizen passive/verbal resistance.

Beyond this, what seems to happen (as illustrated in the example provided above) in encounters involving nonresistant citizens is that officers issue a command and then apply a threat or physical restraint. In encounters involving a resistant citizen a similar pattern of behavior often unfolds, but the citizen resists after the initial command. Thus, the behavior on the officers' part is the same, but in the latter case it is interrupted by citizen resistance. When this occurs, therefore, the added element of a threat or physical force then falls in line with the continuum. For example:

> *Encounter (traffic ticket and tow)*
> O1 informed C1 he would have to have the car towed due to the circumstances. C1 became upset, and stated it was his mom's boyfriend's car. O1 informed him he shouldn't be driving while suspended. C1 stated he was on his way to work, and tried numerous times for a negotiation. O1 finally told C1 and C2 to hit the road. C1 shook his head and stated this was bullshit. O1 told C1 and C2 they both better go now while they had the chance.

The other interesting finding involves initial physical resistance. Officers were less likely to refrain from *and* less likely to jump the continuum when citizens were initially more aggressive at the outset. In these cases, officers stick close to the continuum. Recall from the earlier example that when a citizen flees, officers generally chase him or her down and apply physical restraint, which is in accordance with following the continuum criteria. It is rare for an officer to allow citizens to "act up" in the form of physical resistance.

However, when such citizen resistance does occur, it appears that officers generally do not go to the extreme of jumping the continuum, either. That is, they match physical resistance with physical force, but not in the form of extreme force, for the most part. Of course, there is a "topping off" effect at work in the measurement here to some extent. A citizen who displays the highest form of resistance (level five, active) cannot be subjected to a jump in the continuum unless the citizen lowers the level of resistance afterward and the officer continues with more force.[14]

Interaction Effects

As was done with nonresistant citizens, as well as in the last chapter with the highest level of force, interactions were tested through a series of three separate elaboration models. In each case, three of the four interaction terms were introduced while one was excluded. LSite1, LSuper1, and LWork1 served as the reference category in each of the respective models. Results from these analyses are presented in Tables 7-7 and 7-8.

Table 7-7 shows results from officers holding back from following the continuum, while those involving a jump in the continuum are shown in Table 7-8. It was hypothesized that the impact of force decisions may be better determined by looking across levels of explanation. In other words, officers with certain proclivities may be more inclined to act on these when placed in a context that promotes such behavior. More specifically, each assumes that officers with an inclination toward viewing legal guidelines negatively may be further influenced by the organizational context in which they find themselves, which may more readily permit them to resort to forceful ways. Each assumes a different level of influence: site (department), supervisor (first-line), and workgroup (peer).

As seen in Table 7-7, none of the interactions were significantly related to officers refraining from the continuum. Looking at instances when officers jump the continuum (Table 7-8), only one of the interactions was significant controlling for other independent effects. Encounters involving officers who do not believe overlooking legal guidelines is necessary in the course of their duties and who work with officers who believe overlooking legal guidelines is necessary in the course of their duties (LWork3) were significantly more likely to result in a jump of the continuum. In total, the posited interactions had little to no effect on officer deviations from the continuum.

Table 7-7: Estimates from Multinomial Logit Model - Interaction Effects
Resistant Citizens Refrain

	Site Model			Supervision Model			Workgroup Model		
	Coeff.	*SE*	*p*	*Coeff.*	*SE*	*p*	*Coeff.*	*SE*	*p*
Citizen:									
Male	- .086	.372	.069	- .141	.374	.706	-.081	.376	.828
NonWhite	- .358	.362	.817	- .367	.363	.312	-.412	.358	.250
Age	- .053	.131	.323	- .057	.132	.665	-.047	.134	.724
Wealth	.163	.289	.681	.188	.290	.515	.231	.295	.434
Anger/Fear	.139	.357	.572	- .096	.358	.787	.112	.362	.756
Drug/Alcohol	- .330	.342	.696	.276	.345	.423	-.259	.346	.454
Mental Impairment	.464	.699	.335	.412	.705	.558	.327	.704	.642
Disrespect	.064	.348	.854	.039	.348	.909	.052	.352	.881
Officer:									
Male	.476	.434	.273	.503	.433	.245	.480	.432	.265
White	.728	.435	.093	.772	.432	.074	.668	.435	.124
Experience	.013	.031	.663	.013	.032	.674	.015	.032	.634
Education	.088	.099	.378	.104	.099	.293	.117	.101	.244
Verbal Training	- .176	.162	.275	- .123	.162	.447	-.159	.160	.321

Table 7-7: Estimates from Multinomial Logit Model - Interaction Effects
Resistant Citizens Refrain (cont.)

	Site Model			Supervision Model			Workgroup Model		
	Coeff.	*SE*	*p*	*Coeff.*	*SE*	*p*	*Coeff.*	*SE*	*p*
Officer:									
Crimefighter	-.121	.245	.621	-.136	.247	.581	-.094	.247	.704
Citizens Trust	-.207	.213	.331	-.184	.214	.389	-.194	.214	.364
Legal Guidelines	--	--	--	--	--	--	--	--	--
Organization:									
Indianapolis	--	--	--	.671	.406	.098	-.739	.406	.068
Supervision	.062	.230	.786	--	--	--	.025	.237	.915
Workgroup	-.204	.241	.397	-.153	.247	.535	--	--	--
911 Officer	-.838	.660	.204	-.796	.675	.238	-.664	.655	.310
Control:									
# Officers	-.176	.035	.054	-.169	.072	.020	-.197	.073	.007
# Bystanders	.010	.012	.167	.009	.019	.610	.011	.018	.556
Anticipate Violence	.368	.200	.447	.290	.498	.559	.297	.503	.554
Proactive	-.155	.105	.000	-.180	.354	.611	-.152	.360	.671
Type Problem	.095	.102	.310	.073	.332	.824	-.093	.333	.779

Table 7-7: Estimates from Multinomial Logit Model - Interaction Effects
Resistant Citizens Refrain (cont.)

	Site Model			Supervision Model			Workgroup Model		
	Coeff	*SE*	*p*	*Coeff*	*SE*	*p*	*Coeff*	*SE*	*p*
Control:									
Pattern1	- .126	.386	.742	- .140	.388	.717	-.065	.389	.866
Pattern2	- .538	.577	.350	- .532	.582	.361	-.460	.586	.432
Pattern3	- 1.23	.541	.022	- 1.22	.541	.023	-1.18	.552	.031
Missing	- .405	1.22	.741	- .491	1.19	.679	.147	1.15	.898
Hybrid:									
Site2	1.289	1.13	.139						
Site3	.363	.546	.506						
Site4	.665	.612	.284						
Super2				- .398	.901	.665			
Super3				- .003	.512	.994			
Super4				- .444	.726	.540			

Table 7-7: Estimates from Multinomial Logit Model - Interaction Effects
Resistant Citizens Refrain (cont.)

	Site Model			Supervision Model			Workgroup Model		
	Coeff.	*SE*	*p*	*Coeff.*	*SE*	*p*	*Coeff.*	*SE*	*p*
Hybrid:									
Work2							-.974	.757	.198
Work3							.104	1.01	.301
Work4							-.457	.413	.268
Constant	3.289			3.901			3.460		
Log Likelihood	-210.484			-210.363			-209.056		
Chi Square (p=.010)									
N	343			343			343		

Table 7-8: Estimates from Multinomial Logit Model - Interaction Effects
Resistant Citizens Jump

	Site Model			Supervision Model			Workgroup Model		
	Coeff	*SE*	*p*	*Coeff*	*SE*	*p*	*Coeff*	*SE*	*p*
Citizen:									
Male	1.55	.836	.062	1.46	.833	.078	1.54	.838	.065
NonWhite	-.705	.628	.261	-.603	.621	.331	-.699	.616	.256
Age	-.253	.231	.273	-.253	.234	.279	-.253	.233	.278
Wealth	-.149	.531	.779	-.098	.524	.851	-.002	.533	.996
Anger/Fear	1.36	.681	.044	1.55	.698	.025	1.40	.689	.041
Drug/Alcohol	.418	.645	.516	.461	.652	.479	.421	.649	.516
Mental Impairment	1.35	1.07	.207	1.29	1.08	.232	1.22	1.07	.253
Disrespect	-1.11	.645	.085	-1.05	.643	.100	-1.11	.656	.090
Officer:									
Male	31.5	136	1.00	31.5	138	1.00	31.6	136	1.00
White	1.28	.738	.082	1.32	.739	.072	1.12	.739	.129
Experience	.037	.052	.467	.042	.051	.415	.037	.054	.495
Education	.083	.190	.661	.099	.187	.593	.077	.193	.687
Verbal Training	.071	.299	.811	.126	.294	.667	.081	.301	.786

Table 7-8: Estimates from Multinomial Logit Model – Interaction Effects

Resistant Citizens Jump (cont.)

	Site Model			Supervision Model			Workgroup Model		
	Coeff.	*SE*	*p*	*Coeff.*	*SE*	*p*	*Coeff.*	*SE*	*p*
Officer:									
Crimefighter	.112	.472	.812	-.055	.466	.905	.060	.467	.896
Citizens Trust	-.451	.411	.272	-.403	.402	.315	-.404	.420	.336
Legal Guidelines	--	--	--	--	--	--	--	--	--
Organization:									
Indianapolis	--	--	--	.051	.733	.943	-.097	.731	.893
Supervision	.459	.391	.240	--	--	--	.442	.395	.263
Workgroup	-.209	.388	.589	-.244	.393	.534	--	--	--
911 Officer	.154	1.50	.918	-.008	1.45	.995	.398	1.48	.787
Control:									
# Officers	.069	.138	.612	.096	.140	.490	.053	.141	.703
# Bystanders	-.040	.045	.366	-.051	.046	.265	-.046	.045	.305
Anticipate Violence	.710	.818	.385	.776	.808	.336	.654	.824	.427
Proactive	.388	.656	.554	.480	.654	.462	.329	.662	.619
Type Problem	-.964	.648	.136	-1.01	.651	.121	-.996	.651	.125

Table 7-8: Estimates from Multinomial Logit Model - Interaction Effects
Resistant Citizens Jump (cont.)

	Site Model			Supervision Model			Workgroup Model		
	Coeff	*SE*	*p*	*Coeff*	*SE*	*p*	*Coeff*	*SE*	*p*
Control:									
Pattern1	-1.73	.664	.009	-1.83	.672	.006	-1.63	.662	.013
Pattern2	-2.78	1.33	.037	-3.12	1.37	.023	-2.72	1.34	.042
Pattern3	-3.02	1.01	.002	-3.10	1.03	.002	-2.91	1.03	.004
Missing	.370	2.39	.873	-.436	2.17	.840	.714	2.10	.734
Hybrid:									
Site2	-29.6	276	1.00						
Site3	1.38	.854	.105						
Site4	1.36	1.01	.177						
Super2				-29.7	323	1.00			
Super3				1.34	.827	.105			
Super4				1.39	1.11	.210			

Table 7-8: Estimates from Multinomial Logit Model - Interaction Effects
Resistant Citizens Jump (cont.)

	Site Model			Supervision Model			Workgroup Model		
	Coeff.	*SE*	*p*	*Coeff.*	*SE*	*p*	*Coeff.*	*SE*	*p*
Hybrid:									
Work2							-.429	1.67	.797
Work3							2.62	1.32	.047
Work4							.941	.784	.230
Constant	31.895			31.280			32.725		
Log Likelihood	-210.484			-210.363			-209.056		
Chi Square (p=.010)									
N	343			343			343		

7.3 OPPOSITE ENDS OF THE CONTINUUM

In addition to the 343 encounters involving a resistant citizen where the officer chose to *either* hold back from following or jumped the continuum, another 87 cases involved *both* behaviors. An argument can be made that these encounters involved the most erratic behavior. In essence, officers in these cases swing from one end of the continuum to another as the incident unfolds. In an attempt to uncover how these encounters played out, this section examines the 87 encounters in two ways, both in the context of examining which behavior precedes the other. First, the analysis examines what factors are related to each initial behavior by looking at bivariate relationships. Do officers tend to hold back initially more often on certain individuals (e.g., females) while jumping the continuum right away on others (e.g., males)? Second, the analysis examines possible reasons for why officers chose to move in opposite directions at different points during the encounter. For instance, what would prompt an officer to initially hold back, but later jump the continuum and vice versa?

I begin by asking which behavior occurred first: refrain or jump? Of the 87 cases, officers refrained from moving up the continuum prior to jumping it in 54 (62.0%). In 21 of the 54 cases, officers held back more than one time (e.g., in more than one sequence) before choosing to jump. Conversely, in 33 (38.0%) of the 87 cases the reverse occurred: officers initially jumped the continuum and then held back in subsequent sequences. In five of the 33 cases the officer jumped the continuum more than once prior to holding back. Clearly, when both behaviors are present, officers most often hold back first and jump second. In addition, in many instances officers hold back multiple times before jumping.

Differences in Initial Police Action
I examine the relationship between each of the two initial behaviors (refrain and jump) and the factors previously used to examine how officers move about the continuum. For example, are officers more likely to start out with refraining behavior on whites as opposed to nonwhites before moving on to a jump in the continuum? Table 7-9 presents the relationship between each of these factors and whether the officer began

by refraining from or jumping the continuum. The most pronounced differences are found on citizen characteristics. Most of these variables move in the predicted direction. For example, of the 53 cases involving an emotional citizen, officers begin with jumping the continuum in 23 (43.4%) compared to only 10 of the 34 (29.4%) cases where the citizen was not emotional. However, two of the factors move in the non-predicted direction. Looking at citizen race, we see that officers jumped the continuum more readily in encounters involving whites. We also see that a rather substantial difference is found with disrespect. Five of 19 (26.3%) cases where disrespect was present the officer jumped the continuum compared to 28 of the 40 (41.2%) cases where the citizen was not disrespectful.

Turning to officer characteristics, the most surprising differences are found on gender and race. Encounters involving female and nonwhite officers were both more likely to result in a jump of the continuum initially. While the differences between the two are not overly large, the mere fact that females and nonwhites are more apt to jump at first is somewhat surprising. Scanning the narratives it is difficult to get a sense for why this may be the case. For instance, none of the cases make reference to why these individuals would be more likely to jump first and refrain second.

With the exception of the workgroup legal guideline measure, little differences are found on the organizational variables. Those encounters involving officers who felt that all or most of the officers within their workgroup felt constrained by legal guidelines were more likely to result in the use of more force (63.6%) compared to those who felt that none of the officers in their workgroup perceived such a constraint (40.9%). However, as with all comparisons made here, these percentages are based on a relatively small number of cases.

Looking at the control variables, encounters involving three officers (46.2%) as opposed to one (35.3%) were more likely to result in an initial jump. This pattern is reversed for the number of citizens present. When three citizens were present, officers only jumped initially in five of 15 (33.3%) cases. When only one citizen was present, officers jumped in eight of the 12 cases (66.7%).

Table 7-9: Bivariate Relationships by Continuum
(Refrain and Jump)
Initial Police Action (N=87)

Citizen:	Refrain	Jump
Gender		
Male (77)	46 (59.7)	31 (40.3)
Female (10)	8 (80.0)	2 (20.0)
Race		
White (22)	12 (54.5)	10 (45.5)
Nonwhite (65)	42 (64.6)	23 (35.4)
Age		
Pre-School, 0-5 years (0)	--	--
Child,6-12 years (5)	5 (100)	--
Young Adult, 13-17 years (4)	3 (75.0)	1 (25.0)
Older Teen, 18-20 years (9)	5 (55.6)	4 (44.4)
Young Adult, 21-29 years (25)	15 (60.0)	10 (40.0)
Adult, 30-44 years (34)	21 (61.8)	13 (38.2)
Middle-Aged, 45-59 years (7)	3 (42.9)	4 (57.1)
Senior, 60+ years (3)	2 (66.7)	1 (33.3)
Wealth		
Chronic (5)	2 (40.0)	3 (60.0)
Low (63)	40 (63.2)	23 (36.5)
Middle (19))	12 (63.2)	7 (36.8)
Above Middle (0)	--	--
Emotional State		
Fear/Anger (53)	30 (56.6)	23 (43.4)
No (34)	24 (70.6)	10 (29.4)

Table 7-9: Bivariate Relationships by Continuum
(Refrain and Jump)
Initial Police Action (N=87) (cont.)

	Refrain	Jump
Drug/Alcohol Use		
Yes (39)	20 (51.3)	19 (48.7)
No (48)	34 (70.8)	14 (29.2)
Mentally Impaired		
Yes (4)	4 (100)	--
No (83)	50 (60.2)	33 (39.8)
Disrespectful		
Yes (19)	14 (73.7)	5 (26.3)
No (68)	40 (58.8)	28 (41.2)
Officer:		
Gender		
Male (73)	46 (63.0)	27 (37.0)
Female (14)	8 (57.1)	6 (42.9)
Race		
White (63)	40 (63.5)	23 (36.5)
Nonwhite (24)	14 (58.3)	10 (41.7)
Experience (Years on Job)		
One (2)	--	2 (100)
Five (4)	2 (50.0)	2 (50.0)
Ten (5)	3 (60.0)	2 (40.0)

Table 7-9: Bivariate Relationships by Continuum
(Refrain and Jump)
Initial Police Action (N=87) (cont.)

	Refrain	Jump
Education		
< than High School (2)	2 (100)	--
High School Grad/GED (15)	11 (73.3)	4 (26.7)
Some College, no degree (14)	7 (50.0)	7 (50.0)
Assoc. Degree (4)	2 (50.0)	2 (50.0)
>2 years college, no B.S. (11)	8 (72.7)	3 (27.3)
B.S./B.A. (29)	16 (55.2)	13 (44.8)
Some Graduate, no degree (4)	2 (50.0)	2 (50.0)
Graduate Degree (0)	--	--
Verbal Training		
None (37)	24 (64.9)	13 (35.1)
<1 day (15)	7 (46.7)	8 (53.3)
1-2 days (13)	10 (76.9)	3 (23.1)
3-5 days (9)	4 (44.4)	5 (55.6)
>5 days (6)	4 (66.7)	2 (33.3)
Crimefighter		
Agree Strongly (25)	14 (56.0)	11 (44.0)
Agree Somewhat (42)	26 (61.9)	16 (38.1)
Disagree Somewhat (10)	6 (60.0)	4 (40.0)
Disagree Strongly (3)	3 (100)	--
Distrust		
Agree Strongly (2)	--	2 (100)
Agree Somewhat (23)	15 (65.2)	8 (34.8)
Disagree Somewhat (27)	18 (66.7)	9 (33.3)
Disagree Strongly (22)	14 (63.6)	8 (36.4)

Table 7-9: Bivariate Relationships by Continuum
(Refrain and Jump)
Initial Police Action (N=87) (cont.)

	Refrain	Jump
Individual Legal Guidelines		
Agree Strongly (1)	1(100)	--
Agree Somewhat (14)	6 (42.9)	8 (57.1)
Disagree Somewhat (17)	12 (70.6)	5 (29.4)
Disagree Strongly (47)	29 (61.7)	18 (38.3)
Organization:		
Site		
Indianapolis (57)	35 (61.4)	22 (38.6)
St. Pete (30)	19 (63.3)	11 (36.7)
Assignment		
911 (80)	50 (62.5)	30 (37.5)
CPO (7)	4 (57.1)	3 (42.9)
Supervisor Criticism		
Agree Strongly (50)	32 (64.0)	18 (36.0)
Agree Somewhat (19)	11 (57.9)	8 (42.1)
Disagree Somewhat (8)	4 (50.0)	4 (50.0)
Disagree Strongly (3)	2 (66.7)	1 (33.3)
Workgroup Legal Guidelines		
All of most (11)	4 (36.4)	7 (63.6)
About half (11)	7 (63.6)	4 (36.4)
A few (35)	24 (68.6)	11 (31.4)
None (22)	13 (59.1)	6 (40.9)

Table 7-9: Bivariate Relationships by Continuum
(Refrain and Jump)
Initial Police Action (N=87) (cont.)

	Refrain	Jump
Control:		
Number of Officers		
One (17)	11 (64.7)	6 (35.3)
Two (33)	23 (69.7)	10 (30.3)
Three (13)	7 (53.8)	6 (46.2)
Number of Bystanders		
One (12)	4 (33.3)	8 (66.7)
Two (15)	10 (66.7)	5 (33.3)
Three (15)	10 (66.7)	5 (33.3)
Anticipate Violence		
Yes (18)	11 (61.1)	7 (38.9)
No (69)	43 (62.3)	26 (37.7)
Proactive Encounter		
Yes(30)	20 (66.7)	10 (33.3)
No (57)	34 (59.6)	23 (40.4)
Potentially Violent Problem		
Yes (49)	31 (63.3)	18 (36.7)
No (38)	23 (60.5)	15 (39.5)

Changing Directions
The fact that officers often refrain first and jump second tends to mirror what was found in the other 343 encounters involving a resistant citizen. Officers seem inclined to hold back more readily as opposed to jumping. Although in this subset of cases officers do jump the continuum at some point during the encounter, the jump usually occurs only after holding back. The following examples illustrate how some of these cases unfold:

Encounter 1 (domestic dispute, officers looking to see if suspect is in the house)
O1 walked through the tiny efficiency back to the bathroom. O1 saw the pants of a man in the bathroom and *told him to come out.* The man, C2(WM 31) whose weekly rented efficiency suggests that he is lower class, *did not reply.* O1 stated firmly "*You better show me your hands*" C2 did. *O1 grabbed his hand and pulled him out of the bathroom. O1 pushed the man against the wall* and with the assistance of O2 and O3 hand cuffed him.

Encounter 2 (open container)
O1 while still in the vehicle, told C1 (BM-mid 20s, lower class based on dress and lack of response) to dump his beer out. C1 did not react. O1 yelled again for C1 to dump the beer out. C1 did not react or look at O1 but made a slight effort to hide the beer by his side. O1 stopped the vehicle and went over to C1, who was still not reacting to O1. O1 stepped on his foot, grabbed the beer and pressed his shoulder down.

Encounter 3 (drug traffic stop)
O1 arrives at a convenience store/gas station located outside of the assigned CPA. The store is located at an intersection on the main drag of the city. The neighborhood is part of a seedy hotel district that houses many drug dealers and prostitutes. O2 has made the traffic stop with O3. Shortly after O1 arrives, O3 leaves. There is a young black male in the back of the patrol car. C1 (BM, 25, MC based on expensive designer clothing and respectable vocabulary) is leaning against the stopped vehicle. O1 asks C1 if this is his car. C1 is polite--but quiet and business-like saying that it is a rental car. C2 (BM, 18, MC based on clean expensive clothing) walks up from a group of young black bystanders that are about 50 feet away. C2 asks C1 what's going on, why he is being hassled by the police. O1 jumps in and tells C2 that this incident is none of his business (politely) and he should just stand away from the car and not interfere. C2

complies, but has an annoyed face. C1 explains that C2 is his cousin. O1 says that's okay, buy he shouldn't get involved.

O2 searches the stopped vehicle and finds a blunt (large cigar full of marijuana) under the seat of the stopped vehicle. O1 aks C1 if that was his blunt in the car. C1 is very evasive and says he doesn't know what a blunt is. O1 is playing his game and just avoids confrontation by changing the conversation--talking now about cigars. O1 and C1 chat about where O1 gets good cigars etc. O2 explains to O1 that the juvenile in the back seat of the car has a $10,000 warrant for his arrest-so he's going to take him in. O2 continues to tell O1 that when he stopped the juvenile he tried to "dip" (run away). As O2 explains this as he is opening the patrol car door. The juvenile overhears O2 saying that he tried to dip and the juvenile starts screaming at O2 saying he didn't try to run away...what is the officer talking about. O2 reiterates that the juvenile tried to dip. The juvenile calls C1 over to the patrol car screaming that O2 claims that he tried to run away. C1 walks to the patrol car. *O1 tells C1 to stand back by the car, he doesn't need to be a part of this argument.*

C1 continues to walk toward the car. O1 continues to tell C1 to stay away from the juvenile--but C1 begins to speak to the juvenile. The juvenile is frantic, screaming to C1 that O2 is lying saying he tried to run away. C1 is annoyed when he hears this and says "WHAT??" looking at O2 with disgust. C1 cuts the juvenile off and tells him to shut up--don't say a word [admit anything] to the officers about the incident. The juvenile takes C1's advice and quits screaming. O2 is very angry with this and slams the police door shut so that C1 and the juvenile can no longer talk. O2 shouts at C1 saying that he is disrespectful for telling the juvenile to not say anything [admit anything] to the police. *C1 finally obeys O1's orders to walk away from the patrol vehicle and stand by the rental car. O1 and O2 quickly search C1 by patting him down and checking his pockets.* C1 seems disgusted with this, but does not put up a fight. O2 tells

C1 that he can take off, but he should make arrangements for the vehicle to be picked up.

Encounter 4 (dispatch man with gun)
O2 (from event 6) was on the scene seconds before O1. C1 was a lower class black male in his mid thirties. He was sitting in his rusted car outside of the complainants home. C1 wasn't wearing a shirt and his pants fell well below his waist revealing his briefs and crack to the world. There was a group of five people sitting on the porch.

O1 had his gun and CS out and ready. O2 had turned his spotlight on the car and had his gun drawn as well. O2 yelled at the citizen to remain still. O2 approached from the back of the car and O1 approached from the side. C1 looked stunned. O2 yelled for C1 to get out of the car slowly.

C1 did but began to loudly plead his innocence, "I didn't do nothin. What I do? I didn't do nothin'." He stepped out of the car. O2 asked where the gun was. C1 said that he didn't have a gun. *O1 yelled for C1 to put his hands on the car.*

C1 continued to claim his innocence, repeatedly. O1 repeated himself. C1 looked around confused and began to back peddle slowly away from the car. O1 repeated himself. C1 continued but now screamed like he was crying, "I didn't do nothin." Both officers simultaneously charged C1 and sprayed him with their CS.

C1 shook his head confused but unaffected by the spray. He suddenly turned and began to run. He ran like he was blind. He barreled through the overgrown property and reached the street. He stumbled but continued forward. He was still screaming, saying that he hadn't done anything. O1 and O2 pursued close behind. C1 turned as if realizing he didn't want to run or couldn't run. Just as he began to say that he didn't do anything O2 lunged with his body. He cocked his forearm and leaped into the air. O2's body met C1's big belly. His elbow fell short of its target and barely grazed C1's chin.

O1 caught up and tried a leg sweep. This missed because O2 had gotten behind C1 and began to push him in the opposite direction. O2 had C1's arm held behind his head. He pushed C1 forward and tried to trip him several times. He kept missing. O1 continually tried to swipe C1 with his foot but continually missed. After about three times O2 finally connected with C1's leg.

C1 went crashing down on the side walk. His body half lay in the overgrown weeds, half on the sidewalk. O1 had a cuff on C1's left hand. O2 stepped back for a brief second. C1 was laying on his back. O1 yelled to C1 to let go of his hand. C1 was screaming that he didn't do anything. O1 yelled at him again. O1 began to hit C1's left arm with his free hand. O2 stepped forward and sprayed his CS in C1's eyes. C1 let go. O2pushed C1 over so that O1 could get the other cuff on.

In the first case the officer issued a command to which the citizen did not respond. The officer decides to give him another chance and tells him to come out once again. This time the citizen complies. At this point the officer grabs and gives him a push (this may not have occurred had the citizen initially complied). It seems the added element of force may have been applied to punish the citizen after the officer initially gave him a chance to comply. In the second example, the officer commands the citizen to dump the beer. While the citizen resists the officer repeats the command. When the citizen still does not comply the officer becomes frustrated and goes over and applies physical force. Again, it appears there may be an extra penalty to pay for resisting after the officer gave the citizen a second chance.   The third case provides a similar example. What is the purpose of searching C1 after all this? Is there any indication of him having a weapon?

Finally, the fourth example obviously is the most pronounced. There is no doubt this is a serious situation given the "man with a gun" dispatch, but notice that no intermediate levels of force are attempted; apparently it is either all or nothing. The officers keep trying commands but this clearly is not working. The next step is then to charge and mace him. The interaction proceeds directly to a takedown and macing. Again, some may argue that the force applied is in fact needed given the citizens' repeated resistance. Nonetheless, there was a jump straight from verbal force to impact force. Further, after the suspect fled, stopped, and apparently gave up, additional force was applied. In each of these examples the officer initially tries to gain compliance using no or lower forms of force. When citizens resist and do not take advantage of the officer providing a second chance it seems as if the frustration level builds and instead of slowly (or incrementally) moving up the continuum the officer explodes and comes back with a relatively high form of force.

Turning to those cases where the officer initially jumped the continuum, but then pulled back, it appears this quite often is partially a result of the uncertainty of the initial force in the first place. It seems that officers often quickly resort to higher levels of force (mainly physical restraint) and then one of two things occur. Either the circumstances are rather ambiguous as to the legitimacy of the police intrusion or a decision is made not to pursue any further action. Two examples:

Encounter 1 (dispatch problem with people)
O1 pulled up the location where a problem with people hanging out had been reported. As O1 arrived at the location two other officers pulled in behind O1. O1 stopped the patrol car when he got to C1, a white male middle class in his 50's, the property manager, who was waving him down. C1 said that a group of black males had been hanging around on the property, shooting craps and drinking. C1 said that they wouldn't leave when he told them to and didn't leave until after he had gone to call the police. C1 said that the elderly black people in the area where scared of them. C1 said that the group had moved across the street, but one was still hanging out. C1 pointed to C2, a black male in his 20's middle class, wearing shorts and a shirt, a gold watch, and a gold chain. O1 got out of the car and walked over

to C2 with C1. O1 asked C2 if he lived at the location. C2 said that he was visiting people. O1 then told C2 to place his hands on the car. C2 did that and then *O1 patted him down.*

Afterward O1 asked C2 if he had any identification. C2 gave O1 his license. O1 ran the license and asked C2 who he was visiting. C2 said that his grandmother lived there. O1 asked C2 what his grandmother's address was. *C2 did not respond. O1 asked again* and *C2 asked why he needed to know.* C2 said that the address didn't matter since he was going to be wrong anyway and be told to leave. *O1 told C2 to answer the question.*

C2 began to raise his voice and swing his arms around as he said that it didn't matter because he was wrong because he was black. *O1 told C2 to quit putting on a production and answer the question.* C2 said that the police were putting on production since they were the ones that rolled up on him when he was just trying to visit his people. *O1 told C2 to answer the question.*

C2 finally did. O1 said that they weren't giving him a hard time for being black, they were only hear because the property manager had made a complaint. C1 then said that C2 had been drinking and hanging out on the property where he did belong. C2 began to yell again and said that he wasn't drinking anything and he would take a breathalyser to prove it. C2 said that he didn't care what C1 wanted because C1 didn't ask nicely, he just yelled at him to get off the property and disrespected him for no reason.

O2 then began to yell at C2 and told him that he needed to quit yelling, they had asked him nicely once and would not do so again. C2 ended up not having any warrants out for him. So O1 interrupted and told C2 that regardless of the situation C1 was the manager and he did not want him on the property and that was that. O1 gave C2 his license and told him to go on his way. C2 took the license and walked off with a black female that had been watching the encounter. There were numerous people out on their steps watching this encounter, there were 13 bystanders.

Debriefing O1. O1 commented that he did not like when people started to bring up the whole race thing, because it just wasn't true. O1 said that he expects people to bring it up and they usually do. O1 added that it happens and that he doesn't take things too personally. O1 said that the guy had a lot of attitude before O1 got there and so he didn't really care what C2 said.

Encounter 2 (dispatch domestic argument)
We arrived at the same time O2. Both officers walked right into the house and back to the bedroom where shouts were coming from. C1, a tall, middle-class b/m, was sitting on the side of the bed yelling down at a b/f who was sitting in the corner covering her hands with her head and crying. O2 grabbed C1's arm and stood him up. He put handcuffs on him and *O1 took him by the arm and led him outside.*

A teenage b/m was in the living room looking very scared and confused. As we were walking out, C1 kept saying, "My lady's on crack! But I'm the one going to jail." O1 led C1 to the car and had him lean against. O1 searched his pockets and C1 kept leaning into O1's face and saying, "A man can't get ahead when his lady's on crack, you know what I'm saying, man?" O1 kept saying, "I hear ya." C1 kept repeating it until *O1 told him to chill out a little.*

C1 would be quiet for a minute then *he would lean back into O1's face and say something.* Several times he said that he admitted to drinking, but his lady was on crack.

O2 came out of the house and asked C1 if he had a car to go somewhere. C1 said he did. The b/f was on the porch and yelled to C1 that he couldn't take the car. O2 asked C1 whose car it was and C1 said it was both of theirs. O1 told C1 that he had been drinking so he didn't need to be driving anyway. O1 told C1 that if he had a place to go and they could be sure he wasn't coming back here then they wouldn't arrest him. C1 said he could go to his brother's house and told O1 and O2 the location. O1 commented on how far away it was and asked C1 how he was going to get there. O1 asked if he had any money for a cab. C1 said he did not. O1 and O2 looked at each other for a moment and O2, "If we take you over there, can we be certain you're not gonna come back here?" C1 promised that he would not come back to get his stuff until tomorrow. O2 put C1 in the backseat of his car, and O1 told O2 that he would follow him out there.

Debriefing O1. O1 said that C1's brother lived far enough away so that C1 would not be able to walk back to the house. O1 said that he believed that C1's girlfriend was smoking crack and that' why C1 was so upset. He said C1 probably didn't hit her but pushed her. He said the girlfriend probably told O2 that she didn't want to press charges, she just wanted him to leave.

In the first case, the officer almost immediately does a search on someone suspected of "shooting craps" and "drinking." Then, the officer becomes very tolerant. While there is no direct reference to the legitimacy of the intrusion, especially a pat down search, one has to wonder what influence this had on his tolerance level thereafter. In the second case the officers again immediately grab the suspect and cuff him. While the observed officer is outside waiting for the other officer to find out what is going on, the citizen pledges his case and the officer tells him to "chill out." Had the officer known what the situation was prior perhaps he would not have been so tolerant so as to allow C1 to get in his face after telling him to chill out, or would not have resorted to physical force in the first place.

Finally, while the flow of how these encounters played out was erratic in the sense that officers displayed both forms of behavior (refrain and jump) within the same incident, there was little movement from one behavior to the other and then back to the original behavior. For example, cases where an officer refrained, then jumped, then refrained again. In only 12 (13.8%) encounters did such a pattern occur. This was generally a relatively infrequent occurrence.

7.4 SUMMARY

On the whole, police force tended to closely mirror the level of citizen resistance encountered. When dealing with nonresistant citizens, officers deviated from the continuum (e.g., jump of the continuum) in about one in five encounters. More telling perhaps, is that when this did occur it was usually in the form of what has been characterized as a "minimal" jump - use of a verbal threat or physical restraint. These cases usually unfold with the officer issuing a command first followed by the added element of a verbal threat or pat down search. As discovered when examining the highest level of force, officers are also more likely to demonstrate such behavior on younger and lower class males, as well as those displaying signs of alcohol or drug use. However, officers were *not* more likely to jump the continuum on nonwhite citizens.

In encounters where citizens do exhibit some form of resistance, officers are not only less likely to apply high forms of force, but are actually more likely to refrain from even following the continuum. Regardless of how the numbers are calculated, officers hold back from applying equivalent levels of force in approximately three of every four suspect encounters. When citizens attempt to escalate a situation, officers most often attempt to move in the opposite direction of de-escalation. In effect, officers generally prefer to give resistant citizens a "second chance" to comply. The perception that officers leap at the opportunity to apply force on a resistant citizen is not supported here. However, failure on the citizens part to take advantage of this extra chance does tend to lead to a more forceful outcome. It appears that officers go to great strides in an attempt to resolve resistant encounters in the most noncoercive manner possible. Additionally, such refraining behavior on the officers' part was not reserved for certain individuals or confined to certain officers. For example, officers were not more inclined to hold back or give white citizens a second chance compared to nonwhites.

When officers do resort to a jump of the continuum in encounters with resistant citizens, such a jump was also generally minimal in nature. For instance, rarely did officers respond to passive resistance with a blow to the head. The typical jump case was along the lines of applying low-level physical force on a passively resistant citizen. A jump of the continuum was most likely to occur when citizens are "initially" passively or verbally resistant. While this may appear to contradict the statements above, this is not the case. When officers command a citizen to do something (or not do something) and the citizen resists, the officer tends to re-issue the command, thereby giving the citizen one more opportunity to comply. It is when the citizen starts right off with resistant behavior that prompts an officer to be more aggressive. Additionally, officers were more likely to jump the continuum when resistant citizens were male or emotionally upset. Encounters involving officers with a proclivity to see legal guidelines as a constraint were also more likely to result in a jump of the continuum.

Only one of the 12 interactions tested proved statistically significant. Encounters involving officers who do not believe overlooking legal guidelines is necessary in the course of their duties *and* who work with officers they perceive feel the need to overlook legal guidelines were significantly more likely to result in a jump of the continuum. Hence, the posited interactions had little to no effect on officer deviations from the continuum.

Finally, citizen disrespect had no statistical effect on how the continuum was applied. Based on previous force studies, this came as a surprise. Disrespect (or "demeanor") has been shown to be a fairly consistent predictor of forceful police behavior. Nonetheless, the presence of citizen disrespect here did not produce such a finding.

CHAPTER 8
Conclusions and Implications

At the conclusion of any research endeavor one is inevitably left to ask - so what? What contribution does this research actually make? Comparing the present research to issues presented in the latest and presumably most up to date analysis on force, the NIJ/BJS study discussed in Chapter Two, the answer is - a great deal. Almost all of the issues raised in the NIJ/BJS study were addressed in some fashion by the present research, which is indicative of how this research contributes to the broader research agenda proposed by leading force scholars. The research undertaken and the findings uncovered here not only challenge some of the conventional wisdom of what we think we know about police use of force, but go beyond the rhetoric of what needs to be done by actually doing it. More specifically, this research sought to determine how and why officers use force. It began with three premises:

- all potential acts of force need to be considered - both verbal and physical.
- police force is best understood when conceived and measured along a continuum according to the severity of harm it imposes on citizens.
- the police-citizen encounter needs to be broken down into behavioral sequences and citizen resistance incorporated into these sequences.

It was posited that to fully understand the application of force, *all* forms of force, both verbal and physical, must be examined. Force was defined as acts that threaten or inflict physical harm on citizens. The sampling frame applied was not restricted to only excessive force, or even physical force cases. Rather, all police-citizen encounters were examined. Additionally, the assumption was that force is best understood when conceived and measured along a continuum according to the severity of harm it imposes on citizens. Force was broken down into varying levels ranging from verbal commands to impact methods.

In addition, the police-citizen encounter was broken down into behavioral sequences and citizen resistance incorporated into these sequences. An encounter does not occur instantaneously, but evolves over time. Within each encounter, multiple behaviors by both the police and citizens are possible. An officer may apply force numerous times within an encounter and these applications can vary in terms of severity. Similarly, a citizen may resist, may do so numerous times, and may do so in various ways. Citizen resistance was defined as acts that thwart, obstruct, or impede an officers' attempt to elicit information; failure to respond or responding negatively to an officer's commands or threats; and any physical act, proactive or reactive, against an officer's attempt to control the citizen. Additionally, similar to police force, citizen resistance was conceived and measured along a continuum according to the severity of defiance presented to the officer. Resistance levels ranged from passive to active resistance.

Examining citizen resistance along with police force is critical for understanding the context in which force is used. Virtually any inquiry concerning how or why officers use force is augmented by the inclusion of citizen resistance. Knowing an officer used force tells us very little without knowing the specific type of force used, how many times it was used, and what the citizen behavior was prior to each use. Within this basic operating structure the following research questions were addressed:

- how often do officers use force?
- how does force vary?
- how is force applied in individual encounters?
- what are the causes of police force?
- what factors are related to those instances when officers refrain from moving up the continuum despite resistance, move up and down the continuum incrementally based on resistance, or apply higher forms of force given the level of resistance?

8.1 SUMMARY OF MAJOR FINDINGS

Extent, Variation, and Application of Force

Nearly 60 percent of the observed police-citizen encounters involved some form of force. From this account, police force is clearly not an infrequent event. It actually occurs quite regularly. However, interpretation of this finding requires caution. Many of the previous force studies do not include verbal force, while this study does. If verbal force is excluded from the universe of forceful behaviors, the figure drops to just over 15 percent of all police-citizen encounters. Further, if pat downs and handcuffing are excluded, the percentage drops to about five percent. Nonetheless, if multiple uses of force within individual encounters are considered, the frequency of force is even greater. As demonstrated in Chapter Five, a substantial number of encounters do involve multiple uses of force, which dramatically increases its overall frequency.

Most force occurs at the bottom of the force spectrum. If verbal force is included then most force falls into this category of behavior. If verbal force is excluded, most force still occurs at the bottom of the continuum in the form of physical restraint and control. It was also discovered that force does not tend to fluctuate a great deal as an encounter unfolds. In 80 percent of the observed encounters, officers either remained at the same level of force or moved in only one direction (e.g., started with a command and issued another command; started with a command and increased to a threat; started with a threat and decreased to a command). In only about one in five encounters does the officer move up and then back down the continuum (or visa versa) within the same incident.

Although officers use force quite regularly on resistant citizens, nonresistant citizens are not exempt from forceful police behavior. As demonstrated in Chapter Seven, approximately 20 percent of the encounters involved an officer "jumping" the continuum on a completely nonresistant citizen and not in the course of an arrest. The general form of this jump is through the use of a threat or physical restraint.

Extent, Variation, and Application of Resistance

Citizens demonstrated some form of resistance in about 12 percent of the observed encounters. In comparison to police use of force, this figure is substantially lower. However, like police force, when multiple uses of resistance are considered the frequency drastically increases. While only 446 encounters involved a resistant act, when multiple behaviors are counted 941 resistant acts were uncovered across the 3,544 observed encounters. Also similar to forceful behavior, much of the resistance encountered falls at the bottom of the continuum, generally in the form of passive or verbal resistance. Additionally, citizen resistance remains somewhat stable in most encounters. Again, a similar pattern of stability was found with police force. In only about 10 percent of the encounters do citizens move up and down the continuum or visa versa within the same incident. Citizens tend to remain at the same level of resistance (e.g., start with passive and repeat passive) or move up/down in only one direction (e.g., start with passive and move to verbal or start with verbal and move to passive).

Resistance/Force Interplay

Force and resistance were also examined in combination with one another in an attempt to determine what impact each has on the other as an encounter evolves. Several scholars have posited that what occurs early in an encounter can set the "tone" for the remainder of the encounter. For instance, Bayley and Garofalo (1989) have emphasized that officers sometimes need to take charge at the outset in order to maintain control throughout.

In the current study, beginning an encounter with force led to a greater frequency of citizen resistance. Fifteen percent of the encounters that began with officer force led to some form of citizen resistance as opposed to only five percent of those where the officer did not use initial force. It was also found that the use of initial police force was no assurance that the officer would not apply additional force at some later point during the encounter. Encounters where officers started with some form of force resulted in a 50 percent chance of force being used again. Only 10 percent of the encounters where the officer did not begin with force eventually led to force being used. Thus, initial force generally prompted more force at some later point, regardless of eventual citizen resistance.

Causes of Force

In Chapter 6 numerous determinants of the highest level of force within an encounter were tested. It was discovered that legal factors play a prominent role in the use of force. Officers are most likely to apply greater levels of force when faced with resistant citizens, citizens in conflict with one another, when officer safety is an issue, and in the course of making an arrest. Despite these findings, it was also found that officers respond to several extra legal factors. For instance, Black posits that the application of law can be explained in terms of social space or distance. In the context of police force, Black predicts that the police will be more coercive toward those perceived to have lower status such as minorities, the poor, and those classified as lower class. Evidence from this study shows support for Black's theory. In particular, it was found that officers were significantly more likely to use increased levels of force on males, nonwhites, poor citizens, younger citizens, and those displaying signs of alcohol or drug use.

Perhaps one of the most surprising findings involved citizen demeanor. Citizens who displayed disrespectful behavior toward officers were no more likely to have force used on them than those who were respectful. This runs counter to much of what has been found in previous force studies. Disrespect had been one of the most consistent predictors of police force, yet this was not the case here. Possibly, as discussed in Chapter Six, the increased attention given toward measuring citizen disrespect and resistance may help to explain this finding. Previous work sometimes did not properly distinguish the difference between citizen disrespect and resistance. For example, Reiss talked about "defying police authority" and the effect this had on police use of force. But, defying police authority can take the form of a legal or an illegal justification for force. Defying police authority can be perceived as either disrespect, citizen resistance, or both. In analyzing the Police Services Study (PSS) data, Worden measured demeanor according to whether the citizen was detached, hostile/ antagonistic, or other. What exactly does this mean? Is telling an officer to "screw off asshole" hostile or antagonistic? While there is no question it is disrespectful, whether such a statement is combined with resistant behavior is something else. If the officer asks for the suspect's name and is met with such a statement, then it is both disrespectful and resistant behavior. If the suspect is just angry that he or she was arrested and is sitting in the back of a patrol waiting to be transported to jail then this is just disrespectful behavior. If the officer is not trying to elicit information or control the citizen in some way, then there is no resistance. Smith and Visher also used suspect antagonism taken from the PSS data when looking at determinants of arrest. Here antagonism was defined as displaying a hostile attitude, cursing an officer, or refusing to cooperate. This shows quite clearly the mixing of demeanor with resistance. The bottom line is that it is absolutely crucial that each of these behaviors are properly distinguished since one (disrespect) in an extra legal factor while the other is a legal (resistance) justification for the application of force.

Officer characteristics such a gender, race, and age were all unrelated to force. It was also found, somewhat surprisingly, that officer training in verbal mediation did not have an effect on the level of force applied. However, two officer characteristics, education and experience, were shown to influence force. Encounters involving both younger and more inexperienced officers were significantly more likely to result in higher levels of force compared to those involving more educated and experienced officers.

Of the numerous organizational factors tested only site emerged as a significant predictor. Encounters involving officers from Indianapolis showed higher levels of force compared to those involving St. Petersburg officers. This was predicted given the emphasis placed on more traditional law enforcement duties by officials in Indianapolis.

Finally, a number of interactions were tested involving officer views toward legal constraints. It was believed that officers with a proclivity to see legal guidelines as a constraint may be more inclined toward forceful behavior given their organizational environment. More specifically, it was posited that officers inclined to overlook legal guidelines may be influenced by department level policies, perceived supervision style, and/or the perceived peer culture. Officer proclivity to overlook legal guidelines was tested separately as well, but was not significant. Nonetheless, it was hypothesized that different levels of perceived organizational influence combined with such a proclivity may help tip the scales toward more forceful behavior, but this clearly was not the case here.

Application of the Force Continuum

An important contribution of this work rests with the analysis presented in the preceding chapter on the force continuum. The continuum provides an analytic tool for measuring and examining police use of force relative to citizen resistance. The benefit of examining police force through use of a force continuum is that it allows for the identification of instances when officers fail to escalate and de-escalate force in small increments in relation to resistant behavior. Concern over the proper use of force is most pronounced when it appears the level of police force is not congruent with the level of resistance that preceded it. As a result, citizen and police behavior were linked into sequences in an attempt to determine how often and what factors are related to instances when: officers refrain from moving up the continuum despite resistance, move up and down the continuum incrementally based on resistance, or apply higher forms of force given the level of resistance. Such an approach speaks directly to the transactional nature of the police-citizen encounter, a recommendation made in the NIJ/BJS report.

On the whole, officers tended to escalate and de-escalate force in small increments or in accordance with the force continuum. When faced with nonresistant citizens, officers deviated from the continuum (e.g., jump of the continuum) in about one in five encounters. More telling perhaps, is that when this did occur it was usually in the form of what has been characterized as a "minimal" jump - use of a verbal threat or physical restraint. These cases usually unfolded with the officer issuing a command first followed by the added element of a verbal threat or pat down search. As discovered when examining the highest level of force, officers were also more likely to demonstrate such behavior on younger and lower class males, as well as those displaying signs of alcohol or drug use. However, officers were not more likely to jump the continuum on nonwhites.

In encounters where citizens did exhibit some form of resistance, officers were often not only less likely to apply higher forms of force, but were actually more likely to refrain from even following the continuum. Officers held back from applying equivalent levels of force in approximately three of every four suspect encounters. When citizens attempted to escalate a situation, officers most often attempted to move in the opposite direction of de-escalation. In effect, officers generally preferred to give resistant citizens a "second chance" to comply.

When officers did resort to a jump of the continuum in encounters involving resistant citizens, such a jump was also generally minimal in nature. For instance, rarely did officers respond to passive resistance with a blow to the head. The typical jump case was along the lines of physical restraint on a passively resistant citizen. A jump of the continuum was most likely to occur when citizens were "initially" passively or verbally resistant. When officers command a citizen to do something (or not do something) and the citizen resists, the officer tended to re-issue the command, thereby giving the citizen one more opportunity to comply. It was when the citizen started right off with resistant behavior that prompted an officer to be more aggressive. Additionally, officers were more likely to jump the continuum when resistant citizens were male or emotionally upset. Encounters involving officers with a proclivity to see legal guidelines as a constraint were also more likely to result in a jump of the continuum.

Only one of the 12 interactions tested proved statistically significant. Encounters involving officers who did not believe overlooking legal guidelines was necessary in the course of their duties *and* who worked with officers they perceived believe overlooking legal guidelines was necessary in the course of their duties were significantly more likely to result in a jump of the continuum. Overall though, it is safe to say that the posited interactions had little to no effect on officer deviations from the continuum.

Finally, similar to the analysis on the highest level of force, citizen disrespect had no statistical effect on how the continuum was applied. Again, this came as a surprise. Disrespect has been shown to be a fairly consistent predictor of forceful police behavior. Nonetheless, the presence of citizen disrespect did not produce such a finding here.

8.2 CONCLUSIONS AND IMPLICATIONS: MAKING ADVANCES AND FILLING GAPS

It is difficult to determine how far police have come with respect to force, even after such an exhaustive study. The application of force continues to be anything but a parsimonious process. How and why the police resort to force involves a mixture of complex factors. In large part, the decision to use force has a great deal to do with the interplay between suspect and officer. However, to say that force occurs simply as a result of what goes on during the process of citizen and officer interacting, at least within the context of the immediate situation, is naive. There are many factors that come into play, including who the citizen is, who the officer is, and the organizational environment within which the incident takes place.

Where does this leave us? Perhaps the most pressing question with respect to police force is, and always will be, whether force is a problem? Hence, do the findings uncovered here indicate that force is a problem? In some respects the findings are very encouraging. For example, there were many instances where officers could actually have applied more force, but chose not too. In three of every four encounters involving a resistant citizen, the officer attempted to de-escalate a situation where the citizen was attempting to escalate it. *The perception that officers leap at the opportunity to apply force on a resistant citizen is not supported here. Officers generally go to great strides to resolve resistant encounters in the most noncoercive manner possible.* Additionally, refraining behavior on the officers' part was not reserved for certain individuals or limited to certain officers. For instance, officers were not more inclined to hold back or give white citizens a second chance compared to nonwhites.

It is also encouraging that officers do not generally respond to citizen disrespect with forceful behavior. Whether this is a sign of police progress or simply a result of closer attention to distinguishing citizen disrespect from resistance is impossible to determine. It is probably a little of both. In many cases the officer simply disregarded citizen disrespect, opting to refrain from using force. Given previous findings this is surprising, but given the fact that officers also tended to hold back on resistant citizens, it is not. On the whole, officers were somewhat reserved toward resistant *and* disrespectful citizens. Perhaps such citizens posed more of a challenge or degree of uncertainly, prompting officers to be more cautious and slow to increase force. Such citizens may demonstrate a greater degree of unpredictability in the minds of officers. An unpredictable citizen is generally perceived to be one of the most dangerous citizens an officer has to deal with. Officer disdain for handling domestic disputes underlies this fear. Unfortunately, too few debriefing sessions are available to shed more insight on "why" officers choose to treat such citizens less harshly.

Nonetheless, looking at forceful behavior from another angle sheds a more negative light on the situation. Officers resort to some form of force in well over half of all suspect encounters. The coercive authority granted to the police is used quite frequently, albeit usually in the form of verbal commands. Officers regularly resort to a command nature, which goes beyond the impression that such actions are only a last resort when all else fails. In fact, officers issued a command to a nonresistant citizen in 2,316 separate sequences. While officers may rely on suggestion, requests, or so-called "cajoling" to regulate and maintain the control of suspects, something that was not directly measured or tabulated in this study, it is quite clear that they rely heavily on coercive commands. Further emphasizing the point, when multiple commands are considered, officers use this form of force in 3,152 sequences across the 3,544 observed encounters.

Reliance on verbal commands as a means of control is not on the face of it overly troublesome. In fact, it is generally considered quite appropriate in law enforcement circles. Nonetheless, looking beneath the surface another picture emerges, one that *is* troublesome given the perspective that less force is most desirable. Using verbal commands leads to an increased probability that a suspect will become resistant. Even when this does not occur (e.g., the suspect remains nonresistant), officers are still three and a half times more likely to not only apply an additional command, but to increase the level of force (e.g., use of a threat or physical force). Few administrators would find this acceptable police practice. Use of verbal commands is not a minor nor simple police behavior. It is a coercive act that often leads to more severe coercive acts.

Administrators need to approach such behavior in much the same way many cities began to deal with corruption some 20 years ago. Attention needs to start at the bottom, with the least severe act. In this particular case, with verbal commands. Officials need to rethink exactly why officers are permitted to assume a command nature given no citizen resistance, no threat to personal safety, and no threat to citizen safety. Police officials, street officers, and even some scholars, will argue that the ability to command and order is an essential component to being able to "maintain control," but what exactly needs to be controlled to the point of commanding if the citizen is compliant in the first place?

Another troublesome discovery was that officers jump the continuum in 20 percent of the encounters involving nonresistant citizens. In these cases, officers actually engage in behavior that, as Muir (1977) discussed, can be perceived as an attempt to "jack up" the situation. If the citizen takes the bait, then the subsequent force becomes justified. However, as uncovered here, quite often the citizen does not resist, yet officers continue being forceful to the point that such behavior falls outside the continuum 20 percent of the time. Why do officers choose to apply such force on totally nonresistant citizens? It may be that officers feel such force proves effective. As previously discussed, many times an officer will throw in an additional threat or pat down search in an attempt to make sure the suspect understands whatever message he or she is trying to convey (e.g., "if I have to come back tonight you will be one sorry SOB"). In this case it appears such force has more of a instrumental purpose. However, additional acts of force may also be the result of the very fact that the citizen does not resist [e.g., "stop talking (citizen complies), you're lucky you shut your mouth because I'm just looking for a reason to take you in"]. Officers may feel like they have free reign to deal with nonresistant citizens in a coercive manner, while not having any fears that the citizen is going to create a troublesome situation, let alone complain.

Besides frequency of use, force is clearly problematic as well with respect to who is subjected to it. Males, nonwhites, poor citizens, younger citizens, and those showing signs of alcohol or drug use were all treated more harshly. From a professionalization and community policing perspective this is particularly discouraging. One would hope that officers do not treat certain individuals differently than others simply based on who they are as opposed to what they do, but that was the case here. The only good news that can be taken from this is that much of the differences were found in the form of verbal force or lower level physical force (e.g., restraint and control). Little differences were uncovered at the upper end of the continuum (e.g., striking, macing, kicks, punches, etc.).

Of course, such a debate on whether police force is a problem, or whether they use their coercive powers wisely, presupposes that less force, is in fact, better. This seems to be the most popular perspective. Scholars such as Bittner (1970), Muir (1977), and Klockars (1995) all advocate such an approach, as does the norm inherent within a continuum of force. In fact, it is a virtually uncontested theoretical perspective toward the application of coercion. The best officers are those who use less, not more force. Force is permitted in many situations, but a good officer is one who can handle a situation by not having to rely on force - a necessary evil, but one that should be avoided if at all possible. However, is less force always the most desirable choice? What if the police did not show up to a dispute between two parties and order them to separate for the night? Would such an incident eventually be resolved with more or less force? An argument can be made that by investing the police with the authority to apply force, and to go and issue such a command as in this example, that despite the use of some coercion being applied, the ultimate outcome may actually be less, rather than more force. In this case, the officer only issues a verbal command or threat. It may be that failure for the police to show up at all, or to use no form of coercion, may have led to the two citizens resolving the conflict on their own. If that were the case, what is the probability that it could have been resolved verbally as opposed to physically? Would a verbal command or threat from one of the disputing parties carry the same weight as the officer's command? Or, would it have come down to a physical altercation? Thus, while on the face it, less force on the part of the police is generally perceived to be the most desirable, this may result in more violence on the part of private citizens.

Nonetheless, assuming that less force is indeed the preferred route, results from this study offer numerous policy implications. First, of particular concern, is that officers often use increased levels of force on the most disadvantaged citizens, irrespective of their behavior. Regardless of how one categorizes the meaning of force, the fact that officers use more force on an individual simply based on the status of that person is wholly unacceptable behavior. So, why do officers end up using higher levels of force on such individuals? Perhaps it is because they can get away with it. Maybe it is because such individuals are less likely to complain; and when they do complain, their complaints may not be taken as seriously as if it were a white professional male in his 50s who lives in the Mayor's neighborhood. Deciphering "why" is only speculative, but much of this behavior falls directly in line with Black's theory of law. At the least, officials need to consider cultural diversity training, re-emphasize departmental values, and initiate open discussions on the importance of accountability to the law. Of course, this assumes that officials take such a finding seriously, which may not be the case. It seems almost shocking that officers continue to apply greater force against the most disadvantaged, even after civil disturbances broke out in each city just one year prior to data collection.

Second, verbal mediation training had no statistical effect on either increased levels of force or whether an officer refrains from, or jumps, the continuum. It may be that such training was simply inadequate. It is also possible that those officers who use force most often are also sent to more training in an attempt to rectify the problem, without success. However, assuming this finding is valid, and since verbal mediation training is designed to enhance an officer's verbal ability to handle and control contentious situations, department officials need to revisit this issue. The simple implication here is not to spend money on such training. Nonetheless, officials need to find some way of not only reducing the amount of verbal coercion occurring, but on addressing the often "added" threat that accompanies nonresistant citizens. There are no easy answers here, but in the current setup, verbal mediation training needs to be abolished or refocused.

Third, it was discovered that an official department mandate toward the style of policing practiced does affect the amount of force used at the street level. Indianapolis' mode of operation was self-defined as "get-tough," while St. Petersburg's was more toned down and geared in the direction of a problem-solving model. What does this mean from a policy perspective? It means that if you want less force you emphasize a "kinder-gentler" problem-solving approach instead of emphasizing a "get-tough" approach. This is not to say that a "get-tough" approach will always translate to increased levels of force. What it does say, however, is that officials need to take additional steps (e.g., roll call briefings that address getting tough while ensuring force is not being unnecessarily applied, increased supervisor reviews of use-of-force reports) to make it clear that "getting-tough" is not akin to cobblestone justice.

Surprisingly, site or city was the only organizational variable that had an effect on officer behavior. As mentioned above, assignment did not matter, nor did perceptions of ones' supervisor or workgroup. It makes more intuitive sense that the latter influences would have more of an effect compared to what is being promoted out of the chief's office. Anyone that has spent even a little time observing street-level officers comes to realize that the chief, even when liked by a majority of the troops, is generally viewed as being distant from patrol and what occurs out on the street. Reading of memos from the chief's office at roll call is usually met with sneers and jeers. Officers make regular reference that they could care less what the chief is pushing, usually followed with something along the line of, "that guy hasn't been in a patrol car in 10 years, and he is going to tell me how to handle some scumbag selling on the corner?" Conversely, immediate supervisors and peers are much more respected, and if not respected, at least deemed closer to the situation at hand (e.g., the reality and pressure of street work). Yet perceptions of these two groups had no influence. So why would a chief sponsored mandate have an effect in this case? Probably because the message was viewed as "pro-cop." It was no secret within the Indianapolis Police department that most officers thought the community policing concept was nothing short of complete "crap," and even worse, it was believed to be social work, not real police work. However, bring in a chief advocating a "get-tough" community police approach and all of a sudden you have a message from the top that the troops actually like.

It is also important to recognize yet another alternative explanation for why St. Petersburg officers resorted to less force. By all accounts, the St. Petersburg civil disturbance (discussed in Chapter Four) was more severe than Indianapolis' (e.g., frequency and intensity of disturbances, newspaper reports, police reports). This, combined with the fact that all St. Petersburg street-officers were required to put in three days of civil disturbance training during the time of data collection, a requirement that stemmed from the 1996 disturbance, may help to partially explain why less force was found in St. Petersburg. The sweeping effect force can have may have been more in the forefront on St. Petersburg officers' minds. However, on the whole, there is no evidence to suggest this. If observations would have directly followed those incidents there may have been more concern. Further, the disturbances were not an overly discussed topic of conversation for officers on the street in either city. Additionally, officers made no mention (e.g., in the debriefing session) of the disturbances in terms of how it may have influenced their decisionmaking. For instance, there were no instances where an officer said he held back from using force because he feared another disturbance or that he would get into trouble with his supervisors.

Fourth, it is curious that no differences were found between 911 and community policing officers. One would expect that officers charged with community policing duties would rely on coercion less often, but this was not the case. The view of community policing as noncoercive is more a mis-perception than reality. Officials would be wrong to assume that a move toward a community policing approach automatically translates to less coercion. Assignment and delivery of service decisions should exclude issues of force

Fifth, more educated and experienced officers were found to use less force than their counterparts. Departments that currently stipulate an educational requirement should continue the practice. Those who do not should institute one. While educated officers moved about the continuum in a similar fashion to less educated officers, they did, on average, use slightly lower levels of force (e.g., commands as opposed to threats, threats as opposed to physical restraint). Although much has been made of the down side of verbal coercion, it must be remembered that when it comes to applying verbal as opposed to physical force, few could argue against preferring verbal.

Sixth, it is more difficult to determine how departments might utilize the finding that more experienced officers use less force. Patrol assignments are traditionally determined by seniority. The implication of this finding is that departments need to consider assigning more experienced officers to patrol duties, something many seasoned officers and police unions would resist. Such an arrangement could have beneficial effects much beyond a less coercive force. As most agencies are currently set-up, the officer who knows how to handle disputing neighbors, the fleeing felon in a stolen car, and the fast-talker picked up for shoplifting, is also the most likely to be taking a long lunch after hours of morning meetings on the new parking meters being installed downtown. There is little doubt that such an officer may have become tired and possibly even a little lazy over the years, but it is difficult to argue that a 21-year-old rookie is better equipped to handle such situations.

8.3 FUTURE RESEARCH

Future research should continue to focus on the transactional nature of the police-citizen encounter. Four specific areas require special attention. First, the differential impact that initial verbal commands play in the overall outcome of an encounter needs to be examined more fully. The fact that officers tend to jump the continuum on nonresistant citizens while holding back on resistant citizens is particularly curious. Detailing an officer's motivation for applying an "added" element of force on a nonresistant citizen can shed light on why officers choose this tactic. Officers probably believe this is necessary to "hammer home" the point they are trying to make. Also, issuing a final threat or conducting a pat down search is not seen as using inappropriate force, while resorting to a very high level of force (e.g., impact method) on a passive or verbally resistant citizen is.

Second, additional research should focus on measuring and incorporating noncoercive tactics into sequencing as well as examining the interplay between such tactics and force. Just as citizen resistance and force were sequenced out, noncoercive tactics can be added in a similar manner. This would take the transactional approach a step further. Third, future research should attempt to more adequately incorporate backup officer actions into analyses. The application of force is often a group process as opposed to a one-on-one process. Backup officer actions were accounted for here but only in an attempt to more adequately explain the observed officers' actions.

Fourth, there continues to be a lack of substantive theory in the application of force. This research attempted to partially fill the void by looking at several interactions across different levels of determinants. However, make no mistake, this study was slanted in favor of new ways to measure and conceive the application of force as opposed to advancing theoretical development.

Finally, scholars ranging from Bittner (1970) to Muir (1977) to Klockars (1995) have observed that the best police work is accomplished when carried out in the least coercive manner possible. Applying force sparingly ultimately serves to enhance the legitimacy of the institution as a whole. The norm inherent within the continuum applied in this study is that force will be applied in small increments. By examining force within this context, a better understanding of how and why the police go about applying force in a conservative fashion has been developed.

Notes

Chapters One through Eight

Chapter One

1. This definition is similar to the National Academy of Sciences definition of violence. According to Garner and colleagues, "[t]here is no similarly explicit definition of the meaning of 'force' in the police literature, but the Academy's definition of violence, which incorporates threats, attempts, and actual physical force, adequately captures what the research literature on police use of force typically means by 'force'" (Garner et al., 1995: 152).

2. Ranking force along continuum is well established. See Desmedt (1984); Parsons (1988); Connor (1991); McLaughlin (1992); Garner et al. (1995); Klinger (1995); and Alpert and Dunham (1997).

3. Unlike an explicit threat (e.g., "do this or else"), in the case of commands the threat to do harm is implicit (e.g., "drop the frying pan"). Garner and colleagues (1995), Klinger (1995), and Alpert and Dunham (1997), all similarly recognize that verbal force does not have to include an explicit threat outright. For example, Klinger defines verbal force as "verbal orders that officers issue to citizens" (1995: 173). Garner and colleagues consider verbal force to include instances when "officers shouted or used a command voice" (1995: 158). Alpert and Dunham place verbal force in their minimal force classification, which includes "strong directive language" (1997: 3). Further, when a threat is issued, it does not have to explicitly involve physical force (e.g., do this or I'll mace you). Rather, like the issuance of a command, a threat may implicitly refer to the use of physical force that may follow. For instance, a common threat applied is that of arrest. Such a threat is included in the definition of force applied in this research since this generally implies the use of physical force to follow in relation to such an arrest. A final point on verbal force involves the threatened use of a firearm. While the use of a firearm has the "potential" to inflict the greatest degree of physical harm to a citizen, this study is concerned with the "impact" of harm actually delivered. Therefore, the threatened use of a firearm is also classified within this category of force.

4. Both figures were derived using arrests as the denominator.

5. According to McLaughlin, "[a] force continuum is a guideline representing the appropriate amount of force that should be utilized by a law enforcement officer in generic situations. It should provide a means for escalating force when the subject shows non-compliance and a means for de-escalating force when the subject complies. A force continuum gives and officer a clearer picture of the type of force that may be used legitimately in a given situation, which usually is

not accomplished through the reading of the appropriate legal statute" (1992: 65).

6. I again turn to situational, individual, and organizational theoretical explanations.

7. I do not attempt to make an *explicit* judgement concerning excessive or abusive force, only that which is not in accordance with the level of resistance officers encounter.

Chapter Two

1. Bayley and Garofalo defined "potentially violent mobilizations" as those that involved disputes, intervention by the police to apply the law against specific individuals, and attempts to question suspicious persons.

2. Fyfe defined "potentially violent situations" as those that involving routine traffic stops, high-risk traffic stops, crimes in progress, and disputes.

3. It should also be noted that these studies computed force rates based on suspect or potentially violent encounters only. Therefore, if one were to compute a force rate based on all encounters observed, the rate would be even lower than characterized here. For example, Bayley and Garofalo's observers recorded 1,059 total police-citizen encounters. Therefore, computing a force rate based on this figure, force was only used 3.5 percent of the time by police.

4. Croft reports that the increase from her earlier study is most likely a result of better reporting procedures and officer compliance filling out forms.

5. Adams (1995) provides a detailed discussion of calculating the use and abuse of police force, and the factors that may account for different reporting rates.

6. See also Worden, 1989.

7. See also Black, 1980.

8. Despite this, Reiss found that in only 1 of every 6 cases did an officer exhibit excessive force behavior when faced with an antagonistic citizen.

9. Garner et al. (1996) tested numerous predictors, including officer experience, on three different measures of force: physical force, a continuum of force, and maximum force. They classified each predictor as falling into one of three categories: consistent predictors, inconsistent predictors, or non-predictors.

10. They did examine the number of years since the officers' last "arrest" training (which had an effect), but did not examine the potential influence of use of force or alternative (e.g., verbal mediation) use of force training tactics.

11. It is important to recognize that most of these studies were structured in a way that may not have provided an ideal test. From an organizational perspective, only PSS involved more than three departments, thus the others had a small number of cases. Regarding the lack of support for individual explanations, again the design may have had an impact Each of the observational studies used the shift as the sampling unit, which over sampled busy shifts to maximize the likelihood of observing police-citizen encounters. Ideally, examining the effects of individual determinants would be best tested if officers were used as the sampling selection method.

12. See Muir for a description of "avoidance" behavior, 1977.

13. Muir (1977) refers to such cases as "critical incidents." Fyfe (1988) and Bayley and Garofalo (1989), refer to them as "potentially violent" encounters. Reiss (1968) and Worden (1995) classified potential force cases as any that involved a suspect.

Chapter Three

1. See Chapter Four for a full description and definition of each type of force.

2. See Chapter Four for a full description and definition of each type of resisance.

3. See Fyfe, 1996, pg 339-40.

4. See department descriptions in Chapter Four for further detail on the style of policing promoted by leaders in both departments.

5. See Worden (1995) for further discussion on potential interaction effects and use of police force.

6. Note that for the second and third hypotheses, organization is measured by the "officers" perception of the organization. Thus, these variables are *about organization*, but were not measured at the organizational level, unlike the site variable. The intent here is to test whether officers with a proclivity to overlook legal guidelines are more likely to apply force based on their "perception" of organizational context. For instance, If I feel overlooking legal guidelines is necessary and also feel that my supervisor is not going to intervene in my decision making, am I more inclined to use force as opposed to those who do not? It may very well be that my supervisor does or would interject, but it is my perception of his interference that is key here.

7. In addition to examining the aforementioned determinants, nine factors are used as controls (e.g., citizen resistance, officer safety, citizen safety, arrest, number of officers present on scene, number of bystanders present, anticipation of violence, proactivity, type of problem).

Chapter Four

1. See Mastrofski et al. (1998) for a more detailed account of social systematic observation.

2. The National Institute of Justice (NIJ) funded POPN in late 1995. Principal Investigators included Professor Stephen Mastrofski, Michigan State University; Roger Parks, Indiana University; Robert Worden, State University of New York (SUNY) at Albany; and Albert Reiss, Jr., Yale University. I served as Site Director for the Project.

3. Although geographically concentrated, each district was headed by a separate district chief who tailored services to the unique needs of the district.

4. Stephens received a promotion to city administrator and Davis was named chief in June, 1997.

5. In both cities, community policing officers were relieved of calls for service responsibility. Further, it is important to note that officials in both cities stressed the need for *all* officers to engage in community policing, not just those designated as community policing officers.

6. Forty-eight were assigned to each of the 48 community policing areas (traditionally known as beats). The remaining 12 were assigned to the downtown business district.

7. Community policing officers set their own hours so as to work during problem periods as well as with patrol officers from all shifts.

8. Field researchers accompanied their assigned officer during all activities and encounters with the public during the shift, except on those rare occasions when the officer instructed the researcher not to do so because of danger or because it would impede police business. Field researchers were instructed to minimize involvement in police work (except for minor assistance or emergencies) and to refrain from expressing views about police work in general or what was observed on the ride. The researcher's function was not to judge the officer, only to note what happened during the observation session and to note how the officer interpreted situations he or she encountered - officer interpretation of the situation was conducted through a "debriefing" session where the observer would inquire as to the officers' thoughts and motivation for handling the encounter (see Mastrofski and Parks for explicit protocol on this technique, 1990).

9. Selection based on the Indianapolis distribution as field research there preceded field research in St. Petersburg. The selection of patrol areas in St. Petersburg was made to closely match the Indianapolis distribution.

10. See Appendix A for further detail on beat selection.

11. The data do not capture any effects of seasonal variation, an important limitation in a city that experiences a large tourist influx during winter months. However, this study concentrated on policing in residential neighborhoods, where fluctuations in numbers of tourists visiting the city are less likely to have an impact.

12. POPN Principal Investigators had a great deal of prior experience in conducting police field research. In particular, three of the four had extensive experience with designing and carrying out large scale police observational studies. In 1966, Reiss conducted the first large scale observational study. In the 1977 Police Services Study (PSS), Parks was one of three Principal Investigators and Mastrofski served as a Site Director. In 1993, Mastrofski conducted a pilot-study in Richmond aimed at perfecting the techniques used for POPN.

13. POPN researchers promised confidentiality to individual officers observed. This is a requirement of the federal government and the universities conducting the research.

14. Encounter passages are taken directly from narrative accounts from observer accounts. Several points on narrative accounts. First, O1 refers to the observed officer. O2, O3, O4 and so on refer to other officers on the scene. C1, C2, C3 refer to citizen one, two, three and so on. Observers also used shorthand to describe citizen characteristics (e.g., WM meant white male). Second, relevant passages are taken verbatim (except for spelling errors) from the observers' narrative account, minus any information that might make it possible for the officer to be identified (e.g., the age and race of the officer combined with the area he or she was working). Third, encounter examples are placed into context by listing the problem in italics prior to listing the example. Fourth, passages are often italicized to help the reader identify the most important actions. Finally, in some cases a debriefing session is included. Observers were asked to elicit the officer's motivation when possible. Hence, the debriefing is included when provided by the observer.

15. There were an additional sixteen suspect-disputant encounters in the original POPN database. However, narrative descriptions of these cases were too incomplete to provide the necessary information for inclusion. This was mainly a result of unobserved events (e.g., officer instructs observer to stay in car).

16. See Section 4.6 for further description.

17. A citizen may verbally disagree with police actions, plead innocence or non-involvement in an incident, question an officers' behavior, or be disrespectful, and still be considered nonresistant as long as none of the above three behaviors were present.

18. All three approaches were eventually examined during the analyses phase, but the third option proved most useful. Splitting cases posed severe difficulty with trying to distinguish misdemeanors and felonies. The manner in which problem codes were originally coded by observers was not in the form of such a classification. The second option, splitting codes into a series of different problem types and entering as separate dummy variables, was attempted but made interpretation exceedingly difficult, given attempts to compare each type to a given reference category. Further, the addition of several more variables into an already large model proved unwise.

19. It is important to note that backup officer force actions are included in the patterns variables. How an encounter unfolds is often dependent not only on the observed officers actions but other officers' actions on the scene as well. For example, another officer on the scene may issue a threat to a citizen in which the citizen may resist. The observed officer may respond to this resistance with physical restraint as a result. Failure to account for the other officers actions would certainly misrepresent what occurred prior to the observed officer using force in this situation. In effect, encounters sometimes evolve as a group process and not in isolation between just the observed officer and citizen. Therefore, this was taken into account.

20. For instance, Pattern1 was coded into a dummy of 0 (pattern did not occur) and 1 (pattern did occur) and used as a determinant like any other in the model.

21. Conceptualization of the various pattern variables was done according to what was believed to be most theoretically relevant. An alternative approach would have been to use the most frequently occurring patterns as predictors. However, there was no theoretical reason for such an approach. Instead, it was hypothesized (as others have) that the use of police force early in an encounter may result in the necessity of having to use force (most notably greater force) later in the encounter. Similarly, it was hypothesized that early citizen resistance may cause an officer to be more coercive. Since the "type" of resistance and force were coded, this allowed me to go a step further and distinguish not only instances of resistance and force prior to a break in the continuum, but the type or level of each. As a result, instead of just using two particular patterns as predictors (citizen initially resists or officer initially uses force), I was able to use four (citizen initially resists with low level resistance, officer initially uses low level force, citizen initially resists with high level resistance, officer initially applies high level of force).

22. This was done simply to achieve as much parsimony as possible given the number of categories.

23. Alpert and Dunham (1997) propose a means for evaluating police force by examining citizen resistance. They develop a 4-point scale for both police force and citizen resistance with 1 being the lowest level of force or resistance and 4 being the highest. They then take the highest level of police force used in the encounter and subtract from it the highest level of citizen resistance. Scores closest to zero indicate that the level of police force was in accordance with the level of citizen resistance.

24. Of the 3,544 encounters, 87 fit into this category.

25. The ordered probit is an extension of the probit model used to evaluate binomial dependent variables.

26. Cases where a citizen never displayed resistance presents a logic problem. If there is never an opportunity to de-escalate (when a citizen is resistant) an officer cannot select this option. To analyze the full compliment of police-suspect encounters within one model would assume that each of the three options were available to the officer.

Chapter Five

1. A complete listing of all combinations is supplied in Appendix B.

2. A complete listing of all combinations is provided in Appendix C.

3. Number in parentheses signifies the number of sequences where a backup officer used force when faced with that level of resistance, while the observed officer did not. For instance, in the 2,019 sequences where the citizen was nonresistant and the observed officer responded with no force, in 772 of the 2,019 another officer *did* respond with force. Thus, in the 2,019 sequences when the citizen was nonresistant resistant, in 1,247 no force was used on him or her at all, while in another 772 force was used on him or her, but was the result of the backup officer's force, not the observed officer's force.

Chapter Six

1. The continuum was reduced to four categories to ensure a sufficient number of cases in each category, particularly with reference to the final category - impact methods.

2. Descriptive statistics, bivariate relationships, and model estimates for the missing case variables are all provided in Appendix D. The size of the current tables were already somewhat cumbersome given the large number of predictors.

3. For each level of force (no force, verbal, restraint, impact) the number of cases is provided followed by the percentage of cases in parenthesis (e.g., there were 979 male suspects where the officer used no force, which accounted for 38.3

percent of all male suspects). The number in parenthesis following each attribute is the number of cases for that particular attribute (e.g. the were 2552 male suspects compared to 992 female suspects).

4. The ordered probit "distinguishes between Y, the dependent variable of theoretical interest, and Z the dependent variable that is observed. There is an assumption that Y is an interval-level variable, but due to deficient measurement, it is represented by an ordinal form, namely Z." (Jarjoura, 1993: 156). Y is thus a latent variable and therefore requires mapping to the observed categories (Long, 1997). As a result, while the aim is to estimate

$$Y = \beta' X + u.$$

Z is used in the form of

$$Z = 0 \text{ if } Y \leq 0$$
$$= 1 \text{ if } 0 \leq Y \leq \mu_1$$
$$= 2 \text{ if } \mu_1 \leq Y \leq \mu_2$$
$$\vdots$$
$$= J \text{ if } \mu_{j-1} \leq Y.$$

The estimate represents the increased probability of falling into a higher level on the dependent measure; in this case, falling into a higher level of force.

5. Calculated for each response category of the dependent measure according to:

$$Prob\,[\,Y = 0] = \Phi\,(-\beta' X\,),$$
$$Prob\,[\,Y = 1] = \Phi\,(\mu_1 - \beta' X\,) - \Phi\,(-\beta' X\,),$$
$$Prob\,[\,Y = 2] = \Phi\,(\mu_2 - \beta' X\,) - \Phi\,(\mu_1 - \beta' X\,)$$
$$\vdots$$
$$Prob\,[\,Y = J] = 1 - \Phi\,(\mu_{j-1} - \beta' X\,).$$

6. As noted in Chapter Four, in addition to the independent variables of interest a series of missing dummy variables are also included in the model. The purpose of these variables is to prevent the process of listwise deletion of missing data. For ease of presentation, missing case estimates from the model are presented in Appendix D. None of the missing case results were significant. In addition to the approach presented here, the model was also run in the traditional manner while employing listwise deletion. These results are presented in Appendix E. Listwise deletion resulted in a loss of 446 (12.5%) cases. As shown in Appendix E, the same predictors were significant as when the missing case variables were included. This was somewhat surprising given a loss of over 12 percent of the cases. It was originally anticipated that such a decrease would result in a loss of statistical power resulting in a lower number of significant factors. However, this was not case, probably because there were still over 3,000 cases in the model.

7. The highest level of resistance that occurred prior to the highest level of force is used.

8. Each was coded and tested as a separate dummy variable with white officer/nonwhite citizen as the reference category.

9. As noted in Chapter Four, with the exception of site, which was already a dichotomous measure, each of the variables were recoded into a dichotomous measure using the top and bottom two responses. For example, officers who agreed (strongly or somewhat) with the individual legal guidelines statement were classified as those who believed legal guidelines served as a constraint; officers who disagreed with the statement (strongly or somewhat) were classified as those who did not. The same approach was used with the supervisor criticism and workgroup legal guideline measures.

Chapter Seven

1. It is important to understand that use of the terms *less/refrain* and *more/ jump* force need to be understood strictly in terms of the "continuum criteria." Less force just means that the officer used less force than what is called for according to the continuum criteria; while more force refers to the use of more force than what is called for according to the continuum criteria. In both instances this is based on citizen resistance, while accounting for officer and citizen safety issues, as well as arrest. There are cases where in one encounter an officer may use physical restraint that is considered less force (e.g., citizen attacks officer), while in another an officer may issue a threat that is considered more force (e.g.,

citizen is nonresistant). On the normal scale of severity physical restraint obviously is more (higher level of force) than a threat, but in the context of the continuum criteria it is quite possible that the reverse is true (as in the previous example) - it depends on what has occurred prior in regard to successive citizen and police actions. Further, use of the phrase *follow* the continuum simply refers to those cases where the officer escalates "or" de-escalates force in small increments, which means in accordance with the continuum criteria.

2. Model 1 (logistic) contains 3,114 cases, while Model 2 (multinomial logit) contains 343 cases. As noted earlier, the remaining 87 cases are analyzed qualitatively. These cases involved *both* refraining and jumping within the same encounter. Such cases did not present an acceptable choice on which to try to predict or explain. Arbitrarily selecting one over the other was deemed unacceptable.

3. Figures exclude the 87 cases where refraining *and* jumping were present within the same encounter. See Section 7.3 below for analysis of these cases.

4. For instance, as opposed to those where an officer strikes a nonresistant or passively resistant citizen.

5. Recall that for the pattern variables backup officer actions are included. Thus, while by definition (according to the continuum criteria established) the use of physical force on a nonresistant suspect would be an immediate use of more force (jump of the continuum) unless applied in the process of arrest or if there was an officer or citizen safety issue, this would not be the case when backup officers use such force. Although only the observed officer behavior is measured in terms of determining whether the continuum was followed, all force used during the encounter (observed officer and backup officers) was considered for purposes of determining what happened prior to any decisions made by the observed officer. Again, as noted in Chapter Four, encounters sometimes evolve as a group process and failure to account for this process provides an artificial look at what actually happened.

6. These are the exponentiated values of the coefficients.

7. This excludes the 87 cases where citizens displayed resistance and officers refrained and jumped the continuum. Analysis of these cases are presented in Section 7.3.

8. By definition this is the case since officers had the opportunity to both refrain from and jump the continuum.

9. Percentages sum to greater than one since both refraining and jumping occurred in these cases.

10. The reader should employ caution when interpreting the findings presented here as a result of the low number of cases within the "more" force category. Percentages are based on only 25 cases.

11.　　　　In this particular case, the Multinomial logit estimates the odds of $y = 1$ (refraining) and $y = 2$ (jumping) relative to $y = 0$ (following). According to Long (1997), given that $\exp(X_i \beta_1) = \exp (X_1 0) = 1$, the model is represented as:

$$\Pr (y_i = 1 \mid x_i) = \frac{1}{1 + \sum_{j=2}^{J} \exp (X_i \beta_j)}$$

$$\Pr (y_i = m \mid x_i) = \frac{\exp (X_i \beta_m)}{1 + \sum_{j=2}^{J} \exp (X_i \beta_j)} \quad \text{for } m > 1$$

12. This raises two issues. First, those factors found to be significantly related to jumping the continuum need to be viewed with caution due to so few cases. Second, although there were a sufficient number of cases within the "follow" and "less" categories to provide confidence in these estimates, it was decided to also estimate a separate model that excluded the 25 "more" cases. Since the dependent measure is reduced to two outcomes - followed and less, a logistic model was estimated predicting the use of less force. In this model, the number of officers variable remained significant. Conversely, pattern3 falls out and citizen emotional state becomes significant.

13. See the first example provided in this chapter. In this particular case, the observed officer was the only officer on the scene when dealing with six suspects, one of which becomes resistant.

14. See Encounter 2 in the last set of examples in this chapter for an illustration.

Appendices

Appendix A: Beat Selection

The below figure shows the distributions of socioeconomic distress scores for all 50 IPD and 48 SPPD patrol beats and for the 12 beats selected in each city. Four of the POPN beats in each city had distress scores that ranged between the 20th and 41st percentiles of the IPD distribution. These four were expected to have crime problems and police activity somewhat lower than the average IPD beat and about average for SPPD beats. Three POPN beats in each city had scores between the 48th and 61st percentiles of the Indianapolis distribution, where crime and police activity where expected to be somewhat above average in both cities. The remaining five POPN beats in each city were selected from those with the most difficult socioeconomic conditions, with scores ranging from the 80th to 100th percentiles of the socioeconomic distress index distribution in Indianapolis and from the 85th to 96th percentiles in St. Petersburg. In this set of study beats high levels of crime and police activity where expected.

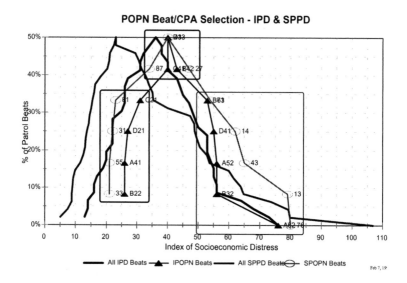

Appendix B: Force Combinations within Encounters

Each number in the force type column represents the following force types: 2=command, 3=threat, 4=physical restraint, 5=pain/takedown, 6=strike with body or external mechanism. Thus, a 22 force type represents a command followed by a command; a 223 represents two commands followed by a threat; a 254 represents a command, followed by a take down, followed by physical restraint.

Force Types	Number of Encounters	Percent of Encounters
2	689	19.4
3	124	3.5
4	207	5.8
5	4	.1
6	3	.1
22	232	6.5
23	67	1.9
24	89	2.5
25	3	.1
32	17	.5
33	14	.4
34	4	.1
35	2	.1
42	53	1.5
43	8	.2
44	53	1.5
54	5	.1
55	1	.0
222	57	1.6
223	22	.6
224	18	.5
232	10	.3
233	2	.1
234	3	.1
242	28	.8
243	4	.1
244	23	.6

Appendix B: Force Combinations within Encounters (cont.)

Force Types	Number of Encounters	Percent of Encounters
246	1	.0
262	1	.0
322	3	.1
323	2	.1
324	1	.0
332	3	.1
333	2	.1
342	3	.1
344	1	.0
422	14	.4
423	2	.1
424	7	.2
442	4	.1
443	3	.1
444	7	.2
462	1	.0
522	1	.0
542	1	.0
543	1	.0
544	1	.0
2222	21	.6
2223	11	.3
2224	6	.2
2226	1	.0
2232	3	.1
2233	1	.0
2242	5	.1
2243	1	.0
2244	8	.2
2254	1	.0
2324	1	.0
2332	2	.1
2422	4	.1
2423	2	.1

Force Types	Number of Encounters	Percent of Encounters
2424	3	.1
2426	1	.0
2442	6	.2
2444	2	.1
2455	1	.0
2542	1	.0
2544	1	.0
2642	1	.0
2644	1	.0
3232	2	.1
3233	2	.1
3244	2	.1
3323	1	.0
3332	1	.0
3334	1	.0
3343	2	.1
4222	6	.2
4223	3	.1
4224	1	.0
4233	2	.1
4242	2	.1
4244	1	.0
4332	1	.0
4422	2	.1
4423	1	.0
4444	1	.0
4454	1	.0
4466	1	.0
5242	1	.0
5442	1	.0
5644	1	.0
22222	12	.3
22223	2	.1
22233	2	.1
22242	1	.0

Force Types	Number of Encounters	Percent of Encounters
22243	1	.0
22244	3	.1
22322	1	.0
22323	1	.0
22342	2	.1
22422	5	.1
22423	1	.0
22442	1	.0
22443	1	.0
22524	1	.0
22532	1	.0
22624	1	.0
23223	1	.0
23224	1	.0
23232	1	.0
23322	1	.0
23463	1	.0
24222	1	.0
24223	2	.1
24224	1	.0
24244	1	.0
24322	7	.2
24422	1	.0
24442	1	.0
24443	1	.0
32454	1	.0
33423	1	.0
42222	1	.0
42334	1	.0
42444	1	.0
44322	1	.0
44433	1	.0
44535	1	.0
46444	1	.0
52434	1	.0

Force Types	Number of Encounters	Percent of Encounters
62436	1	.0
62544	1	.0
222222	4	.1
222223	1	.0
222244	2	.1
222422	2	.1
222423	1	.0
222424	2	.1
222442	2	.1
222646	1	.0
222664	1	.0
223333	1	.0
223422	1	.0
223654	1	.0
224233	1	.0
224422	1	.0
226445	1	.0
232332	1	.0
242222	1	.0
242224	1	.0
242242	1	.0
242456	1	.0
243222	1	.0
243525	1	.0
244243	1	.0
245222	1	.0
246646	1	.0
266264	1	.0
422222	1	.0
422224	1	.0
422254	1	.0
425244	1	.0
444535	1	.0
2222222	4	.1
2222224	1	.0

Appendix B: Force Combinations within Encounters (cont.)

Force Types	Number of Encounters	Percent of Encounters
2223222	2	.1
2223334	1	.0
2224322	1	.0
2224423	1	.0
2242222	1	.0
2242542	1	.0
2244432	1	.0
2345325	1	.0
2422233	1	.0
2423234	1	.0
2554226	1	.0
4524422	1	.0
5522242	1	.0
5526662	1	.0
22222223	1	.0
22222333	1	.0
22222424	1	.0
22422222	1	.0
22443642	1	.0
22445465	1	.0
23224422	1	.0
24243524	1	.0
25552422	1	.0
44222334	1	.0
44422225	1	.0
55464356	1	.0
66622323	1	.0
222222442	1	.0
222224224	1	.0
432223232	1	.0
2222244223	1	.0
22222222422	1	.0
22242225544	1	.0

Appendix B: Force Combinations within Encounters (cont.)

Force Types	Number of Encounters	Percent of Encounters
625266425245	1	.0
2222223322244	1	.0
Force (201combinations)	2068	58.4
No Force	1476	41.6
Total	3544	100.0

Appendix C: Resistance Combinations within Encounters

Each number in the resistance type column represents the following resistance types: 2=passive, 3=verbal, 4=defensive, 5=active. Thus, 22 resistance type represents passive resistance followed by passive resistance; a 223 represents two passives followed by verbal resistance; a 254 represents passive, followed by active, followed by defensive resistance.

Resistance Types	Number of Encounters	Percent of Encounters
2	120	3.4
3	95	2.7
4	30	.8
5	1	.0
22	21	.6
23	9	.3
24	1	.0
25	1	.0
32	6	.2
33	30	.8
34	1	.0
42	3	.1
44	11	.3
45	1	.0
54	1	.0
55	1	.0
222	9	.3
223	2	.1
225	1	.0
232	1	.0
244	3	.1
322	2	.1
323	3	.1
332	1	.0
333	14	.4
334	1	.0

Resistance Types	Number of Encounters	Percent of Encounters
335	1	.0
422	1	.0
432	1	.0
444	3	.1
454	1	.0
455	1	.0
2222	7	.2
2233	1	.0
2322	1	.0
2333	1	.0
2334	1	.0
3233	2	.1
3332	1	.0
3333	5	.1
3334	1	.0
3344	1	.0
3345	1	.0
4432	1	.0
4433	1	.0
4442	1	.0
4444	1	.0
22222	1	.0
22233	2	.1
22244	1	.0
22334	1	.0
23232	1	.0
23322	1	.0
32435	1	.0
33233	1	.0
33332	1	.0
33333	2	.1
42333	1	.0
54433	1	.0
55422	1	0

Appendix C: Resistance Combinations within Encounters (cont.)

Resistance Types	Number of Encounters	Percent of Encounters
55444	1	.0
55544	1	.0
223444	1	.0
324444	1	.0
333333	1	.0
333353	1	.0
344444	1	.0
345244	1	.0
2222222	3	.1
2222233	1	.0
2232433	1	.0
2333333	1	.0
2444444	1	.0
3333333	3	.1
5454444	1	.0
22222223	1	.0
33322223	1	.0
33454333	1	.0
44444444	1	.0
444323232	1	.0
2222222224	1	.0
2222244444	1	.0
444444422224	1	.0
3333332324333	1	.0
Resistance (84 combinations)	446	12.6
No Resistance	3098	87.4
Total	3544	100.0

Appendix D: Missing Cases - Chapter 6 - Ordered Probit Analyses

Descriptive Statistics

Variables	Range	Mean	S.D.
Missing1	0-1	.005	.220
Missing2	0-1	.005	.224
Missing3	0-1	.006	.239
Missing4	0-1	.005	.227
Missing5	0-1	.009	.291
Missing6	0-1	.007	.257
Missing7	0-1	.006	.239
Missing8	0-1	.006	.251
Missing9	0-1	.007	.268
Missing10	0-1	.007	.259

Bivariate Relationships

Variables	No Force	Verbal	Restraint	Impact
Missing1 (182)	63 (34.6)	76 (41.8)	39 (21.4)	4 (2.2)
Missing2 (188)	65 (34.6)	78 (41.5)	41 (21.8)	4 (2.1)
Missing3 (216)	80 (37.0)	85 (39.4)	47 (21.8)	4 (1.9)
Missing4 (193)	70 (36.3)	79 (40.9)	40 (20.7)	4 (2.1)
Missing5 (332)	144 (43.4)	126 (38.0)	57 (17.2)	5 (1.5)
Missing6 (253)	84 (33.2)	108 (42.7)	55 (21.7)	6 (2.4)
Missing7 (217)	72 (33.2)	97 (44.7)	44 (20.3)	4 (1.8)
Missing8 (241)	80 (33.2)	99 (41.1)	56 (23.2)	6 (2.5)
Missing9 (277)	86 (31.0)	126 (45.5)	59 (21.3)	6 (2.2)
Missing10 (257)	87 (33.9)	108 (42.0)	56 (21.8)	6 (2.3)

Ordered Probit Model Estimates - Main Effects

Variables	Coefficient	S.E.	Significance
Missing1	.087	.835	.916
Missing2	- .130	.654	.842
Missing3	.297	.267	.265
Missing4	- 1.235	.699	.077
Missing5	- .146	.136	.281
Missing6	.108	.366	.767
Missing7	.333	.329	.312
Missing8	.643	.367	.079

Ordered Probit Model Estimates - Site Model

Variables	Coefficient	S.E.	Significance
Missing1	.176	.835	.833
Missing2	- .116	.657	.858
Missing3	.310	.266	.245
Missing4	- 1.43	.701	.040
Missing5	- .163	.136	.230
Missing6	- .035	.352	.919
Missing7	.359	.330	.277
Missing8	.763	.361	.034

Ordered Probit Model Estimates - Supervision Model

Variables	Coefficient	S.E.	Significance
Missing1	.122	.863	.883
Missing2	- .163	.655	.803
Missing3	.299	.267	.263
Missing4	- .886	.617	.150
Missing5	- .148	.136	.275
Missing8	.464	.286	.104
Missing9	.265	.242	.273

Ordered Probit Model Estimates - Workgroup Model

Variables	Coefficient	S.E.	Significance
Missing1	.067	.837	.935
Missing2	- .099	.656	.879
Missing3	.293	.266	.270
Missing4	- 1.06	.694	.124
Missing5	- .143	.136	.296
Missing7	.362	.330	.272
Missing10	.568	.166	.006

Appendix E: Estimates from Ordered Probit Model - Using Listwise Deletion

Citizen:	Coefficient	S.E.	Significance
Male	.266	.052	.000
NonWhite	.120	.046	.009
Age	- .093	.017	.000
Wealth	- .131	.037	.000
Anger/Fear	.047	.050	.347
Drug/Alcohol Use	.328	.052	.000
Mentally Impaired	- .475	.129	.712
Disrespect	- .065	.078	.403
Resistance	.356	.035	.000
Officer:			
Male	.095	.065	.142
White	.033	.055	.550
Experience	- .013	.004	.001
Education	- .041	.013	.003
Verbal Training	.028	.020	.169
Crimefighter	- .019	.030	.521
Citizens Trustworthy	.013	.027	.625
Legal Guidelines	.022	.028	.419
Organization:			
Indianapolis	.195	.053	.000
911 Officer	- .112	.067	.095
Supervision	- .025	.031	.419
Workgroup	- .004	.028	.860

Appendix E: Estimates from Ordered Probit Model - Using Listwise Deletion (cont.)

Control:	Coefficient	S.E.	Significance
# Officers	.061	.014	.000
# Bystanders	- .000	.004	.941
Anticipate Violence	.022	.076	.771
Proactive	237	.043	.000
Type Problem	.011	.043	.791
Arrest	1 .251	.062	.000
Officer Safety	.583	.186	.001
Citizen Conflict	.104	.044	.020

Intercept	- .1056
Log Likelihood	- 3027.410
Chi-Square	948.8096 (.0000)
N	3098

References

Adams, Kenneth (1995). "Measuring the Prevalence of Police Abuse of Force." In William A. Geller and Hans Toch (Eds.), *An Justice for All: Understanding and Controlling Police Abuse of Force*. Washington, D.C.: Police Executive Research Forum.

Aldrich, John H. and Forrest D. Nelson (1984). "Linear Probability, Logit, and Probit Models." *Sage University Papers: Quantitative Applications in the Social Sciences, 07-045*. Beverly Hills, CA: Sage.

Alpert, Geoffrey P. and Roger G. Dunham (1997). *The Force Factor: Measuring Police Use of Force Relative to Suspect Resistance*. Washington, D.C.: Police Executive Research Forum.

Babbie, Earl (1995). *The Practice of Social Research, Seventh Edition*. New York: Wadsworth.

Bayley, David H. (1986). "The Tactical Choices of Police Patrol Officers." *Journal of Criminal Justice* 14: 329-348.

-------- and Harold Mendelsohn (1969). *Minorities and the Police: Confrontation in America*. New York: Free Press.

-------- and James Garofalo (1989). "The Management of Violence by Police Patrol Officers." *Criminology* 27 (1): 1-27.

Binder, Arnold and Peter Scharf (1980). "The Violent Police-
    Citizen Encounter." *The Annals of the American Academy
    of Political and Social Science* 452: 111-121.

Bittner, Egon (1970). *The Functions of Police in Modern Society.*
    Washington, D.C.: U.S. Government Printing Office.

-------- (1974). "Florence Nightingale in Pursuit of Willie Sutton:
    A Theory of the Police." In Carl B. Klockars and Stephen
    D. Mastrofski (Eds.), *Thinking About Police:
    Contemporary Readings.* New York: McGraw-Hill.

Black, Donald (1976). *The Behavior of Law.* New York: Academic
    Press.

-------- (1980). *Manners and Customs of the Police.* New York:
    Academic Press.

Brown, Michael K. (1981). *Working the Street: Police Discretion
    and the Dilemmas of Reform.* New York: Russell Sage
    Foundation.

Campbell, Angus and Howard Schuman (1968). "Racial Attitudes
    in Fifteen American Cities." *Supplemental Studies for the
    National Advisory Commission on Civil Disorders.* New
    York: Praeger.

Cascio, Wayne F. (1977). "Formal Education and Police Officer
    Performance." *Journal of Police Science and
    Administration* 5: 89-96.

Chevigny, Paul (1969). *Police Power: Police Abuses in New York
    City.* New York: Pantheon Books.

Cohen, Bernard and Jan M. Chaiken (1972). *Police Background
    Characteristics and Performance.* New York: Rand.

Connor, Gregory (1991). "Use of Force Continuum: Phase II." *Law
    and Order* (March): 30-32.

Cook, Thomas D. and Donald T. Campbell (1979). *Quasi-Experimentation: Design and Analysis Issues for Field Settings*. Chicago: Rand-McNally.

Croft, Elizabeth Benz (1985). "Police Use of Force: An Empirical Analysis." *Unpublished Ph.D. Dissertation*. University of Michigan.

-------- and James Austin (1987). Police Use of Force in Rochester and Syracuse, New York 1984 and 1985. *Report to the New York State Commission on Criminal Justice and the Use of Force* (Vol III, May: 1-128). Albany, NY: New York State Commission on Criminal Justice and the Use of Force.

DeJong, Christina (1997). "Survival Analysis and Specific Deterrence: Integrating Theoretical and Empirical Models of Recidivism." *Criminology* 35 (4): 561-576.

-------- and Kenneth C. Jackson (1998). "Putting Race into Context: Race, Juvenile Justice Processing, and Urbanization." *Justice Quarterly* 15 (3): 487-504.

Desmedt, John C. (1984). "Use of Force Paradigm for Law Enforcement." *Journal of Criminal Justice* 12 (2): 170-176.

Dugan, John R. and Daniel R. Breda (1991). "Complaints About Police Officers: A Comparison Among Types and Agencies." *Journal of Criminal Justice* 19 (2): 165-171.

Fridell, Lorie A. and Arnold Binder (1992). "Police Officer DecisionMaking in Potentially Violent Confrontations." *Journal of Criminal Justice* 20: 385-399.

Friedrich, Robert J. (1977). "The Impact of Organizational, Individual, and Situational Factors on Police Behavior." *Unpublished Ph.D. Dissertation*. University of Michigan.

-------- (1980). "Police Use of Force: Individuals, Situations, and
      Organizations." *The Annals of the American Academy of
      Political and Social Science* November, 82-97.

Fyfe, James J. (1979). "Administrative Interventions on Police
      Shooting Discretion: An Empirical Examination." *Journal
      of Criminal Justice* 7: 303-323.

-------- (1988). *The Metro-Dade Police-Citizen Violence Reduction
      Project, Final Report, Executive Summary.* Washington,
      D.C.: Police Foundation.

-------- (1989). "Police-Citizen Violence Reduction Project." *FBI
      Law Enforcement Bulletin* 58 (May): 18-25.

-------- (1996). "Methodology, Substance, and Demeanor in Police
      Observational Research: A Response to Lundman and
      Others." *Journal of Research in Crime and Delinquency*
      33 (3): 337-348.

-------- (1997). "The Split-Second Syndrome and Other
      Determinants of Police Violence." In Dunham, Roger G.
      and Geoffrey P. Alpert (Eds.), *Critical Issues in Policing:
      Contemporary Readings.* Prospect Heights, IL: Waveland
      Press.

Gallup, George (The Gallup Organization) (1991). "Americans Say
      Police Brutality Frequent But Most Have Favorable
      Opinion of Their Local Police." *The Gallup Poll Monthly*
      (March): 53-56.

Garner, Joel H.; Schade, Thomas; Hepburn, John; and John
      Buchanan (1995). "Measuring the Continuum of Force
      Used By and Against the Police." *Criminal Justice Review*
      20 (2): 146-168.

--------; Buchanan, John; Schade, Thomas; and John Hepburn
      (1996). "Understanding the Use of Force By and Against
      the Police." *National Institute of Justice: Research in
      Brief.*

Goldstein, Herman (1990). *Problem-Oriented Policing*. New York: McGraw Hill.

Indianapolis Police Department Interdepartmental Memo (November, 1995). *The Safe Street Initiative*.

Jarjoura. G. Roger (1993). "Does Dropping Out of School Enhance Delinquent Involvement? Results from a Large-Scale National Probability Sample." *Criminology* 31 (2): 149-171).

Klinger, David A. (1995). "The Micro-Structure of Nonlethal Force: Baseline Data from and Observational Study." *Criminal Justice Review* 20 (2): 169-186.

Klockars, Carl B. (1995). "A Theory of Excessive force and its Control." In William A. Geller and Hans Toch (Eds.), *An Justice for All: Understanding and Controlling Police Abuse of Force*. Washington, D.C.: Police Executive Research Forum.

Liao, Tim F. (1994). "Interpreting Probability Models: Logit, Probit, and Other Generalized Linear Models." *Sage University Papers: Quantitative Applications in the Social Sciences*, 07-045. Beverly Hills, CA: Sage.

Long, J. Scott (1997). *Regression Models for Categorical and Limited Dependent Variables*. Thousand Oaks, CA: Sage Publications.

Lundstrom, Ross and Cynthia Mullan (1987). "The Use of Force: One Department's Experience." *FBI Law Enforcement Bulletin*: 6-9.

Manning, Peter K. (1989). "The Police Occupational Culture in Anglo-American Societies." In William G. Bailey (Eds.), *Encyclopedia of Police Science*. Dallas: Garland.

Mastrofski, Stephen A.; Roger B. Parks; Albert J. Reiss Jr.; and Robert E. Worden (1995). "Community Policing at the

Street Level: A Study of the Police and the Community."
Proposal submitted to the National Institute of Justice.
Washington, D.C..

-------- ; Roger B. Parks; Albert J. Reiss Jr.; Robert E. Worden;
Christina DeJong, Jeffrey B. Snipes, and William Terrill
(1998). *Systematic Observation of Public Police: Applying
Field Research Methods to Policy Issues.* National
Institute of Justice Research Report: NCJ 172859

-------- and Ritti, R. Richard (1996). "Police Training and the
Effects of Organization on Drunk Driving Enforcement."
Justice Quarterly 13 (2): 291-320.

McEwen, Tom (1996). *National Data Collection on Police Use of
Force.* Washington, D.C.: Bureau of Justice Statistics.

McKelvey, Richard D. and William Zavoina (1975). "A Statistical
Model for the Analysis of Ordinal Level Dependent
Variables." *Journal of Mathematical Sociology* 4: 103-
120.

McLaughlin, V. (1992). *Police and the Use of Force: The
Savannah Study.* Westport, CT: Praeger.

Muir, William Ker, Jr. (1977). *Police: Streetcorner Politicians.*
Chicago: University of Chicago Press.

National Commission on Law Observance and Enforcement (1931).
Report on Lawlessness in Law Enforcement. Washington
D.C.: U.S. Government Printing Office.

National Institute of Justice Research Report (October, 1999). *Use
of Force By Police: Overview of National and Local Data.*
U.S. Department of Justice, Office of Justice Programs,
NCJ 176330.

Niederhoffer, Arthur (1967). *Behind the Shield: Police in Urban
Society.* Garden City, New York: Anchor Books,
Doubleday.

Parks, Roger B. and Michael D. Reisig (1998). "Community Policing and Perceived Safety: Psychological and Ecological Effects." *Paper presented to the American Society of Criminology.* Washington D.C.

Parsons, Ken (1988). "Use of Force Tactics and Non-lethal Weaponry." *Alert* 3: 1-8.

Pate, Anthony and Lorie Fridell (1993). *Police Use of Force: Official Reports, Citizen Complaints, and Legal Consequences Vol. 1.* Washington D.C.: Police Foundation.

Reiss, Albert J., Jr (1966). "Police Observation Report Instructions." *Internal Document of the Center for Research on Social Organization.* University of Michigan, Ann Arbor, Michigan.

-------- (1968). "Police Brutality--Answers to Key Questions." *Trans-action* 5: 10-19.

-------- (1971). *The Police and the Public.* New Haven: Yale University Press.

Riksheim, Eric C. and Steven M. Chermak (1993). "Causes of Police Behavior Revisited." *Journal of Criminal Justice* 21: 353-382.

Sherman, Lawrence W. (1980a). "Perspectives on Police and Violence." *The Annals of American Academy of Political and Social Science* 452 (Nov): 1-12.

-------- (1980b). "Causes of Police Behavior: The Current State of Quantitative Research." *Journal of Research in Crime and Delinquency* 17: 69-100.

-------- and Ellen G. Cohn (1986). *Citizens Killed by Big-City Police, 1970-1984.* Washington D.C.: Crime Control Institute.

Smith, Douglas A., and Christy A. Visher (1981). "Street-Level
    Justice: Situational Determinants of Police Arrest
    Decisions." *Social Problems* 9 (2): 167-177.

Sykes, Richard E. and Edward E. Brent (1980). "The Regulation of
    Interaction by Police: A Systems View of Taking Charge."
    Criminology 18: 182-197.

-------- (1983). *Policing: A Social Behaviorist Perspective.* New
    Brunswick, NJ: Rutgers University Press.

Toch, Hans (1969). *Violent Men: An Inquiry into the Psychology of
    Violence.* Chicago: Aldine.

Westley, William A. (1953). "Violence and the Police." *American
    Journal of Sociology* 59: 34-41.

White, Susan O. (1972). "A Perspective on Police
    Professionalization." *Law and Society Review* 7: 61-85.

Wilson, James Q. (1968). *Varieties of Police Behavior: The
    Management of Law and Order in Eight Communities.*
    Cambridge, MA: Harvard University Press.

Winick, Charles (1987). "Public Opinions on Police Misuse of
    Force: A New York Study." *Report to the Governor: Vol
    III (Consultant Reports).* Albany, New York State
    Commission on Criminal Justice and the Use of Force.

Winship, Christopher. and Robert Mare. (1984). "Regression
    Models with Ordinal Variables." *American Sociological
    Review* 49: 512-525.

Worden, Robert E. (1989). "Situational and Attitudinal
    Explanations of Police Behavior: A Theoretical
    Reappraisal and Empirical Assessment." *Law and Society
    Review* 23: 667-711.

-------- (1995). "The 'Causes' of Police Brutality: Theory and Evidence On Police Use of Force." In William A. Geller and Hans Toch (Eds.), *An Justice for All: Understanding and Controlling Police Abuse of Force*. Washington, D.C.: Police Executive Research Forum.

Subject Index

Author Index